C0-ARD-498

**fundamental
programming
concepts**

**harper's series in
computer and information science**

*under the advisory editorship of
Alan J. Perlis, Yale University*

fundamental programming concepts

JONATHAN L. GROSS

WALTER S. BRAINERD

Columbia University

Harper & Row, Publishers

New York Evanston San Francisco London

QA
76.6
.G76

fundamental programming concepts

Copyright © 1972 by JONATHAN L. GROSS *and* WALTER S. BRAINERD.

*Printed in the United States of America. All
rights reserved. No part of this book may
be used or reproduced in any manner
whatsoever without written permission except
in the case of brief quotations embodied
in critical articles and reviews. For
information address Harper & Row, Publishers,
Inc., 49 East 33rd Street, New York, N.Y. 10016.*

Standard Book Number: 06–042531–8

Library of Congress Catalog Card Number: 74–181539

To
Aaron, Jessica, and Joshua
Lisa, Pamela, and Julie

contents

preface

IMAGINATIVE APPLICATIONS by computer users and increased
versatility of the machines themselves have aroused interest in
programming among students in just about every discipline. In
teaching the essentials of programming in the BASIC language,
this book reflects the vast variety of current applications in topics
such as ecology, political science, and archaeology. It is the
outgrowth of the authors' course at Columbia University, which
they designed to meet the needs of a highly diversified group
of students, including majors in the sciences, social sciences,
humanities, business, engineering, and education.

The programs used as examples are drawn from the experience
of the students and provide an entertaining and motivating
approach to communicating underlying concepts. Formulating
problems for programming solution is a central theme, and the
exercises at the end of each section reinforce the ideas presented.

High school algebra is the only prerequisite for understanding
the material here. Because of the variety of examples, a course
based on this book might equally well be taught by a professor of
biochemistry, sociology, music, or accounting, as long as he or
she is interested in teaching the principles of programming.
Naturally, an instructor who is expert in the area of certain
problems might develop additional examples in that area.

This book is the appropriate length for a concentrated semester
course and could also be used as a self-teaching guide for a
motivated person who has time-sharing service available. A more
leisurely course might omit some of the mathematical examples

in Chapter 5 or the discussion of other programming languages in Chapter 10.

Time-sharing systems and the language BASIC were pioneered at Dartmouth College under the direction of Professors John G. Kemeny and Thomas E. Kurtz. For educational purposes, time-sharing has a clear advantage over batch-processing because of its capability for immediate response. The language BASIC is ideal for an introductory course because its simplicity allows a student to begin writing programs immediately, while its generality permits discussion of loops, subroutines, data structures, recursion, and other key topics. A BASIC programmer can quickly learn another language if the need should ever arise.

Nearly every major computer manufacturer supports BASIC, so it is a widely available language. If a college has a research or administrative computer facility, it probably offers BASIC or can be modified to do so. Even if no computer is available, there are many commercial time-sharing service vendors who can install a remote terminal and an acoustic coupler beside the nearest telephone on short notice. The cost is only a few dollars per terminal hour and it decreases with increased usage.

The authors would like to thank Sally Anne Ford Gross for her contribution to the jacket design, Ann Fox of Harper & Row for her professional help with the manuscript, Mrs. Beatrice Williams, Miss Florence Armstrong, and Mrs. Betty Lim for typing and other assistance in preparation of the manuscript, IBM and the ACM for providing photographs used in this book, and Mr. Samuel Glazer for preparing and running the COBOL program in Chapter 10.

All BASIC programs were run on a commercial system operated by Computer Solutions, Inc., of East Orange, New Jersey. (Any errors are the authors' responsibility.) The authors wish to thank Computer Solutions for their courtesy in providing excellent facilities and service.

JONATHAN L. GROSS
WALTER S. BRAINERD

**fundamental
programming
concepts**

1

elementary BASIC

A COMPUTER is a device that can perform a variety of jobs, ranging from simple arithmetic calculations to solving difficult problems in mathematics, the sciences, the humanities, and the social sciences. This book considers computer applications to problems in all of these areas.

To tell a computer what to do, it is necessary to devise a complete and unambiguous list of instructions called a *program*. Since natural languages (e.g., Chinese, English, Turkish) contain idioms that permit more than one interpretation, special languages with no ambiguities have been created for writing computer programs. The language BASIC is chosen here because, of all the widely available general-purpose computer languages, it is the one most easily understood by humans.

This chapter is written to teach a person with no previous knowledge of programming or of computers how to write some simple programs in BASIC and how to run them on a computer.

A programmer who is using IBM CALL/360-OS BASIC should read Appendix A for a description of some essential differences between that dialect and the ordinary version described here.

1 | some simple programs

This section describes how to write some elementary programs that perform arithmetic computations. The first example is a program to compute the sum of two numbers.

LIST
SUM2

```
100   LET X=84.12
110   LET Y=13
120   LET Z=X+Y
130   PRINT Z
140   END
```

    The program consists of the lines numbered from 100 to 140. Its name SUM2 was chosen to give a brief indication of the purpose of the program, but changing the name would not affect what the program does, which is solely determined by the content of the numbered lines. The word LIST, just above the name SUM2, indicates that what follows is a listing of the lines of a program. Some additional significance of the word LIST is explained in Section 3.

    The LET statement in line 100 tells the computer to assign the value 84.12 to the variable X. The LET statement in line 110 tells the computer to assign the value 13 to the variable Y. The computer executes the LET statement in line 120 by setting the value of the variable Z to the sum of the values of X and Y, in this case to 97.12, which is the sum of 84.12 and 13. The PRINT statement in line 130 directs the computer to print the value of Z, and the END statement at line 140 terminates execution of the program. The highest numbered line of any BASIC program must be an END statement.

    The following printout results from running the program SUM2 (the next two sections tell how to run a program) on the computer.

```
RUN
SUM2

  97.12

DONE
```

    The word RUN over the name SUM2 indicates that what follows is the result of running the program SUM2 on the computer. Further explanation of RUN is given in Section 3. The computer prints only 97.12, the value of Z, when line 130 is executed, and not the values of X and Y, because it has only been instructed to print the value of Z. The word DONE at the bottom signifies that the execution of the program is complete.

    The line numbers are somewhat arbitrary. There is no necessity either to begin at 100 or to space lines ten numbers apart. The important fact is that the computer executes the statements of the program SUM2 in the order of ascending line number. The language BASIC accepts any line number between 1 and 9999.

To add any two other numbers, one need only replace lines 100 and 110 of SUM2 by different LET statements. For example, if one makes the replacement

```
100   LET X=139.26
110   LET Y=4.1
```

then the variables X and Y would assume the values 139.26 and 4.1, respectively, when lines 100 and 110 are executed, and the computer would execute the PRINT statement at line 130 by typing out the number 143.36.

Many persons would be able to add two numbers together more quickly than to write the program SUM2. They would have good reason to object that the program SUM2 offers them no advantage. However, more complicated arithmetic can be performed by programs that are no more difficult to write than SUM2, as shown by the next program, PROD3.

```
LIST
PROD3

200   READ A,B,C
215   DATA 32,6.4,.96
228   LET P=A*B*C
374   PRINT P
999   END

RUN
PROD3

  196.608

DONE
```

The computer executes line 200 by assigning to the variables A, B, and C the values 32, 6.4, and .96, respectively, which are given in the DATA statement at line 215. It is as if, instead of the present lines 200 and 215, the program used the three lines

```
200   LET A=32
210   LET B=6.4
215   LET C=.96
```

The asterisk (*) denotes multiplication in BASIC. Therefore, line 228 of PROD3 directs the computer to assign the product of the values of the three variables A, B, and C to the variable P. Line 374 makes the computer print the value of P, and line 999 terminates execution, causing the word DONE to appear.

concerning data

To calculate the product of any three numbers other than those
given in line 215 of PROD3, the programmer simply writes a new
line 215 which contains the three new numbers. This is an
immediate advantage of using a READ statement and a DATA
statement instead of three LET statements.

numbers, variables, and expressions

The grammar for BASIC is quite precise. Perhaps the reader has
observed that the quantity to the left of the equality symbol in each
LET statement is always a variable, whereas the quantity to the
right is sometimes a number and sometimes an expression. It is
simply not permitted to place a number or an expression on the left
of the equality symbol in a LET statement.

The quantities following the word DATA in a DATA statement
must be numbers, not variables or expressions (such as sums or
products) containing numbers. If there are two or more such
numbers in the same data statement, they must be separated by
commas. The quantities following the word READ in a READ
statement are always variables. Two or more of them in the same
READ statement must be separated by commas.

two-line programs

It is possible to perform certain computations with programs
consisting of only two lines, because the operand (i.e., what follows
the word PRINT) of a PRINT statement may be a moderately
complicated expression. For instance, the program AVG4
determines the average of four numbers.

```
LIST
AVG4

1    PRINT (92+72+83+89)/4
2    END

RUN
AVG4

  84

DONE
```

The diagonal slash in line 1 of the program AVG4 is the notation
for division. The computer executes line 1 by first adding the four

numbers 92, 72, 83, and 89 together, then dividing the sum by 4, and finally by printing the result. Line 2 terminates execution. No variables are used in the program AVG4, and it is clear that the use of variables might have been avoided in performing the computations of the programs SUM2 and PROD3. Two-line programs like AVG4, consisting of a PRINT statement and an END statement, would have been sufficient.

Perhaps the program AVG4 makes the reader wonder what limitations there are on the content of a PRINT statement. The restrictions will be explained soon, but for the time being it is hoped that the reader will experiment on a computer if one is available.

The problems at the end of this section require only a simple knowledge of the arithmetic operators

+ (addition)
− (subtraction)
* (multiplication)
/ (division)

and use of the BASIC statements READ, DATA, LET, PRINT, and END. The reader is reminded not to concern himself with what name to give a program, since the name will not affect the computation.

problems

1 Write a two-line program that performs the computation of SUM2.

2 Write a two-line program that performs the computation of PROD3.

3 Write a five-line program, modeled after SUM2, that computes the difference of two numbers.

4 Write a program that computes the average of the following numbers: 104, 80, 46, 573, 2, 2527, 61, 68, 612, 153, 988, 3101, 945, 95, 84, 37, 8, 901, 62, 847, 299, 85, 591, 93, 676, 325, 378, 766, 28, 779, 19, 205, and 4154. The language BASIC does not permit a single statement to contain more than 72 characters, including blanks, nor does it permit a single statement to occupy more than one line.

5 State why each of the following lines is not a valid BASIC instruction.

```
100   LET 5.7=F
200   LET A+B=5
300   DATA 3,B,7.2,-4
400   DATA 1,5+3.1,7.02
500   READ B,4
600   READ A;J
```

2 | *remote access*

The language BASIC was specifically designed for operation from
remote-access terminals called teletypewriters. The teletypewriter
is not a computer but, rather, a device which enables a person to
communicate with a computer. The computer itself might be in
another room, or even several hundred miles away. The technical
details of computers and of the communication between a
teletypewriter and a computer are quite complicated. The present
concern is not with these matters of electronics. Rather, the
discussion here is about what a computer does and how a
programmer directs its actions from a teletypewriter.

connecting to the computer

The first step in remote operation of a computer is connecting the
teletypewriter to the electrical power line. The teletypewriter is
plugged into a standard electrical outlet, and a switch is moved or a
button is pushed to turn it on. At some installations, moving the
switch or pushing the button automatically completes the
connection with the computer. At others, it is necessary to dial the
telephone number of the computer from a telephone dial attached
to the keyboard. Sometimes the teletypewriter has an acoustic
coupler instead of a telephone dial, and the connection is effected
using an ordinary telephone.

Computers have ordinary telephone numbers, consisting of a
three-digit area code, a three-digit exchange code, and a four-digit
number. When a computer is called from within the same area, the
area code is omitted, just as it is when a person is called. Computer
phone numbers are rarely listed in the public directory. Generally,
either they are posted near the teletypewriter or they are given to a
person who is authorized to use them.

After the number is dialed, either a busy signal or a ring will be
heard from the earpiece of the handset. If it is a busy signal, then
the programmer should hang up and call back in a few minutes.
If it is a ring, then the computer will soon answer and give a
steady medium high-pitched tone. If the dial is attached to the
teletypewriter, then the connection is complete. If the teletypewriter

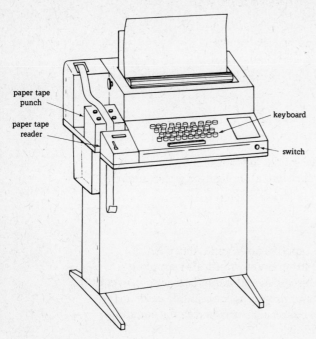

paper tape
punch

paper tape
reader

keyboard

switch

Figure 1   Teletypewriter.

has an acoustic coupler attached, then the handset should be placed
in the coupler, properly aligned, which completes the connection.
Naturally, if the handset is placed in the wrong direction, there is
no connection.

logging in

Before going to the teletypewriter, a programmer must obtain a
user code. After the teletypewriter is connected to the computer,
the programmer logs in by supplying this user code. The procedure
for logging in varies erratically from one computer installation to
another and, therefore, a programmer needs to learn the precise
details for supplying a user code to the computer he is operating.
Two examples of possible procedures are given here.

Example 1   Suppose that 123456 is the user number. The
programmer might type

HELLO-123456

and push the keyboard button labeled RETURN. The computer
might respond by causing the teletypewriter to type

```
GREETINGS...TIME-SHARING SYSTEM AT YOUR SERVICE
```

Example 2 Suppose again that 123456 is the user number. The
programmer might type

```
HELLO
```

and push the RETURN button on the keyboard. The computer
might reply by typing on the next line a request for a user number.

```
USER NUMBER?
```

The programmer should then type the user code and push the
RETURN key. Sometimes the programmer must also supply a
"password". The purpose of user codes and passwords is to prevent
unauthorized usage and to assure proper accounting of costs and
proper billing. If an invalid user core is transmitted to the computer,
then it will print a message such as

```
INVALID USER CODE
```

It may even sever the telephone connection (hang up), so that a
programmer will have to dial the phone number of the computer
again in order to log in.

programming languages

Many computer systems are capable of executing programs in any
of several languages. There are other popular languages besides
BASIC, such as ALGOL, FORTRAN, PL/I, and SNOBOL. Each
has specific advantages and limitations. If a programmer is working
with a system that accepts other languages besides BASIC, then,
after logging in, he might have to tell the computer which
programming language he will write in. For example, he might type

```
LANGUAGE-BASIC
```

and push the RETURN key.

Like logging in, the procedure for indicating a language preference varies so widely from one system to another that a programmer will have to be instructed how to do this at any particular computer installation.

time-sharing

Many computers in use today can virtually achieve the simultaneous processing of programs. Whereas 4 programmers, each at his or her own terminal, might simultaneously access a small system, 50 or more programmers might simultaneously access a large system. Each programmer has the sensation of control of a "private" computer, although, in fact, the computer is shared. Through a complicated scheduling arrangement, the computer gives one programmer its full attention for a fraction of a second and then gives a turn to another programmer. The net effect is that no programmer has to wait very long for service. The service may be brief, but each programmer feels the comforting sensation of constant attention. Furthermore, the computer accomplishes a lot in a fraction of a second.

A possible analogy to a computer time-sharing system is a waiter attending to many tables in a restaurant while a chef cooks for everyone. When the diners arrive at a table, the waiter brings menus as soon as possible. He leaves to attend other tables. When diners seem ready to order their meal, the waiter reappears as soon as possible. He relays the message to the chef and attends to the other tables. He serves the meal when it is ready, and so on. At the various tables he is attending, the service is in different stages of completion. Perhaps some of his tables are empty or maybe all are occupied. The speed of service may depend on the number of occupied tables.

If a waiter attends to only one table, then much of his time is spent uselessly while the diners eat. If a computer is responding to only one terminal, then some of its time may be wasted while it awaits input. If the program involves a lot of printing, then the computer's computational capacity will be wasted. Under a time-sharing system, the computer can compute for one program while it prints for another. This is like the chef preparing one meal while the waiter is serving another.

A computer servicing only one terminal is said to be operating in "batch mode". If a single program requires a great deal of computing, which often happens in engineering and scientific problems, then batch mode may be better, because the computer cannot actually compute two problems simultaneously (even though it can overlap printing and computing). Perhaps the reader should imagine a diner who requires all of the chef's facilities and also, perhaps, the waiter's constant attention. A computer completes a program more slowly in its time-sharing mode than in its batch mode, both because it is also servicing other programs and because it loses "overhead" time in switching from one program to another.

3 | *writing and running programs*

After the logging-in procedure and the determination of a computer language, the programmer may begin transmitting a program.

keyboard

The teletypewriter keyboard resembles the keyboard of a typewriter. However, the alphabetic characters on a teletypewriter are all capitals. Pushing the shift button simultaneously with a character key which has an upper-case marking will usually produce the upper-case character. For certain special characters, such as the bell (upper-case G) one pushes the control key labeled CTRL instead of the shift key.

giving a name

The program considered in this section converts a distance in meters to a distance in yards. The name METERS is chosen for the program, but certainly it might just as well be called YARDS. Not every computer system requires the programmer to name each program but many do. On some systems the programmer gives the name by typing NAME— followed by the name of the program, in this case,

```
NAME-METERS
```

and then the RETURN key. Other systems may follow the logging-in procedure or the selection of a computer language by immediately printing out the question

```
NEW OR OLD?
```

Until the programmer has saved some programs (as described later in this chapter) in disk storage, the correct response is

followed by the RETURN key. The system may then request a
name by printing

NAME?

The programmer should type the name of the program and then the
RETURN key.

transmitting a line

After the computer knows the name of the program it is ready to
receive the lines of code (i.e., the numbered statements). Suppose
that the distance to be converted to yards is 120 meters. The
programmer might begin by typing the line

10   READ M

then the RETURN key, and then the line

20   DATA 120

followed by the RETURN key.

After correctly typing any numbered statement, the programmer
transmits it to the computer by pushing the RETURN key. If the
line of code is long, a bell may ring to signal that the teletypewriter
carriage is nearing the right-hand margin. On most systems a
single numbered statement must occupy only one line.

erasing a line (escaping)

A line of code is not actually recorded by the computer as part of
the program until the RETURN key is pushed. Before then, the line
may be erased by pushing the escape key, which is usually labeled
either ESC or ALT MODE. A reverse slash (\) will appear at the
end of the line, and the carriage will restore. Obviously, the printed
symbols on the erased line cannot vanish from the paper, but they
are not recorded in the program.

For example, in attempting to convert the distance in meters to a
distance in inches, the programmer might type

then the escape key when the error is noticed, and finally the correct line. The printout paper would show the following program lines.

```
10   READ M
20   DATA 120
30   LET I=M*37.37\
30   LFT I=M*39.37
```

Only the latter line 30 would be recorded by the computer.

backspacing

It is not always necessary to erase an entire line. One may erase a single character by typing the backspace key (marked ←). Several consecutive wrong characters may be erased by typing the backspace key several times. Thus, the following four lines are equivalent.

```
40   LET Y=I/36
40   LEE←T Y=I/36
LET←←←40   LETT← Y=I/36
40   LET I←Y=M←I/366←
```

Line 40 converts the distance in inches into a distance in yards.

deleting or replacing a line

If the RETURN key is already pushed, it is still possible to delete or replace a line. To delete it from the program, simply type the line number and then the RETURN key. This may be done even if other lines have been transmitted after the one that should be removed.

To replace a statement, simply type another statement with the same number. Suppose, for example, that the programmer has already typed lines 10 to 40 of the program METERS when he discovers that he meant to convert the distance 180 meters into yards. He simply transmits the line

```
20   DATA 180
```

blank characters in statements

The running of a BASIC program is not affected by the insertion or the omission of blank characters in any numbered line. The following three lines, therefore, are equivalent.

```
50   PRINT Y
50P RI   NTY
5    0 PR  INTY
```

Line 50 prints the distance in yards.

listing a program

A listing of the lines of a program may be obtained at any time by typing the "system command" LIST. The program need not be complete or correct. For example, the program METERS as described so far does not contain an END statement. On the line immediately below the one on which the programmer types LIST, the name of the program will appear. Then the lines of the program will be typed. Thus, typing LIST at this time during the writing of METERS yields the following.

```
LIST
METERS

10   READ M
20   DATA 180
30   LET I=M*39.37
40   LET Y=I/36
50   PRINT Y
```

No record of erasures, deletions, or alterations appears in a new listing, only the present content of the program.

If the programmer now transmits an END statement as line 60 followed by another LIST command, he obtains a listing of his complete program.

```
LIST
METERS

10   READ M
20   DATA 180
30   LET I=M*39.37
40   LET Y=I/36
50   PRINT Y
60   END
```

ascending line number

The statements of a BASIC program are executed in the order of ascending line number. The computer actually "forgets" the order in which they were written. Because of the rule for replacing a line, it is impossible for two lines to have the same number. The command LIST always causes the computer to print out a listing of the lines of the program in the order of ascending line number.

The great advantage of this convention on order of execution is that it makes it possible to insert lines. For example, if the programmer had already transmitted the lines

```
10  READ M
20  LET I=M*39.37
30  LET Y=I/36
40  PRINT Y
50  END
```

he could obtain a correct meters-to-yards conversion program by transmitting the line

```
15  DATA 180
```

Skipping numbers between lines is a good way to facilitate modifications and corrections of programs.

error messages about lines

Sometimes a programmer will inadvertently type a line, such as

```
10  READ 180
```

which cannot be interpreted by the computer. In BASIC, the instruction READ must be followed by the name of a variable, such as M, or by a series of variable names separated by commas. The computer might respond

```
INVALID VARIABLE NAME
```

to such an error.

The content of error messages varies greatly from one computer system to another. Some BASIC installations provide a large collection of valuable messages, while others only print the word ERROR for each mistake.

The computer does not record lines containing errors, so they need not be deleted. The correct procedure after an error message is simply to type a valid line.

The computer does not have extrasensory perception, so it cannot detect errors of meaning, like adding the wrong number or naming the wrong variable. It can only detect errors of syntax (grammatical errors), such as an invalid name for a variable or the omission of an arithmetic operator. Sometimes the diagnostic will not seem to fit the mistake, because the computer does not know what the programmer intended. For example, the error message for the line

```
175 LET P=7Q
```

might be either

```
MISSING OPERATION SYMBOL
```

to indicate that the computer believes some arithmetic operation symbol should go between 7 and Q, or

```
CHARACTERS AFTER END OF LINE
```

to indicate the computer's belief that the programmer wanted to set the value of the variable P to 7 and that the letter "Q" was inadvertently typed after the line was completed.

running a program

Once the entire program has been transmitted to the computer, the programmer may order the computer to execute it by transmitting the system command RUN, as shown for the program METERS.

```
RUN
METERS
 196.85
DONE
```

Running a program does not change it in any way. Afterward it may still be listed (by giving the command LIST) or it may be rerun. The programmer may even insert lines, delete lines, or change lines as desired. These alterations in the program will be effective in any subsequent listing or running.

compilation and execution

The RUN command instructs the computer to compile and execute the program. *Compilation* consists of reserving sufficient computation space in the computer memory and converting each

line of the BASIC program into an internal computer code called
machine language (see Chapter 9).

Not every sequence of BASIC instructions can be compiled into a
machine language program. The absence of an END statement will
always prevent successful compilation, as will numerous other
errors. However, if a program can be compiled, then each BASIC
line is converted into a distinct group of machine language
instructions. Execution of a line of a BASIC program is properly
identified with execution of the corresponding machine language
instruction group. Execution of a BASIC program really means
execution of the machine language program.

Whether or not a programmer knows the machine language, it is
necessary to be aware that a compilation process precedes
execution.

In a certain sense, machine language is more fundamental than
BASIC. However, there are many reasons for beginning the study of
BASIC first. BASIC is a lot easier to learn because it is more
closely related to the everyday language of mathematics. Learning
a modern machine language requires a lot of patience and
perseverance. Also, there are already thousands of different
computers whose machine languages often bear little resemblance
to each other. Whereas a given computer may quickly achieve
obsolescence, the language BASIC can operate on new and different
models, provided that a compiler is created. Thus, a programmer
who knows BASIC can use a new computer without learning a new
language. An old program in BASIC may be executed on the new
machine. A machine language program is generally restricted to one
model of computer.

This argument for BASIC is also an argument for ALGOL,
FORTRAN, SNOBOL, and other "higher level languages" over
machine language. However, someone needs to know machine
language to write the compilers for the machine that permit other
programmers to use BASIC or other languages.

error messages about programs

It has been mentioned that the computer prints a diagnostic
message immediately after a programmer transmits a line with a
syntax error. But it is possible that no particular line of a program
contains any syntax error while the entire program is still invalid
(i.e., it cannot be compiled). For example, the highest numbered
statement might not be an END statement. After the command
RUN, in such a case, the computer would print an error message
about the program, such as

The computer certainly has no way of knowing whether a given program suits the intent of the programmer. It can only detect such syntax errors as a missing END statement.

logging out

After finishing work at the computer, the programmer may log out by transmitting the system command GOODBYE on some systems or BYE on others. The computer then stops charging the programmer's user number for processing time and connection time. (The computer charges a user for being connected to the system even if his teletypewriter is idle, that is, not running, not listing, and not receiving any instructions from the programmer. The reason for this is that simply by logging in, a programmer blocks access by others to the system.) If the teletypewriter has an acoustic coupler, the programmer should hang up the telephone. To resume using the system, the programmer reconnects and logs in again.

problems

1 Take your solution to any problem at the end of Section 1 of this chapter and run it on the computer.

2 Write and run a program that converts a distance in meters into a distance in feet.

3 Write and run a program that converts a distance in feet and inches into a distance in meters.

4 There are 453.6 grams in a pound, 16 ounces in a pound, and 1000 grams in a kilogram. Write and run a program that converts a weight given in pounds and ounces into an equivalent weight in kilograms.

5 The area of a circle is the product of π (approximately 3.14) and the square of its radius. Write and run a program that computes the area of a circle from its radius.

6 Write and run a program that computes the annual interest on a loan if the rate is 7.75 percent.

7 Write and run a program that computes the total interest accumulated on a 4-year deposit if the interest rate is 5.25 percent, compounded annually.

8 Each Fahrenheit degree corresponds to $5/9$ of a centigrade degree. Furthermore, 100° centigrade corresponds to 212° Fahrenheit. Write and run a program that converts a centigrade temperature to a Fahrenheit temperature.

4 | deleting an entire program

The facility of a computer that records the lines of a program is called its *memory*. The portion of memory allotted to a particular teletypewriter connected to the system is called the *scratch area* for that terminal (or for the programmer at that terminal).

  A programmer can record only one program in his scratch area at a time, so that if he finishes work on a first program and wants to begin work on a second, he must delete every line of the first program. According to the previous section, he might accomplish this by typing every line number. A quicker way is to transmit the system command

SCRATCH

The command SCRATCH does not affect the name of a program. It only deletes the instructions. To change the name on some systems, transmit the command NAME followed by a dash and the name of the new program. On other systems, transmit the systems command NEW and the computer will request a new name, which should then be given.

5 | decisions and transfers

This section introduces the first programs in which the statements are not executed in the order of ascending line number. Any statement that causes the computer to vary from its ordinary execution sequence is called a *transfer statement*.

conditional transfer

The language BASIC includes a simple device for making a decision, as illustrated in the program DIVIDE, whose purpose is to determine if one given integer (a whole number) divides another evenly (i.e., it decides whether the quotient is a whole number).

```
LIST
DIVIDE

100   PRINT "GREETINGS"
110   PRINT
120   READ X,Y
130   DATA 512,8192
140   IF INT(Y/X)=Y/X THEN 170
150   PRINT X;" DOES NOT DIVIDE ";Y
160   STOP
170   PRINT X;" DIVIDES ";Y
180   END


RUN
DIVIDE

GREETINGS

 512    DIVIDES   8192

DONE
```

Line 100 is an example of how a PRINT statement may be used to type out a message. Whatever is inside the quotation marks will be printed. A PRINT statement with no operand, as in line 110, tells the computer to skip a line. Thus, the computer begins the execution of the program DIVIDE by printing the word "greetings" and then skipping a line. Line 120 instructs the computer to assign the values in the DATA statement at line 130 to the variables X and Y.

Line 140 is an example of a conditional transfer that involves a decision. The notation INT( ) stands for what is commonly called "the greatest integer function". It associates to its argument (whatever number lies within the parentheses) the greatest integer that is less than or equal to that argument. For example,

$$INT(3.1) = 3 \quad INT(5.97) = 5 \quad INT(17) = 17$$
$$INT(-2.4) = -3$$

Evidently, $INT(N) = N$ if and only if the number N is an integer. Therefore, $INT(Y/X) = Y/X$ in line 140 if and only if Y/X is an integer, that is, if and only if X divides Y. Since 512 (the present value of X) divides 8192 (the present value of Y), the computer takes its next instruction at line 170. If the condition did not hold, then the computer would have proceeded in the order of ascending line number to line 150.

Line 170 is a PRINT statement with three operands, which are separated by semicolons. As shown in the printout above, it causes the computer to first print the value of the variable X, then the word "divides", and then the value of the variable Y, all on the same line. Line 180 terminates the program.

If the data in line 130 were different, then there might be some changes in the execution of the program. For instance, suppose that line 130 were

```
130   DATA 317,17239
```

Then the result of running the program DIVIDE would be

```
RUN
DIVIDE

GREETINGS

 317   DOES NOT DIVIDE   17239

DONE
```

Since, in this case, the value of X (317) does not divide the value of Y (17239), the computer does not transfer from line 140 to line 170. It proceeds, instead, in the order of ascending line number to line 150. The execution of the program terminates with the STOP statement in line 160.

By changing only line 130 of the program DIVIDE, a programmer can test any pair of numbers to see if the first number divides the second.

stopping without ending

Most versions of BASIC do not prohibit the usage of more than one END statement in a program, but it is standard practice to use a STOP statement to terminate execution, as at line 160 of the program DIVIDE, except in the highest numbered line.

relation symbols

Six possible relations may occur in an IF statement. The relation = (equals), as used in line 140 of the program DIVIDE, the relation > (is greater than), and the relation < (is less than) are all denoted by the usual mathematical symbols. The relation >= (is greater than or equal to) and the relation <= (is less than or equal to) are both represented by two consecutive symbols. This is because neither the symbol $\geq$ nor the symbol $\leq$ appears on the teletypewriter keyboard. The relation <> (is not equal to or, equivalently, is less than or greater than) is also represented by two symbols, because the symbol $\neq$ is not on the keyboard.

Thus, when the computer executes the statement

it will transfer to line number 2041 if the values of B and F are unequal. Otherwise, the computer will proceed with the line whose number is next higher than 1396.

Any number, variable, or arithmetic expression may occur on either side of the relation in an IF statement.

flowcharts

The logical design of a program, particularly one which includes a decision, may be depicted by what is called a flowchart. Many programmers prefer to draw a flowchart before writing a program because the flowchart enables them to visualize what is going on. A flowchart is simply a series of descriptive blocks with some interconnecting arrows. For example, the flowchart in Figure 2 describes the program DIVIDE.

A reasonable requirement for a flowchart is that it should explain the problem to someone who is not a programmer. Therefore, it

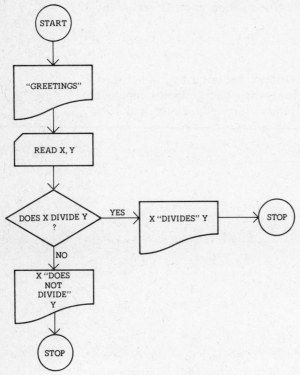

Figure 2   Flowchart of the program DIVIDE.

should not be dependent upon the language BASIC or upon any other particular language. A good flowchart rarely has one distinct block for each statement of the program. When a flowchart is drawn before the program it describes is written, it can be a great help in creating a correct program, particularly if that program contains logical complexities.

The circular block at the top of Figure 2 tells where to start. The language BASIC has no "START" instruction because execution generally begins at the lowest numbered line. However, anyone looking at a flowchart needs to know where processing begins, and using a starting block is a good way to indicate this.

Circular blocks are also commonly used to indicate possible places for termination of execution.

unconditional transfer

Suppose that a programmer wishes to specify at some line of his program that a transfer should always occur, regardless of the values of any variables or anything else. He might accomplish this by inserting an unconditionally true relation in an IF statement such as

```
140  IF 1=1 THEN 160
```

or, better, by inserting a GOTO statement, as at line 140 of the program PARITY, which determines whether a number supplied as data at line 110 is odd or even, prints a farewell message, and halts.

```
LIST
PARITY

100   READ X
110   DATA 212
120   IF INT(X/2)=X/2 THEN 150
130   PRINT X;" IS ODD"
140   GOTO 160
150   PRINT X;" IS EVEN"
160   PRINT "GOODBYE"
170   END


RUN
PARITY

 212    IS EVEN
GOODBYE

DONE
```

As illustrated by Figure 3, a GOTO statement does not require a block in a flowchart. Instead, it simply corresponds to a path from one block to another.

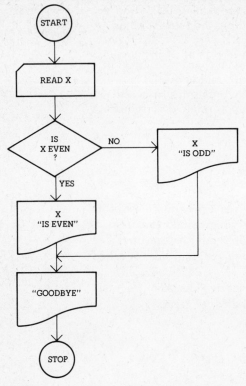

Figure 3   Flowchart of the program PARITY.

problems

1 Draw a flowchart for a program that decides if two numbers given as data are equal or unequal and prints out the word "equal" or the word "unequal" accordingly.

2 Write the program described in Problem 1.

3 Draw a flowchart for a program that determines which of three numbers supplied as data is smallest and prints that number followed by the words "is smallest" on the same line.

4 Write the program described in Problem 3.

5 Draw a flowchart for a program that accepts three numbers as data and prints them out in ascending order.

6 Write the program described in Problem 5.

7 A certain bank pays interest at an annual rate of 4.5 percent on accounts with less than $500, 4.75 percent on accounts with $500 to

$1,000, and 5 percent on accounts with more than $1,000. Draw a flowchart and write a program for computing the interest on an account whose balance is supplied as data.

8 A city devises an air pollution index such that less than 36 is "acceptable", from 36 to 58 is "unpleasant", and above 58 is "hazardous". Draw a flowchart and write a program that accepts an air pollution index as data and prints the appropriate description of the air.

6 | *loops*

The ability to make a decision is what gives a program most of its power because that capacity enables the programmer to specify that a particular collection of lines of code should be executed a large number of times. Such a collection of program lines is called a *loop*.

The first example of a loop is somewhat frivolous. The program HAPPY prints the message "happy birthday" 17 times.

```
LIST
HAPPY

100   LET I=1
110   PRINT "HAPPY BIRTHDAY"
120   LET I=I+1
130   IF I <= 17 THEN 110
140   END

RUN
HAPPY

HAPPY BIRTHDAY
HAPPY BIRTHDAY
HAPPY BIRTHDAY
HAPPY BIRTHDAY
HAPPY BIRTHDAY
HAPPY BIRTHDAY
HAPPY BIRTHDAY
HAPPY BIRTHDAY
HAPPY BIRTHDAY
HAPPY BIRTHDAY
HAPPY BIRTHDAY
HAPPY BIRTHDAY
HAPPY BIRTHDAY
HAPPY BIRTHDAY
HAPPY BIRTHDAY
HAPPY BIRTHDAY
HAPPY BIRTHDAY

DONE
```

Line 100 assigns to the variable I the initial value 1. Line 110 prints the message "happy birthday". Line 120 increases the value of the variable I by 1. If at the time that line 130 is executed the value of the variable I is less than or equal to 17, then the computer takes the transfer back to line 110. Otherwise, it proceeds with line 140 and halts execution. Although lines 100 and 140 are each executed but once, lines 110, 120, and 130 are each executed 17 times.

Some serious applications of loops occur in the programmed solutions to certain mathematical problems. One such problem is determining whether a given positive integer is a prime number. The reader will recall that a positive integer greater than 1 is called prime if its only divisors are 1 and itself. The number 5 is prime because it is not divisible by any of the numbers 2, 3, and 4. The number 49 is not prime, however, since it is divisible by 7. The program PRIME determines if a number supplied as data in line 110 is prime.

```
LIST
PRIME

100   READ N
110   DATA 11213
111   IF INT(N)=N THEN 115
112   PRINT N;" IS NOT AN INTEGER"
113   STOP
115   IF N >= 2 THEN 120
116   PRINT N;" IS LESS THAN 2"
117   STOP
120   LET I=2
130   IF I>N-1 THEN 170
140   IF INT(N/I)=N/I THEN 190
150   LET I=I+1
160   GOTO 130
170   PRINT N;" IS PRIME"
180   STOP
190   PRINT N;" IS NOT PRIME"
200   END

RUN
PRIME

  11213     IS PRIME

DONE
```

The procedure that the program PRIME uses to determine if the number in the DATA statement at line 110 is prime is to attempt to divide that number by all possible integers between (but not including) 1 and the number. Since the number 11213 is prime, the computer executes lines 130 to 150 exactly 11211 times, prints a message at line 170 and halts.

checking data

Lines 111 to 113 print an error message and halt execution of the program if the number supplied at line 110 is not an integer. Lines 115 to 117 print an error message and halt execution if the number supplied is less than 2. It is a good programming principle to check the data, as illustrated by lines 111 to 117 of PRIME, rather than carelessly assuming that correct data will be supplied in all future applications of a program.

infinite loops

A common mistake in programming is to indicate the wrong line in a transfer statement. The result of such a mistake might be a program that never stops. For example, if line 160 of the program PRIME were

```
160   GOTO 120
```

then the program would run forever (for N = 11213 or other odd integer values of N $\geq$ 3).The problem is that lines 120 to 150 would form an infinite loop, that is, a collection of instructions which the computer is doomed to repeat endlessly. Each time, line 120 would set the value of I at 2. Line 130 would determine that 2 does not exceed 11212 and omit the transfer. Line 140 would not transfer because 2 does not divide 11213. Line 150 would increase the value of I to 3. And line 160 would transfer back to line 120. Line 120 would reset the value of I at 2, and so on.

If a program is running and the computer does not complete execution within a reasonable time, then the program might contain an infinite loop. To regain control of the computer, push the keyboard button labeled BREAK. The computer will print the word STOP and halt execution. The program may now be corrected by inserting, deleting, or changing lines in the usual manner.

FOR–NEXT loops

The language BASIC includes a pair of instructions, FOR and NEXT, which make it particularly easy to design loops. The program PRIME*, whose purpose is the same as the program PRIME, illustrates the use of FOR and NEXT.

A FOR statement always specifies a FOR-variable, in this case I, which appears after the word FOR; a lower limit, in this case 2, which is the value of the expression preceding the word TO; and an upper limit, in this case 1536, which is the value of the expression following the word TO. Whenever a program has a FOR statement, it must also have a NEXT statement in which the FOR-variable follows the word NEXT.

The computer begins to execute a FOR statement by assigning the lower limit to the FOR-variable. If the lower limit exceeds the

```
LIST
PRIME*

100    READ N
110    DATA 1537
111    IF INT(N)=N THEN 115
112    PRINT N;" IS NOT AN INTEGER"
113    STOP
115    IF N >= 2 THEN 120
116    PRINT N;" IS LESS THAN 2"
117    STOP
120    FOR I=2 TO N-1
140    IF INT(N/I)=N/I THEN 190
150    NEXT I
170    PRINT N;" IS PRIME"
180    STOP
190    PRINT N;" IS NOT PRIME"
200    END


RUN
PRIME*

   1537       IS NOT PRIME

DONE
```

upper limit, then there is an immediate transfer to the line following the NEXT statement. Usually, as in the program PRIME*, the lower limit is less than or equal to the upper limit, and the computer takes its next instruction from the line immediately following the FOR statement.

When execution reaches the NEXT statement, the FOR-variable is incremented by 1. If the value of the FOR-variable is still less than or equal to the upper limit, then the computer transfers back to the line following the FOR statement. Thus, the statements in the loop will be reexecuted, with a new value for the FOR-variable. This process is repeated each time the NEXT statement is reached, until the FOR-variable becomes greater than the upper limit. The computer then leaves the FOR–NEXT loop by going to the line following the NEXT statement for its next instruction.

The obvious advantage of using the statements FOR and NEXT over creating any other sort of loop is that the position of a FOR–NEXT loop in the program is so completely clear. The statements FOR and NEXT can only indicate a loop.

flowcharts with loops

The FOR statement in BASIC is so powerful that it requires two blocks in a flowchart. Generally, one uses a rectangular block and a diamond-shaped block, as shown in Figure 4. The rectangular block assigns the lower limit to the FOR-variable and the diamond-shaped block tests to see if the FOR-variable exceeds the upper limit. The NEXT statement requires only a rectangular block

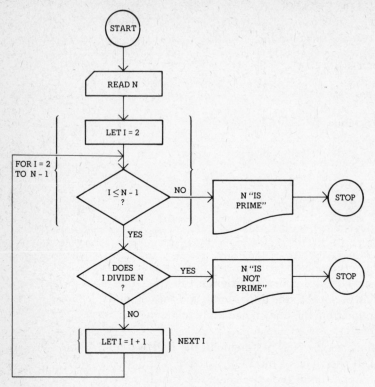

Figure 4   Flowchart of the program PRIME*.

which increments the value of the FOR-variable by 1. The arrow
leading from this block goes back to the diamond-shaped block
belonging to the FOR statement.

FOR *without* NEXT

A program containing a FOR statement without a corresponding
NEXT statement will be rejected by the compiler. The RUN
command will yield an error message, and the computer will not
attempt to execute any part of the program. Similarly, the compiler
will reject any program containing a stray NEXT statement that
is not properly paired with some FOR statement.

problems

1   Write a program that prints each of the integers from 7 to 39.

2   Write a program that prints each of the odd integers from 7
to 39.

3 Write a program that prints all the divisors of a number supplied as data. For example, the number 12 has the divisors 1, 2, 3, 4, 6, and 12.

4 Write a program that determines the least common multiple of two numbers supplied as data. For example, the multiples of the number 4 are 4, 8, 12, 16, . . . , and the multiples of the number 6 are 6, 12, 18, ... The least common multiple of 4 and 6, that is, the smallest number which is a multiple both of 4 and of 6, is 12.

5 The greatest common divisor of two positive integers is the largest positive integer that divides both of them. Write a program that determines the greatest common divisor of two numbers supplied as data.

6 The Fibonacci sequence 1, 1, 2, 3, 5, 8, 13, . . . has the property that each number (except for the first two) is the sum of the two preceding numbers. Write a program that prints the first 30 numbers in the Fibonacci sequence.

7 Write a program that computes the sum of the numbers
$1 + \frac{1}{2} + \frac{1}{3} + \frac{1}{4} + \cdots + \frac{1}{100}$.

8 Write a program that computes the sum of the numbers
$\frac{1}{2} + \frac{2}{3} + \frac{3}{4} + \frac{4}{5} + \cdots + \frac{99}{100}$.

7 | *numbers, variables, and expressions*

The early sections of this chapter try to avoid overburdening the reader with definitions. This section fills in some of the omitted details. It provides precise terminology required for a thorough understanding of the language BASIC.

numbers

Numbers occur in BASIC in any of three possible forms. The numbers 45 and −317, for example, are said to be in *integer form.* The numbers 41.37 and −16.2 are in *decimal form.* And the numbers 15 E 6 and 7.2 E −8 are in *exponent form.* To evaluate a number in exponent form, multiply the number to the left of the letter "E" times 10 to the power given at the right of the letter "E". Thus, 15 E 6 means 15×10^6 (15000000) and 7.2 E −8 means 7.2×10^{-8} (.000000072). The exponent part (the number at the right of the letter "E") must be an integer written without a decimal point.

The BASIC numbers 41, 41., 41.0, and 4.1 E 1 all have the same internal meaning to the computer. For most purposes, the programmer may use them interchangeably in his program. (One exception is that a line number must be in integer form.) A programmer may be unable to force the computer to print a particular number in the form he desires.

Some BASIC systems permit numbers to have only six significant digits. Others allow more. A programmer can determine by experimentation how many significant digits are available in the system he is using. To do this, log in on the computer and begin writing the following lines.

```
400   PRINT 1111
500   PRINT 11111
600   PRINT 111111
700   PRINT 1111111
ERROR-TOO MANY DIGITS
```

The error message occurs here because the system used by the authors allows only six significant digits and line 700 has a number with seven. If, on some other system, it were possible to write the number 11111111 but not the number 111111111 without getting an error message, then the programmer would know that the maximum number of significant digits on that system was eight.

A programmer can also determine by experimentation the maximum and minimum absolute values of numbers in a BASIC system. This is accomplished by typing lines which include the numbers 1 E 30, 1 E 40, 1 E 50, and so on, until an error message is obtained. If 1 E 50 causes the error message, then try 1 E 41, 1 E 42, and so on, until another error message appears. If, for example, 1 E 47 causes the error message, then 1 E 46 is the approximate maximum absolute value of a number in the system. A similar method yields the approximate minimum absolute value. (The *absolute value* of a positive number or zero means the number itself. The *absolute value* of a negative number means the number obtained by dropping the minus sign.)

variables

The only kind of variable which has occurred so far is a simple variable. (Subscripted variables and string variables are discussed in later chapters.) In BASIC, a simple variable is represented either by a single letter, such as C or X, or by a letter followed by a digit, such as A7 or Z3.

A variable may assume many different values during the execution of a program, but each must be a valid BASIC number. The limitations on the number of significant digits and on maximum and minimum absolute values apply not only to constants and printed numbers but also to intermediate values of variables during computations.

Unassigned variables occasionally cause a novice programmer some difficulty. For example, running the program UV results in an error message.

```
LIST
UV

100   PRINT X
999   END


RUN
UV

UNDEFINED VALUE ACCESSED IN LINE 100
```

The computer is unable to execute line 100 because it cannot print the value of a variable which has never been assigned a value. Errors involving unassigned variables are usually more subtle than the one in the program UV, but the error message shown always indicates that the first time the computer tried to execute the specified line some variable in that line had no value.

exponentiation operation

The first section of this chapter introduced symbols for the operations of addition, subtraction, multiplication, and division. The language BASIC includes one additional operation, exponentiation, which is denoted by an arrow pointing upward.
Thus,

$2 \uparrow 3$ means $2^3 = 2 \times 2 \times 2 = 8$

and

$1.1 \uparrow 4$ means $1.1^4 = 1.1 \times 1.1 \times 1.1 \times 1.1 = 1.4641$

In BASIC, the only permitted exponents are integers, including zero and negative numbers. Although fractional exponents have a well-defined mathematical meaning, they are not allowed.

simple numeric expressions

A *simple numeric expression* in BASIC is a finite sequence of BASIC numbers with interspaced BASIC operation symbols.
For example,

5 $5 * 3$ $5 * 3 - 2$ $5 * 3 - 2 \uparrow 4$ $5 * 3 - 2 \uparrow 4 + 7.1$

are all simple numeric expressions. A number following the exponentiation symbol ↑ must be an integer.

A simple numeric expression is evaluated according to the usual mathematical rules.

1 Apply every exponentiation (↑) operator, proceeding from left to right.
2 Then apply every multiplication (*) and division (/) operator, proceeding from left to right.
3 Then apply every addition (+) and subtraction (−) operator, proceeding from left to right.

The following two examples illustrate the evaluation procedure.

Example 1   5 * 3 − 2 ↑ 4 + 7.1.
Apply rule 1 to obtain 5 * 3 − 16 + 7.1.
Apply rule 2 to obtain 15 − 16 + 7.1.
Apply rule 3 to obtain −1 + 7.1; we then have 6.1.

Example 2   4 + 12/2 − 1 + 5 * 3 ↑ 2.
Apply rule 1 to obtain 4 + 12/2 − 1 + 5 * 9.
Apply rule 2 to obtain 4 + 6 − 1 + 5 * 9; we then have
4 + 6 − 1 + 45.
Apply rule 3 to obtain 10 − 1 + 45; we then have 9 + 45, which gives us 54.

The "left to right" part of each rule is essential. It means that

10 − 1 + 45

is evaluated as

9 + 45 = 54

instead of

10 − 46 = −36

compound numeric expressions

A *compound numeric expression* is one that involves parentheses. For the usual mathematical reasons, there must be exactly as many right parentheses as there are left parentheses, and a pair of parentheses should enclose a legitimate numeric expression, either compound or simple. A compound expression is evaluated by the usual mathematical method of first evaluating the simple expressions contained in the innermost pairs of parentheses and proceeding outward until all parentheses are gone.

Example $(8 \uparrow (3 * 2 - 5) - 6) * (4 - 3 \uparrow (8/4))$. The innermost pairs of parentheses contain the simple expressions

$3 * 2 - 5$ and $8/4$

These are evaluated as

$3 * 2 - 5 = 6 - 5 = 1$ and $8/4 = 2$

and the result is used to simplify the original compound expression

$(8 \uparrow 1 - 6) * (4 - 3 \uparrow 2)$

The new set of innermost pairs of parentheses contains expressions to be evaluated.

$8 \uparrow 1 - 6 = 8 - 6 = 2$ and $4 - 3 \uparrow 2 = 4 - 9 = -5$

This information is used to further simplify the original expression to the form

$2 * (-5)$

whose value is

-10

arithmetic expressions

An *arithmetic expression* is almost the same as a numeric expression, except that some of the numbers are represented by variables. For example,

$B \uparrow (5 - Q)$ and $J * 7.09 + D$

are arithmetic expressions. To evaluate an arithmetic expression, first replace each variable name by its value and then evaluate the resulting numeric expression.

Being able to recite definitions of "simple expression" or "compound expression" is not very important to the reader. What matters is knowing how the computer will evaluate whatever expressions occur in practice, as indicated by the reader's success in doing the problems at the end of this section.

round-off error

In mathematical theory the expressions

$(2/7) * 21$ and $(2 * 21)/7$

are both evaluated as 6. Regrettably, a limitation to six significant digits may result in the evaluations

$(2/7) * 21 = .285714 * 21 = 5.99999$ and $(2 * 21)/7 = 42/7 = 6$

Other examples of round-off error may occur in a computation. The programmer is cautioned not to expect absolute accuracy.

checking answers to problems

Answers to the problems at the end of this section may be checked on the computer. To check an answer to the first part of Problem 2, transmit the line

```
100  PRINT 1E-20
```

If no error message appears, then 1 E -20 is a valid BASIC number. To check (or to obtain) an answer to the second part of Problem 4, run the program

```
100  PRINT 12/6*2↑2
999  END
```

problems

1 Write each of the following BASIC numbers in its integer form if possible. Otherwise write it in decimal form.

3 E -2 1.07 E 2   .15 E 1   .00712 E 4   .01175 E 5
81.00

2 Which of the following are not valid BASIC numbers? Give reasons.

1 E -20 E -2 3.4 E 7   5 E $(2 * 3)$ -2.9 E 0
4 E .5   4 E 0.5

3 Which of the following are not simple variable names in BASIC? Give reasons.

G12   AT7   B5   I

4 Evaluate each of the following expressions.

$12 * 6/2 \uparrow 2$ $12/6 * 2 \uparrow 2$ $12/2 \uparrow 2 * 6$ $2 \uparrow 2 * 6/12 - 7 + 3$

5 Evaluate each of the following expressions.

$2 \uparrow (5 - 3)$ $((6 * 2) \uparrow (5 - 3)/(16 * 3 \uparrow 2)) * 4$
$(1 + 3) \uparrow ((-2) * ((6 * 2) \uparrow (5 - 3)/(16 * 3 \uparrow 2)))$

6 Evaluate each of the following expressions assuming that the value of X is 3 and the value of Y is −4.

$$7 - X - Y \qquad (X + Y) * 7 \qquad (X - Y)/7 \qquad 3 - X + Y - X * Y$$

8 | *storing programs for later use*

The contents of the scratch area vanish when the teletypewriter is disconnected from the system, whether by the logging-out procedure or otherwise. They also vanish when the programmer transmits the system command SCRATCH. It is possible, however, to save a copy of the program in the scratch area by transmitting the system command

SAVE

This causes the computer to place a copy of the program in disk storage.

retrieving programs

If a program has been placed in disk storage, there is an easy way to obtain a copy of it in the scratch area at a later time. On some systems this is accomplished by transmitting the system command

GET-

followed by the name of the program. For example, if the program of an earlier section has been saved in disk storage, the command

GET-DIVIDE

would cause a copy of DIVIDE to be placed in the scratch area. On some systems, instead of GET, the programmer uses the command

OLD

When the computer responds with the question

NAME?

the programmer types the name of the program in disk storage that he wants copied into the scratch area.

A unique region in disk storage is associated with each user number so that a programmer has access only to his own programs. He need not worry that the computer will be confused if some other programmer has given a program the same name as one of his own programs. It is not possible, however, for a programmer to store two programs with the same name under the same user number.

Retrieving a program from disk storage with the GET command or otherwise does not affect the copy of the program in disk storage. That copy is not destroyed or altered. However, it totally obliterates the previous contents of the scratch area.

If there is a copy of a program in disk storage and another copy in the scratch area, then only the copy in the scratch area will be affected by insertions, deletions, or changes of lines or by the command SCRATCH. How to change the copy in disk storage is described later in this section.

catalog

Transmitting the command CATALOG causes the computer to print the name of every program saved under a programmer's user number. For example, if the programs DIVIDE and PRIME* are saved, then the command CATALOG yields the following.

```
CATALOG

DIVIDE      PRIME*
```

erasing a program in disk storage

Suppose that a programmer wants to erase the copy of a program, say, the program DIVIDE, in disk storage. Then he transmits the command

```
KILL-DIVIDE
```

This procedure does not affect the contents of the scratch area. On some systems the more euphemistic word UNSAVE is used instead of KILL. Since disk storage is usually a scarce resource, a programmer should periodically remove programs that have become obsolete.

The procedure for changing the lines of a program in disk storage is slightly complicated. First, retrieve the program from disk storage and place it in the scratch area. Then, make all necessary changes in the scratch area copy. Next, kill the disk storage copy. And finally, save the corrected copy lying in the scratch area.

public library

Most BASIC systems include a "public library" containing programs of general interest. Whereas a programmer cannot retrieve programs stored under someone else's user number, anyone can retrieve a program in the public library. To determine the contents of the public library, transmit the command

```
LIBRARY
```

The computer will print the names of the programs available. The programmer must either know the contents of a library program or determine them by listing, after he has placed it in his scratch area. Public library programs are retrieved by the usual retrieval procedure, except that the name of the library program is preceded by a dollar sign, as in the example

```
GET-$FTBALL
```

that (on many systems) retrieves the famous football-playing demonstration program created by John G. Kemeny, now president of Dartmouth College.

2

advanced BASIC

THE LANGUAGE BASIC includes several features beyond the elementary ones already presented. The first section of this chapter describes the INPUT statement, which instructs the computer to interrupt program execution in order to receive additional information. The second and third sections discuss how to create functions and subroutines, which circumvent the task of writing repetitious code. The fourth section gives a method for reusing the data on the data stack. The fifth section discusses the use of subscripted variables. The sixth section summarizes the present description of BASIC. Some special features of BASIC and a few minor details are introduced in later chapters as the need for them arises.

Users of IBM CALL/360 BASIC should continue to consult Appendix A.

1 | supplying input

The programs of this section are designed to teach arithmetic to a child. Although this facility was not demonstrated by any program of the previous chapter, the computer is able to interrupt its execution of a program in order to receive information from the teletypewriter and then to use this information when it resumes execution. In this section, the information to be received during the interruption is the child's answer to a problem in arithmetic.

computer-assisted instruction

The flowchart in Figure 1 depicts a scheme for teaching addition of
two integers between 0 and 10. Immediately below the circular
starting block is a rectangular block indicating that the computer is

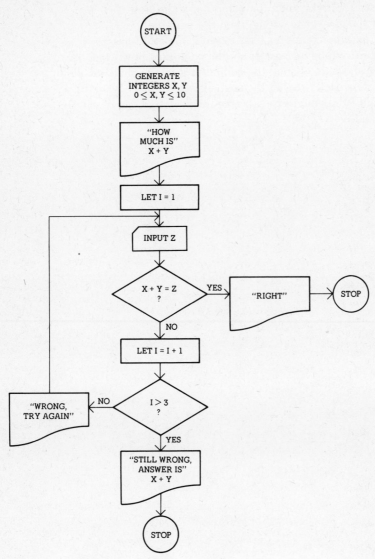

Figure 1   Flowchart of the program ADD.

to generate two such numbers. The next block calls for the computer to print on the teletypewriter a message to the child asking for their sum.

The rectangular block assigning the value 1 to the variable I sets up a loop which will allow the child three chances to get the correct answer. The next block, labeled "input Z", is the place where the computer is supposed to interrupt execution and wait for the child's answer. If the answer is right, then the computer so informs the child and halts. If the answer is wrong, then the variable I is incremented by 1 and the computer tests to see if the child has given his or her third wrong answer. If so, the computer prints out the correct answer and halts. If not, the computer asks the child to try again and transfers back to await the next answer.

The program ADD implements the ideas of the flowchart.

```
LIST
ADD

100   LET X=INT(11*RND(1))
110   LET Y=INT(11*RND(2))
120   PRINT "HOW MUCH IS ";X;" AND ";Y
125   LET I=1
130   INPUT Z
140   IF X+Y=Z THEN 170
142   LET I=I+1
144   IF I>3 THEN 150
146   PRINT "WRONG. TRY AGAIN."
148   GOTO 130
150   PRINT "STILL WRONG. THE ANSWER IS ";X+Y
160   STOP
170   PRINT "RIGHT. VERY GOOD."
180   END


RUN
ADD

HOW MUCH IS  4      AND  7
?9
WRONG. TRY AGAIN.
?13
WRONG. TRY AGAIN.
?12
STILL WRONG. THE ANSWER IS   11

DONE


RUN
ADD

HOW MUCH IS  4      AND  7
?9
WRONG. TRY AGAIN.
?13
WRONG. TRY AGAIN.
?12
STILL WRONG. THE ANSWER IS   11

DONE
```

random numbers

Line 100 of the program ADD uses the built-in functions RND and INT to generate a random integer between 0 and 10. The term RND(1) in line 100 means a random number between (but not including) 0 and 1. It follows that 11 * RND(1) is a random number between (but not including) 0 and 11. Since the built-in function INT drops the fractional part of its argument, the term INT(11 * RND(1)) means a random integer between 0 and 10.

The value produced by applying RND to a number does not depend on that number. That is, RND(3.14) and RND(−2) are also random numbers between 0 and 1. What is important is that every time the function RND appears in a BASIC program, no matter what its argument, the computer produces a new random number. It is understood that the likelihood of the occurrence of any one particular random number between 0 and 1 is as great as the likelihood of the occurrence of any other random number.

Thus, line 100 assigns to the variable X a random integer between 0 and 10. Any of these integers is equally likely. Similarly, line 110 assigns to the variable Y a random integer between 0 and 10. As in line 100, the chance of any particular one of these integers occurring is 1/11.

INPUT *statement*

The INPUT statement at line 130 interrupts the running of the program ADD. The computer begins the execution of line 130 by printing a question mark. It then waits for a response from the teletypewriter. The child sees the following

```
HOW MUCH IS  4     AND  7
?
```

The computer is in no particular hurry for the child to answer. Under a time-sharing system the computer can execute programs submitted at other terminals, so its patience is unlimited. When the child has an answer, he types it and pushes the RETURN button. The computer completes the execution of line 130 by assigning the child's answer to the variable Z.

The child is not expected to know anything about programming. It is sufficient for the teacher to demonstrate the use of the numbered buttons at the top of the keyboard and the RETURN button.

In general, the program ADD follows the flowchart in Figure 1, which was described earlier.

twenty addition problems

A few modifications in the program ADD yield the program ADD*, which gives the child three chances at each of 20 addition problems. The main change needed is the insertion of lines 90 and 172 to create a FOR–NEXT loop. Another important change is the replacement of the STOP statement in line 160 of ADD by a transfer to the NEXT statement in line 172. Leaving the STOP statement would have a very undesirable effect, terminating execution of the program after any addition problem that the child cannot do correctly within three tries. In other words, the program would refuse to educate the child who most needed the practice!

```
LIST
ADD*

80   REM TWENTY ADDITION PROBLEMS
90   FOR J=1 TO 20
100   LET X=INT(11*RND(1))
110   LET Y=INT(11*RND(2))
115   PRINT
120   PRINT "HOW MUCH IS ";X;" AND ";Y;" ";
125   LET I=1
130   INPUT Z
140   IF X+Y=Z THEN 170
142   LET I=I+1
144   IF I>3 THEN 150
146   PRINT "WRONG. TRY AGAIN. ";
148   GOTO 130
150   PRINT "STILL WRONG. THE ANSWER IS ";X+Y
160   GOTO 172
170   PRINT "RIGHT. VERY GOOD."
172   NEXT J
175   PRINT "GOODBYE NOW."
180   END


RUN
ADD*

HOW MUCH IS  4     AND  7 ?10
WRONG. TRY AGAIN. ?11
RIGHT. VERY GOOD.

                    •
                    •
                    •
          18 more problems
                    •
                    •
                    •

HOW MUCH IS  8     AND  6 ?14
RIGHT. VERY GOOD.
GOODBYE NOW.

DONE
```

The reader might wonder, however, why line 160 of ADD* is not

```
160  NEXT J
```

The reason is that the language BASIC insists that FOR and NEXT statements be paired, and line 172 is the NEXT statement that is paired with the FOR statement in line 90.

remarks

It is often helpful for a program to include a remark about the purpose of the program or of a group of statements within the program. For one thing, a remark can make it easier for someone other than the original programmer to understand the program. For another, it reminds the original programmer himself of certain information about one program that he might forget while he is working on several others. A remark in BASIC is given as the text of a REM statement, as seen at line 80 of the program ADD*.

A REM statement does not cause the computer to do any work during program execution. Although the computer prints the remark in a program listing, it simply ignores the remark during program execution and proceeds to the next statement in the usual order of ascending line number. Unlike certain other languages, BASIC allows a program to transfer to a remark.

more about PRINT statements

The PRINT statement at line 115 with no operand causes a carriage return and linefeed. Its purpose is to skip a line between two consecutive problems. The PRINT statement at line 175 gives a farewell message to the child after the 20 problems. These two forms of the PRINT statement have been discussed previously. Lines 120 and 146 contain a new variation. The semicolon at the end of the line tells the computer to suppress the carriage return and linefeed that would usually follow the printing of the line. Thus, the question mark generated by the INPUT statement at line 130 and the answer supplied by the child appear on the same line of the run printout as the output from either line 120 or line 146.

teaching subtraction, multiplication, and division

It is easy to modify the program ADD* so that it can teach a child a great deal of arithmetic. For example, to teach the addition of two numbers between 0 and 100, replace lines 100 and 110 by

```
100   LET X=INT(101*RND(1))
110   LET Y=INT(101*RND(2))
```

To teach subtraction, replace lines 120, 140, and 150 by

```
120   PRINT "HOW HUCH IS ";X;" - ";Y;"  ";
140   IF X-Y=Z THEN 170
150   PRINT "STILL WRONG.   THEN ANSWER IS ";X-Y
```

and to avoid negative answers insert the line

```
111   IF X<Y THEN 100
```

To teach multiplication, replace lines 120, 140, and 150 of ADD* by
the lines

```
120   PRINT "HOW MUCH IS ";X;" TIMES ";Y;"  ";
140   IF X*Y=Z THEN 170
150   PRINT "STILL WRONG.   THE ANSWER IS ";X*Y
```

Teaching division without remainder requires the generation of a
dividend which is an integral multiple of the divisor. While it is
possible to wait for an appropriate pair of random numbers, it is
more efficient to obtain two random numbers X and Y and to ask
the child to divide X into the product X * Y. It is important that X
is not zero, because division by zero is undefined. Determining the
coding changes to ADD* needed to produce a program that teaches
division without remainder is left as a problem at the end of this
section.

more about the function RND

In most BASIC systems the program ADD* will produce the same
20 problems every time it runs. The reason for this is that a
computer operating under BASIC depends on a fixed sequence of
random numbers for its supply.

One way to overcome this limitation is to deliberately jump
ahead in the sequence before obtaining any addition problems. For
example, the programmer might place the following instructions at
the beginning of the program.

```
10   PRINT "CHOOSE A NUMBER FROM 1 TO 1000"
20   INPUT N
30   FOR I=1 TO N
40   LET T=RND(1)
50   NEXT I
```

Whatever number N is typed by the teacher or the child in response to line 20, the computer will skip the first N random numbers in the sequence. Thus, by choosing different values of N, the teacher or child can select different collections of 20 problems.

Some BASIC systems will start at different places in the random number sequence if the program writes the special statement

```
1   RANDOMIZE
```

in which case he may omit lines 10 to 50 above. Such systems choose a starting point in the sequence by computing a number based on the time of day, calibrated in fractions of a second.

problems

1 Write a LET statement that uses the functions INT and RND to assign to the variable X a random integer between −7 and 15.

2 Write a LET statement that uses the functions INT and RND to assign to the variable X a random odd integer between 3 and 21.

3 Write a program that asks for a number as input and then computes and prints its cube.

4 Write a program that computes and prints the sum of the squares of three numbers supplied as input.

5 Draw a flowchart for the program ADD*, which is listed in this section.

6 Write a program that teaches division without remainder.

7 Write a program that teaches division with remainder.

8 Write a program that gives a multiple-choice history examination consisting of one question.

9 The game of matchsticks begins with 15 matchsticks in a row. There are two players and they take alternate turns. On each turn a player may remove 1, 2, or 3 matchsticks. Whoever takes the last stick wins. Write a program that allows a person to play the game of matchsticks against the computer. (Let the computer choose its plays randomly.)

10 Write a program that plays the game of matchsticks (see Problem 9) so that whenever the computer goes first it is sure to win.

11 The rules for "reverse matchsticks" are the same as for matchsticks, except that whoever takes the last stick loses. Write a program that plays reverse matchsticks.

2 | BASIC *functions*

The built-in functions INT and RND have already appeared in several programs. This section introduces three more built-in functions of general interest. It also explains how a programmer may create special-purpose functions himself.

absolute value

The *absolute value* of a number X is defined to be the number X itself if X is either positive or zero and to be $-X$ if X is negative. The usual mathematical notation for the absolute value of X is $|X|$. In BASIC, the notation is ABS(X). For instance,

ABS(5) = 5   ABS(-18.01) = 18.01   ABS(0) = 0

sign

The *sign* of a number X is defined to be 1 if X is positive, 0 if X is 0, and -1 if X is negative. Thus,

SGN(0) = 0   SGN(5) = 1   SGN(-18.01) = -1

square root

If the product of a number Y with itself is a number X, then Y is called a *square root* of X. Every positive number has a positive square root and a negative square root whose absolute values are the same. For example,

$1.2 * 1.2 = (-1.2) * (-1.2) = 1.44$

The language BASIC prefers the positive square root and denotes it by SQR(X). If X = 0, then SQR(X) = 0. If X is a negative number, then SQR(X) is undefined, because BASIC does not admit the so-called imaginary numbers.

Some additional built-in functions, including the trigonometric functions, are discussed in Chapter 5.

programmer-defined functions

The program POLY illustrates the feature of the language BASIC that permits a programmer to create additional functions beyond the built-in functions.

```
LIST
POLY

50   DEF FNF(X)=X↑3+4*X↑2-6*X+11
100    READ A
110    DATA 2
120    PRINT FNF(A)
999    END


RUN
POLY

 23

DONE
```

Line 50 of POLY tells the computer that whenever it encounters the function FNF in the rest of the program, it should apply the polynomial function given in line 50 to the argument. Since

$$2^3 + 4 \times 2^2 - 6 \times 2 + 11 = 8 + 16 - 12 + 11 = 23$$

the computer prints the number 23 in the execution of line 120.

The definition of a function by a DEF statement may include one or more built-in functions. For example, the line

```
75   DEF FNR(X)=INT(X+.5)
```

defines FNR to be a function that rounds a number to the nearest integer. A number whose fractional part is ½ is rounded upward. Thus,

$$FNR(2.1) = 2 \quad FNR(8.5) = 9 \quad FNR(1.67) = 2$$

Also, the line

```
70   DEF FNA(X)=INT(11*RND(1))
```

defines $FNA(X)$ to be a random integer between 0 and 10.

Every programmer-defined function has a three-letter name, the first two of which are F and N. In any particular program, a programmer may define as many as 26 functions with DEF statements.

The definition of a function by a DEF statement may include not only built-in functions but also functions created by the programmer in DEF statements elsewhere in the program, preferably with lower line numbers to avoid the possibility of circularity.

Functions of more than one variable do not exist in BASIC but they may be effectively obtained by using subroutines, as described in the next section.

problems

1 Write a DEF statement that creates a function which for any positive integer argument N produces a random integer between 0 and N.

2 Write a DEF statement that creates a function which associates to a nonnegative number X its fourth root, that is, a number Y such that $Y^4 = N$.

3 The "ramp function" assigns to the number X the value 0 if X is negative and the value X itself, otherwise. The name "ramp function" is derived from the appearance of its graph, which slopes upward at a 45° angle in the first quadrant, as seen in Figure 2. Write a DEF statement which uses the built-in function ABS to create the ramp function.

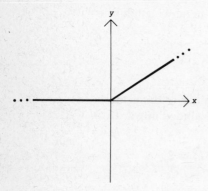

Figure 2   The graph of the ramp function.

The *characteristic function* (sometimes called the *indicator function*) of a set of real numbers is the function whose value on any argument in the given set is 1 and whose value on all other arguments is 0.

4 Write a DEF statement that uses the built-in functions SGN and ABS to create the characteristic function of the set {0}, that is, the function whose value on the argument 0 is 1 but whose value is otherwise 0.

5 Write a DEF statement creating the characteristic function of the set {1, 2, 3}. Hint: The value of the polynomial $(X - 1) * (X - 2) * (X - 3)$ is 0 if and only if X is 1, 2, or 3. Use the solution to Problem 4.

6 Write a DEF statement defining the characteristic function of the nonnegative numbers.

7 Write a DEF statement defining the characteristic function of the set of numbers greater than or equal to 3.

8 Write a DEF statement defining the characteristic function of the set of numbers less than or equal to 4.

3 | subroutines

When a program requires the repeated use of a sequence of statements, the creation of a subroutine may help the programmer to avoid their repetition in writing.

A program that computes binomial coefficients is a good illustration of a case where a subroutine is useful. The process that requires repetition is the computation of factorials. A brief review of the mathematics involved may be helpful.

The binomial coefficient $\binom{n}{j}$ is the coefficient of the term $x^{n-j}y^j$

in an expansion of $(x + y)^n$. For example, $(x + y)^2 = x^2 + 2xy + y^2$
Therefore,

$$\binom{2}{0} = 1 \qquad \binom{2}{1} = 2 \qquad \binom{2}{2} = 1$$

The expansion of $(x + y)^3$ is obtained by multiplication of an expansion of $(x + y)^2$ by $x + y$.

$$
\begin{aligned}
(x + y)^2 = \quad & x^2 + 2xy + y^2 \\
& \quad\quad\; x + y \\
\hline
& x^2y + 2xy^2 + y^3 \\
x^3 + 2x^2y + & \; xy^2 \\
\hline
(x + y)^3 = x^3 + 3x^2y + & 3xy^2 + y^3
\end{aligned}
$$

Therefore,

$$\binom{3}{0} = 1 \qquad \binom{3}{1} = 3 \qquad \binom{3}{2} = 3 \qquad \binom{3}{3} = 1$$

It is known, however, that there is a faster way to obtain binomial coefficients than expansion of $(x + y)^n$ by repeated multiplication. Precisely,

$$\binom{n}{j} = \frac{n!}{j!(n-j)!}$$

where n! ("*n* factorial") means the product of the integers 1, 2, 3, . . . , *n*. For instance,

$$4! = 1 \cdot 2 \cdot 3 \cdot 4 = 24$$

The program BNCOEF obtains binomial coefficients by using factorials.

```
LIST
BNCOEF

100   REM COMPUTE BINOMIAL COEFFICIENT OF  N   AND   J
110   READ N,J
120   DATA 7,4
130   LET X=N
140   GOSUB 300
150   LET B=F
160   LET X=J
170   GOSUB 300
180   LET B=B/F
190   LET X=N-J
200   GOSUB 300
210   PRINT "BIN COEFF OF ";N;" AND ";J;" IS ";B/F
220   STOP
300   REM ** SUBR ** F BECOMES X FACTORIAL
310   LET F=1
320   FOR I=1 TO X
330   LET F=F*I
340   NEXT I
350   RETURN
999   END


RUN
BNCOEF

BIN COEFF OF  7     AND  4     IS  35

DONE
```

Lines 300 to 350 of the program BNCOEF form a subroutine. A subroutine is almost, but not quite, a program in itself. Its last statement is generally RETURN instead of STOP or END. In this particular case, the value of the variable X must be assigned by the main program before it transfers to the subroutine. This subroutine assigns the value X factorial to the variable F before returning to the main program. It is recommended by the authors, but not required by the language BASIC, that the first line of a subroutine be a REM statement which states the purpose of the subroutine.

GOSUB *and* RETURN

The computer executes a GOSUB statement by doing two things. First, it records the line number of the next instruction following the GOSUB statement on a return-address stack. Then it transfers

to the indicated line. For example, the computer executes the
GOSUB instruction at line 140 of BNCOEF by recording the
number 150 on the return-address stack and transferring to line 300,
the REM statement identifying the subroutine.

The computer executes a RETURN statement by transferring to
the line whose number on the return-address stack was most
recently written and deleting that number from the stack. For
example, after line 140 has invoked the subroutine, the computer
executes the RETURN statement at line 350 by transferring back to
line 150 and deleting the number 150 from the stack, leaving it
empty.

The program BNCOEF computes binomial coefficients as follows.
It assigns the value of N to the variable X at line 130. Line 140
causes the subroutine to assign X factorial (i.e., N factorial) to the
variable F. Line 150 initializes the value of the variable B at F (i.e.,

N factorial). The variable B will ultimately have the value $\binom{N}{J}$.

Line 160 assigns the value of J to the variable X. Then the
invocation of the subroutine by line 170 causes the variable F to
assume the value J factorial. Line 180 resets the value of B to N!/J!.

Line 190 resets the variable X at N − J. Calling the subroutine
by the GOSUB statement in line 200 obtains N − J factorial as the
value of F. Finally, the computer executes line 210 by printing the
binomial coefficient and halting at line 220.

nesting subroutines

When one subroutine employs another, that is, when it contains a
GOSUB statement that calls a second subroutine, then the second
subroutine is said to be nested in the first. The program TWO,
which is simply an inefficient way of printing the number 2,
illustrates this concept.

The instructions of TWO are executed in the following order:
100, 110, 120, 200, 210, 220, 300, 310, 320, 230, 240, 130, 140. The
return-address stack is initially empty. After the GOSUB statement
at line 120 is executed it contains the list (130). After the GOSUB
statement at line 220 is executed it contains the list (130, 230). The
first RETURN instruction that is executed is at line 320. The
computer transfers to line 230, the most recently written address on
the list, and erases that address, so the list becomes (130) again.
The execution of the RETURN statement at line 240 transfers to
line 130 and erases the remaining entry on the stack. The maximum
number of entries on the return-address stack in many BASIC

```
LIST
TWO

100   REM ** MAIN PROGRAM IN LINES 100-140 **
110   LET X=1
120   GOSUB 200
130   PRINT X
140   STOP
200   REM ** SUBR **
210   LET Y=X
220   GOSUB 300
230   LET X=X+Y
240   RETURN
300   REM ** SUBR **
310   LET Y=Y
320   RETURN
999   END


RUN
TWO

 2

DONE
```

systems is about ten, so the programmer must be careful not to nest his subroutines too deep.

last-in-first-out stacks

The return-address stack is an example of a "last-in-first-out stack", which is an important concept of programming theory. The underlying principle is that whenever a RETURN statement is executed, the computer transfers to the most recently ("last-in") stored return address and removes that address from the stack.

Another descriptive term, equivalent to last-in-first-out stack, is "push-down stack", which is derived from the familiar clean-plate stack in a cafeteria. Each new plate pushes the stack down into the well so that the last plate in is the first plate out.

The next section describes another kind of stack, the first-in-first-out stack, which is treated like moviegoers in a queue for tickets. The first to arrive is the first to receive a ticket.

problems

1 Write a program that accepts seven positive integers as data and describes each as "odd" or "even". Use a subroutine to determine the parity of each number and print the description.

2 Write a program that considers three positive integers supplied as data and decides if the sum of any two of them is prime. The program should include a subroutine that determines if a number is prime.

3 Write a program that accepts three positive integers A, B, and C as data and determines which two of them have the smallest least common multiple.

4 Write a program that accepts three positive integers A, B, and C as data and computes the number A! + B! + C!. Use the subroutine of the program BNCOEF to compute the factorials.

5 Write a subroutine that computes the sum

$$\frac{1}{1} + \frac{1}{2} + \frac{1}{3} + \cdots + \frac{1}{N}$$

for any positive integer N. Let $h(N)$ denote this sum. Use this subroutine in a program that computes the product $h(A)h(B)h(C)$ for any three positive integers A, B, and C supplied as data.

4 | the data stack

The use of the DATA statement has been severely restricted thus far. First, no program has included more than one DATA statement. Second, the DATA statement in a program has always been immediately preceded by a READ statement. Third, the operand of that READ statement included one variable for each item of data in the DATA statement. None of these restrictions is necessary in a BASIC program. This section explains the technical relationship between DATA statements and READ statements.

subdivisions of the scratch area

When a programmer commands the computer to RUN a valid program in the scratch area, the computer must first perform the process called compilation, which was discussed briefly in Section 3 of Chapter 1. During compilation the computer reserves as many as four subsections of the scratch area. One subsection contains the executable statements of the program, translated into the internal machine language. A second subsection is storage space for the present values of variables. A third subsection is the return-address stack, which is used to execute the GOSUB and the RETURN statements. The fourth subregion is called the data stack, and it is an ordered list of BASIC numbers.

building the data stack

It is emphasized that the computer creates the data stack during compilation, before it begins running the program. It searches the lines of the program in the order of ascending line number. The first time it encounters a DATA statement, the computer begins the list by placing the numbers given in that statement into the data stack in the order in which they appear, from left to right. The computer resumes the search for DATA statements. When it encounters the next one, it continues the list by appending the numbers given in that second DATA statement. This process of building the data stack continues until the last line of the program is encountered.

For example, the program LIST has three DATA statements. The first contains seven numbers, the second contains four numbers, and the third contains four numbers. Therefore, the data stack for the program LIST contains 15 numbers $(15 = 7 + 4 + 4)$.

```
LIST
LIST

100    DATA 1,3,5,7,9,11,13
110    DATA 2,4,6,8
120    DATA 1,6,7,9
130    FOR I=1 TO 14
140    READ X
150    PRINT X;
160    NEXT I
170    END


RUN
LIST

 1      3     5     7     9     11    13    2     4     6     8     1
 6      7
DONE
```

Once the data stack of the program LIST is created, the computer is unconscious of lines 100, 110, and 120. A DATA statement is used only during compilation, not during the running of the program, when the computer refers only to the data stack.

The reader may observe that the computer is not puzzled by the use of the word LIST for the name of a program. From context it distinguishes between the use of LIST as a system command and as a program name.

The computer executes the program LIST by successively assigning to the variable I and then printing the first 14 numbers on the data stack. There is no obligation to read the remaining number. However, if the total number of times that the READ

statements of a program were executed exceeded the number of
items on the data stack, then the computer would terminate the
program with an error message, such as

OUT OF DATA

(unless the program contained a RESTORE statement—see below).

restoring the data pointer

Although no program yet presented has used this facility, it is
possible for items on the data stack to be read and reread as often
as the programmer chooses. This facility is best understood by
conceiving of a data pointer that indicates (at any time during the
running of the program) whatever number on the stack is to be
read next. When the program starts running, the pointer indicates
the first number on the stack. Every time a READ statement is
executed, the pointer moves down the stack by as many items as
there are variables named in the READ statement. Thus the
execution of the statement

250   READ D, E, F2

causes the data pointer to move three items down the stack. If the
same variable is named more than once in a READ statement, then,
for purposes of resetting the data pointer, it counts as more than
one variable. For example, the execution of the statement

375   READ A4, X, X, Y7, X

causes the data pointer to move five items down the stack.
   At any time during the running of a program, the data pointer
may be reset to the first item on the data stack by execution of a
RESTORE statement, as illustrated in the program LIST2.
The data stack for the program LIST2 is the ordered list

1, 2, 3, 4, 5, 6, 7

Line 100 causes three assignments of values to the variable X and
two assignments to Y. First X becomes 1, then Y becomes 2, then
X becomes 3, then Y becomes 4, and finally X becomes 5. Line 110
prints the values of X and Y. The data pointer is then indicating the
sixth item on the stack, but the RESTORE statement at line 120
puts it back at the first item.

```
LIST
LIST2

100    READ X,Y,X,Y,X
110    PRINT X;Y
120    RESTORE
130    READ Y,Y,X
140    PRINT X;Y
150    DATA 1,2,3
160    DATA 4,5,6,7
170    READ X
180    PRINT X
999    END


RUN
LIST2

    5       4
    3       2
    4

DONE
```

The READ statement at line 130 causes the value of Y first to become 1 and then to become 2, and it assigns the value 3 to the variable X. Line 140 prints the values of X and Y. The data pointer is then indicating the fourth item on the stack, which is assigned to X at line 170 and printed at line 180. Line 999 terminates the program.

Whenever the last item on the data stack is read, the pointer moves off the end of the stack. If the computer tries to read another item from the stack before it executes a RESTORE statement, then the program will be terminated with an error message, as mentioned earlier.

The reader may already see a variety of applications for RESTORE statements. Later programs will use RESTORE statements in a more critical way than the examples in this section.

first-in-first-out stacks

The data stack is a variation of a "first-in-first-out stack". The numbers in DATA statements are placed in a queue according to the order of earliest occurrence in the program, and they are used in that order. However, the RESTORE statement is a special device which restarts data usage from the beginning of the queue.

problems

1 Write a program that converts several distances in feet and inches supplied as input into distances in meters. Use a data stack consisting of the number of meters per foot (.3048) and the number of meters per inch (.0254) and a RESTORE statement.

2 Write a program that converts several weights in pounds and ounces supplied as input into weights in kilograms. Use a data stack consisting of the number of kilograms per pound (.4536) and the number of kilograms per ounce (.0284). Also use a RESTORE statement.

3 A calendar date may be expressed as a 5-digit number. For example, 11441 means the 114th day of the year 1941. Another way to express that date is by the triplet 4 24 41, which means the 24th day of the 4th month (April) of the year 1941. Write a program that converts a suitable 5-digit number supplied as data into a triplet expressing the same date. Use a DATA statement containing 12 numbers, the numbers of days in each month. Beware of leap year.

4 Write a program that converts each of six 5-digit numbers into corresponding triplets, as explained in Problem 3. Use a RESTORE statement to reset the data pointer when necessary.

5 Write a program that accepts several pairs of calendar date triplets (as in Problem 3) as input and computes the number of days between the first and second date of each pair. Have the program check each input pair to be sure the second date occurs after the first.

6 Write a program containing only two PRINT statements that produces ten copies of the following array of numbers, leaving an extra blank line between copies.

```
4    9    2
3    5    7
8    1    6
```

5 | subscripted variables

It is possible for a variable in BASIC to stand for a list of numbers. Such a variable is called a single-subscripted variable. If the single-subscripted variable V is a list of seven numbers, they would be denoted

$V[1], V[2], V[3], V[4], V[5], V[6]$, and $V[7]$

The teletypewriter carriage cannot drop half a line to type in subscripted position, so the usual mathematical notation

$V_1, V_2, V_3, V_4, V_5, V_6$, and V_7

is unobtainable.

The program BKWRDS illustrates the use of a single-subscripted

variable. As announced by the REM statement in line 100, the
purpose of the program BKWRDS is to reverse the ordering of a list.
That is, the first element of the subscripted variable V exchanges
places with the last, the second element exchanges places with the
next to last, and so on. The program prints the list in its initial
order, reverses the order, and then prints the reversed list. The
remarks in lines 140, 180, and 240 describe the purpose of the three
program loops.

```
LIST
BKWRDS

100   REM REVERSE LIST ORDERING
110   DIM V[20]
120   DATA 1,2,45,67,89,63,-9,4,9,10
130   DATA 11,12,13,-4,56,67,78,89,93,100
140   REM READ AND PRINT LIST OF NUMBERS ** LINES 150 TO 170
150   FOR I=1 TO 20
160   READ V[I]
165   PRINT V[I];
170   NEXT I
172   PRINT
174   PRINT
176   PRINT
180   REM EXCHANGE ELEMENTS * LINES 190 TO 230
190   FOR I=1 TO 10
200   LET Q=V[I]
210   LET V[I]=V[21-I]
220   LET V[21-I]=Q
230   NEXT I
240   REM PRINT REVERSED LIST * LINES 250 TO 270
250   FOR I=1 TO 20
260   PRINT V[I];
270   NEXT I
999   END


RUN
BKWRDS

 1     2    45    67    89    63    -9     4     9    10    11    12
13    -4    56    67    78    89    93   100


100    93    89    78    67    56    -4    13    12    11    10     9
 4    -9    63    89    67    45     2     1
DONE
```

declaring the dimension

Line 110 of BKWRDS is a declaration that the subscripted variable
V represents a list of 20 components. During compilation, the
computer allots space for 20 numbers which will be assigned values
of the elements $V[1]$, $V[2]$, . . . , and $V[20]$ of the subscripted
variable. The brackets following the variable in a DIM statement
always enclose a positive integer, called the *dimension* of the
subscripted variable. (The word DIM is an abbreviation for
"dimension".) Nonintegral subscripts, zero subscripts, and negative

subscripts are not permitted in BASIC. Every subscripted variable in BASIC is represented by a single letter.

A subscripted variable may be used in any arithmetic expression in the same manner as a simple variable.

parentheses and brackets

In the language BASIC, there is a formal distinction between parentheses and brackets. Arithmetic expressions use parentheses to indicate the order of evaluation. Function arguments are enclosed in parentheses. Subscripts and dimensions are enclosed in brackets. However, many versions of BASIC allow the programmer to use parentheses and brackets interchangeably.

syntax of subscripts

Any positive integer-valued arithmetic expression may serve as a subscript, as demonstrated by the following exotic example.

```
341   READ V[3+INT(4*RND(1))+V[2]*M]
```

The computer executes line 341 by evaluating the expression

$$3 + INT(4 * RND(1)) + V[2] * M$$

and, assuming that the value is a subscript within the bounds declared by the DIM statement for V, assigning a number from the data stack to the appropriate component of V. If the value of the expression violates the declaration in the DIM statement, the computer terminates the program with an error message such as

```
SUBSCRIPT OUT OF BOUNDS IN LINE 341
```

The number inside the parentheses in a DIM statement is not a subscript. It is a declaration of a maximum possible value for subscripts. Since the maximum value is determined during compilation, and not during execution, the maximum value must be given as an integer, not as an arbitrary expression.

A programmer is not obligated to mention every component of a subscripted variable in his program, but if he does not use each component it is likely that he is wasting valuable storage space in the scratch area.

two subscripts

The language BASIC also includes double-subscripted variables. One may think of such a variable as representing a table of numbers. For example, the component M[3, 5] may be regarded as the fifth number from the left in the third row from the top. In general, the syntax for both subscripts of a double-subscripted variable is the same as the syntax for the subscript of a single-subscripted variable.

The program PHONE uses a double-subscripted variable to compute the charge assessed by the local telephone company in a mythical town. The rate is obtained from Table 1. Each row corresponds to the time of day (in the mythical town) that the call originates. Each column represents a possible destination of the call. A component of the table gives the cost of a 3-minute or shorter call. If a call extends beyond 3 minutes, then the charge for the additional time is computed in precise proportion to the amount of additional time, using the 3-minute base rate for the time of origin (even when the call extends into a new time range).

The DIM statement at line 150 declares that the first subscript of M may vary from 1 to 4 and that the second subscript may vary from 1 to 6. The double FOR–NEXT loop on lines 160 to 200 reads the values from the data stack into the appropriate components of the table. Notice that this particular nesting of the loops reads values into the table row by row. The four DATA statements in lines 110 to 140 are arranged so that there are six numbers in each. This arrangement is a convenience, but the same table would be printed out if there were, say, only two DATA statements, one with 15 numbers and the other with 9, as long as the order of the numbers matches the order in which the table components receive values from execution of the READ statement.

table 1 *telephone rates for a 3-minute station–station call from a mythical town to destinations indicated*

	Boston	Chey-enne	Detroit	Fair-banks	Phoenix	San Francisco
7 a.m.–5 p.m.	.90	1.30	1.15	4.75	1.45	1.75
5 p.m.–7 p.m.	.80	1.10	1.05	3.80	1.30	1.45
7 p.m.–12 p.m.	.70	.90	.80	3.05	1.00	1.00
12 p.m.–7 a.m.	.50	.75	.60	2.25	.75	.75

```
LIST
PHONE

100   REM READ TABLE OF TELEPHONE RATES
110   DATA .9,1.3,1.15,4.75,1.45,1.75
120   DATA .8,1.1,1.05,3.8,1.3,1.45
130   DATA .7,.9,.8,3.05,1,1
140   DATA .5,.75,.6,2.25,.75,.75
150   DIM M[4,6]
160   FOR I=1 TO 4
170   FOR J=1 TO 6
180   READ M[I,J]
190   NEXT J
200   NEXT I
210   REM OBTAIN BILLING INFORMATION, 24 HOUR DECIMAL TIME
220   PRINT "TYPE TIMES OF ORIGIN AND COMPLETION, AREA CODE"
230   INPUT B,S,C
240   REM CHECK INPUT: 0 <= B,S <= 24    1 <= C <= 6
250   IF B*(24-B)<0 THEN 276
260   IF S*(24-S)<0 THEN 276
270   IF (C-1)*(6-C)<0 THEN 276
272   IF C=INT(C) THEN 280
276   PRINT "FAULTY BILLING INFORMATION, RESUBMIT"
278   GOTO 210
280   REM DETERMINE CORRECT ROW IN TABLE
290   LET R=4
300   IF B <= 7 THEN 360
310   LET R=1
320   IF B <= 17 THEN 360
330   LET R=2
340   IF B <= 19 THEN 360
350   LET R=3
360   REM DETERMINE COST OF CALL * 370 TO 410
370   IF S>B THEN 390
380   LET S=S+24
390   LET Q=M[R,C]
400   IF S-B <= .05 THEN 420
410   LET Q=(S-B)*(60/3)*M[R,C]
420   PRINT "COST:";Q
999   END


RUN
PHONE

TYPE TIMES OF ORIGIN AND COMPLETION, AREA CODE
? 11.56,12.04,5
COST: 13.92

DONE
```

Lines 210 to 278 obtain and check the billing information for
plausibility, which requires some explanation. The "24-hour decimal
time" system means coding the A.M. times of day as numbers
between 0 and 12, with two decimal places, and coding the P.M.
times of day as numbers between 12.01 and 24, with two decimal
places. The time 7:45 P.M. would be described as 19.75, since
$7 + 12 = 19$ and 45 minutes is .75 of an hour. The times of origin
and completion of the call are submitted to the program via input
variables B and S as times in the 24-hour decimal notation. The area
code for each of the cities listed across the top of Table 1 is simply
the column it heads. Thus, the code for Fairbanks is 4.

The method of checking the plausibility of the input is

noteworthy for its efficiency. The product of B and 24 − B, which is tested in line 250, is greater than or equal to 0 if and only if the value of B lies between 0 and 24. The same reasoning explains the test on the value of S in line 260. These times of origin (B stands for "begin") and completion (S stands for "stop") must lie between 0 and 24. Line 270 verifies that the area code C lies between 1 and 6, while 272 assures that C is an integer. Implausible input draws an error message from line 276 and a request for corrected input values.

The remark in line 280 reveals that the purpose of lines 290 to 350 is to locate the correct row. Lines 370 to 410 actually compute the cost of the call. Although it is assumed that no call lasts as long as 24 hours, it is possible that a call beginning before midnight extends through midnight to the next day. Lines 370 and 380 make the appropriate adjustment.

MAT *instructions*

In order to simplify the coding of programs involving subscripted variables, there are some special statements in BASIC, each of which begins with the word MAT. The word MAT stands for "matrix", which is a mathematical term describing arrays of numbers. The program RATES produces two copies of Table 1.

```
LIST
RATES

100    REM PRINT TABLE OF TELEPHONE RATES
110    DATA .9,1.3,1.15,4.75,1.45,1.75
120    DATA .8,1.1,1.05,3.8,1.3,1.45
130    DATA .7,.9,.8,3.05,1.05,1.05
140    DATA .5,.75,.6,2.25,.75,.75
150    DIM M[4,6]
175    MAT   READ M
210    FOR K=1 TO 2
220    PRINT "BOSTON        CHEYENNE     DETROIT      FAIRBANKS    ";
221    PRINT "PHOENIX       SAN FRAN"
255    MAT   PRINT M;
290    PRINT
300    PRINT
310    NEXT K
999    END
```

```
RUN
RATES
```

BOSTON	CHEYENNE	DETROIT	FAIRBANKS	PHOENIX	SAN FRAN
.9	1.3	1.15	4.75	1.45	1.75
.8	1.1	1.05	3.8	1.3	1.45
.7	.9	.8	3.05	1.05	1.05
.5	.75	.6	2.25	.75	.75

BOSTON	CHEYENNE	DETROIT	FAIRBANKS	PHOENIX	SAN FRAN
•9	1•3	1•15	4•75	1•45	1•75
•8	1•1	1•05	3•8	1•3	1•45
•7	•9	•8	3•05	1•05	1•05
•5	•75	•6	2•25	•75	•75

DONE

The MAT READ instruction in line 175 of RATES is equivalent to the double FOR–NEXT loop in lines 160 to 200 of PHONE. It assigns values from the data stack to components of the subscripted variable M in row order. That is, it reads the first six values into the first row, the next six values into the second row, and so on.

The MAT PRINT statement in line 255 of RATES is equivalent to a double FOR–NEXT loop. A MAT PRINT statement always tries to print a table in its correct shape, in this case 4 × 6. The semicolon at the end of line 255 tells the computer to pack numbers closely on a row. If it were omitted, then the computer would try to maintain the correct shape, but the numbers would spread out more. On certain systems, the six components of a row of the table might require two lines on the printout paper.

The statements MAT READ and MAT PRINT may also be applied to a single-subscripted variable on most systems.

multiple declarations

If a program employs several subscripted variables, the upper limits of all their subscripts may be declared in a single DIM statement such as

110   DIM A[13],M[4,6],V[20],C[12,3]

problems

1   Write a program that finds the largest even integer in a list of ten integers, some of which, possibly, are odd.

2   Write a program that determines the second largest number in a list of 12 numbers supplied as data.

3 Write a program that decides if there are two distinct numbers in a list (of ten numbers supplied as data) whose sum equals 12.

4 Write a program that reorders a list of ten numbers by interchanging the first five numbers with the last five numbers.

5 Write a program that considers a 4 × 4 table of numbers and decides if there are two numbers in any column whose sum is 8.

6 Write a program that interchanges the second and fourth columns of a 4 × 4 matrix.

7 Write a program that subtracts 5 from every element on the main diagonal (top left to bottom right) of a 4 × 4 matrix.

8 Write a program that prints the sums of the rows of a 3 × 5 matrix.

6 | *summary of* BASIC

This section summarizes the main properties of programs in the language BASIC. There are 17 possible statements as listed below. The notation xxxx stands for a line number betwen 1 and 9999.

declaration statements

xxxx DATA $c_1, c_2, \ldots, c_n$

Each c_i is a number. During the compilation of a program, the computer uses all DATA statements to create a single data stack.

xxxx DEF FN$f(u) = e$

The symbol f is one of the letters A, B, . . . , Z. The symbol u may be a simple variable. The symbol e is an arithmetic expression. The programmer uses DEF statements to define special functions.

xxxx DIM $s_1, s_2, \ldots, s_n$

Each s_i is a specification of the limits of subscripts for a subscripted variable, either of the form $a[m]$ or the form $a[m, n]$, where a is a letter and m and n are positive integers.

remarks

xxxx REM t

The symbol t stands for any sequence of teletypewriter characters. The computer ignores the text of the remark. It is permissible to transfer to a REM statement.

executable statements

xxxx END

The highest numbered line of any program is an END statement. The computer executes an END statement by terminating the running of the program.

xxxx FOR $u = e_1$ TO e_2

The symbol u stands for any simple variable. Both e_1 and e_2 are arithmetic expressions. A FOR statement is the first instruction of a loop. The loop must be completed with a NEXT statement (see below).

xxxx GOSUB yyyy

The operand yyyy is the line number of the first instruction of a subroutine. The subroutine must be terminated with a RETURN statement (see below). The computer records the number of the next line on the return address stack and transfers to line yyyy.

xxxx GOTO yyyy

The computer transfer unconditionally to the instruction whose line number is yyyy.

xxxx IF e_1 r e_2 THEN yyyy

Both e_1 and e_2 are arithmetic expressions, and r is a relation symbol. If the condition holds, then the computer transfers to line yyyy.

xxxx INPUT $v_1, v_2, \ldots, v_n$

Each v_i is a variable, either simple or subscripted. The computer begins execution of an INPUT statement by printing a question mark. The teletypewriter operator responds by transmitting n numbers. The computer then assigns these numbers, in order, to the n variables $v_1, \ldots, v_n$.

xxxx LET $v = e$

The variable v, either simple or subscripted, is assigned the value of the arithmetic expression e.

xxxx NEXT u

A NEXT statement completes a loop. The simple variable u must also appear in a FOR statement which starts the loop.

xxxx PRINT p_1; p_2; . . . ; p_n

Each p_i is either an arithmetic expression or a string of characters enclosed by quotation marks. The computer prints the operands $p_1, p_2, \ldots, p_n$ on one line if possible, but more if necessary. Replacing a semicolon between p_i and p_{i+1} by a comma causes wider spacing.

A semicolon or a comma at the end of a PRINT statement (i.e., after p_n) inhibits the carriage return and linefeed after printing.

A PRINT statement with no operand simply causes a carriage return and linefeed.

xxxx READ $v_1, v_2, \ldots, v_n$

The computer executes a READ statement by assigning the next n values from the data stack to the variables $v_1, \ldots, v_n$, which may be either simple or subscripted.

xxxx RESTORE

The data pointer is reset to the first item on the data stack.

xxxx RETURN

The computer transfers to the instruction whose line number on the return address stack was most recently written. It removes that number from the stack.

xxxx STOP

The running of the program is terminated.

7 | *editing commands*

There are two special commands to assist in the writing of programs. They act only on the scratch area and not on any version of the program in disk storage.

The command DELETE is used to erase a collection of consecutive lines from the scratch area. It has two possible forms. An example of the first form is

```
DELETE-300
```

which erases every statement whose line number is 300 or higher. An example of the second form is

which erases every instruction numbered between 500 and 680 inclusive.

The command

RENUMBER

tells the computer to renumber the statements of a program, preserving their order, so that the first statement is numbered 10 and each succeeding line is numbered 10 greater than the previous line. The form

RENUMBER-200

renumbers beginning at 200 in intervals of 10. The form

RENUMBER-250,30

renumbers beginning at 250 with intervals of 30.

For example, if the program RENUM is in the scratch area, then the result of renumbering is as shown.

```
LIST
RENUM

100   REM   WATCH LINE 200
200   GOTO 999
999   END


RENUMBER-311,2

LIST
RENUM

311   REM   WATCH LINE 200
313   GOTO 315
315   END
```

Observe that the text of the remark is not affected by renumbering. A number enclosed in quotation marks in a print statement is also unaffected by renumbering. Notice, however, that the line number which is the operand of a GOTO statement is correctly altered. Similarly, a line number given as an operand of an IF statement would be correctly altered.

suggested readings

Knuth, Donald E. *The Art of Computer Programming: Volume 1, Fundamental Algorithms.* Addison-Wesley, Reading, Mass., 1968.

Lee, J. A. *Anatomy of a Compiler.* Reinhold, New York, 1967.

information processing

APPLICATIONS OF computer technology to information-processing problems are familiar to everyday life. A publisher of a newspaper or a periodical may maintain a list of subscribers on magnetic tape or disk to facilitate distribution. Many large companies maintain payroll information in a computer system for efficiency in printing paychecks. This chapter introduces methods used in computer information systems. Later sections are concerned with techniques for eliminating errors and for documenting programs. These techniques have general application beyond information-processing programs.

1 | *storing and retrieving information*

This section discusses fundamental problems involved in the storage and retrieval of information. A problem concerned with the distribution of university seminar notices illustrates the construction and sequential processing of a simple file of records. Examples in library science and job assignment introduce techniques for handling more complex data structures.

grouping data into records

Although the data stack is essentially a facility for storing a list of individual numbers, there are programming devices that enable the data stack to represent various groupings of data. In many information-processing applications, such groupings are called *records*. A record is really nothing more than a sequence of items within the data stack. The program must somehow distinguish the items of a particular record from the other items on the stack.

fixed record length

It is easiest to process records on the data stack when they are all of the same length. If the length of each record is fixed at a certain number of items, then a single READ statement can extract an entire record, provided that the number of items is not too large.

university seminar notices

The program NOTICE groups items on the data stack into records of length 6. The first item in each record is a decimal number that identifies the office number of someone who receives the seminar notices of a particular department at a university. Since the university has numbered all of its buildings, it is convenient to represent a building by the integer part of the number and an office within that building by the decimal part. Thus, the number 18.301 identifies office number 301 in building 18.

A single seminar meets each weekday afternoon. In addition to students and faculty of the department, many persons from other departments in the university community attend some of the seminars. The Monday afternoon talks are concerned with one specialty, the Tuesday talks with another, and so on. Thus one person might regularly attend the Wednesday seminar, another the Tuesday and Friday seminars, depending on the person's interests.

The second to sixth items in each record are numbers, each either 1 or 0, indicating which seminar notices are to be mailed to the individual whose office number is the first item of the record. If the second item is a 1, the Monday seminar notice is mailed; if the third item is a 1, notice of the forthcoming Tuesday topic is mailed; and so on. The number 0 indicates no notice is to be mailed for the seminar of the corresponding day. Table 1 is a record indicating

table 1 *a record indicating Monday and Thursday seminar notices to be mailed to office 412 in building 8*

8.412	1	0	0	1	0

that the person in office 412 in building 8 wants advance notice of
the topics for the Monday and Thursday afternoon seminars.

Whenever the guest speaker and topic for a seminar are
determined, notices are printed and mailed to a list of offices
generated by the program NOTICE.

```
LIST
NOTICE

100   REM MAILING LIST FOR SEMINAR NOTICES
105   DIM R[6]
110   PRINT "TYPE 2 FOR MON, 3 FOR TUE, ... , 6 FOR FRI"
120   INPUT D
130   PRINT
140   PRINT
150   PRINT "MAILING LIST"
160   REM READ A MAILING RECORD
170   READ R[1],R[2],R[3],R[4],R[5],R[6]
180   REM END OF FILE? IF YES HALT AT 200
190   IF R[1]>0 THEN 210
200   STOP
210   REM IS NOTICE TO BE MAILED? IF YES PRINT ADDRESS
220   IF R[D]=0 THEN 160
230   PRINT R[1]
240   GOTO 160
300   DATA 18.301,0,1,0,0,0
310   DATA 8.412,1,0,0,1,0
320   DATA 3.271,0,1,1,0,1
330   DATA 8.168,1,1,0,0,0
340   DATA 4.424,0,0,1,0,1
980   DATA 0,0,0,0,0,0
999   END


RUN
NOTICE

TYPE 2 FOR MON, 3 FOR TUE, ... , 6 FOR FRI
?3


MAILING LIST
  18.301
  3.271
  8.168

DONE
```

Line 170 of NOTICE reads exactly one record of six items at a
time. If line 190 determines that $R[1] = 0$, which is not an office
number, then line 200 terminates execution. Using a dummy DATA
statement of 6 zeroes in line 980 is an efficient way to mark the end
of the file of records, because it permits the easy test in line 190.
If line 190 discovers an office number instead of a dummy zero,
then line 220 determines whether the individual in that office
receives a notice, in which case line 230 prints the office number on
the mailing list, or whether to go on immediately to the next record.
The abbreviated mailing list on the data stack of NOTICE is
intended for illustration. Obviously, unless the combined list were
much longer, a program like NOTICE would be unnecessary.

files of records

If a program contains more than one kind of record, then the data stack may be subdivided into separate *files* such that within each file all records are of the same type. This is achieved by placing between the two files a number or a sequence of numbers that could not arise as data. For example, in the program BOOKS below, none of the data is negative numbers. Therefore, negative numbers are used to separate the two files.

a small library

The program BOOKS is designed to assist the librarian for a small collection of books. To each title there is assigned a classification number in decimal form, with one to four digits to the left of the decimal point and either one or two digits to the right. Each authorized borrower is identified by an integer code between 1 and 200.

The data stack is separated into two distinct files. The first file, which runs from line 1010 to line 1999, is a catalog of all the classification numbers. Each record in that catalog consists of two numbers: first, the decimal number, and second, an integer

```
LIST
BOOKS

100   REM ** OBTAIN REQUESTED CATALOG NUMBER
110   PRINT "TYPE CATALOG NUMBER";
120   INPUT N
125   PRINT
130   REM ** LET X=NUMBER OF COPIES IN LIBRARY
140   READ W,X
150   IF W>-1 THEN 190
160   REM END OF CATALOG IF W=-1
170   PRINT "BOOK NOT IN LIBRARY"
180   STOP
190   IF W <> N THEN 140
200   REM ** READ DATA STACK TO END OF BOOKLIST
210   READ W,W
220   IF W>-1 THEN 210
230   REM ** LIST BORROWED COPIES
232   PRINT "BORROWER    DUE DATE"
235   LET Y=0
240   READ A,B,M,D
250   IF A>-1 THEN 320
260   REM END OF BORROWED COPIES FILE
270   IF Y=X THEN 300
280   PRINT "COPY AVAILABLE"
290   STOP
300   PRINT "ALL COPIES BORROWED"
310   STOP
320   IF A <> N THEN 240
```

```
 330    LET Y=Y+1
 340    PRINT B;"        ";M;D
 350    GOTO 240
1000    REM ** CATALOG OF BOOKS
1001    REM FORMAT: CATALOG NUMBER, NUMBER OF COPIES
1010    DATA 451.37,3
1011    DATA 99.28,4
1014    DATA 674.01,1
1017    DATA 2416.55,4
1020    DATA 85.96,2
1022    DATA 515.42,6
1024    DATA 742.81,1
1026    DATA 819.22,1
1030    DATA 1041.7,7
1033    DATA 113.35,2
1034    DATA 991.9,5
1037    DATA 425.2,2
1040    DATA 848.42,1
1042    DATA 317.68,3
1043    DATA 2342.1,2
1048    DATA 769.66,3
1999    DATA -1,-1
2000    REM ** BORROWED BOOK LIST
2001    REM FORMAT: CATALOG NUMBER, BORROWER NUMBER, MONTH, DAY DUE
2010    DATA 451.37,31,5,17
2013    DATA 515.42,45,4,30
2017    DATA 451.37,82,5,4
2020    DATA 85.96,17,6,1
2021    DATA 451.37,17,6,1
2022    DATA 2342.1,54,6,3
2032    DATA 1041.7,31,6,5
2038    DATA 742.81,117,6,8
2999    DATA -1,-1,-1,-1
9999    END


RUN
BOOKS

TYPE CATALOG NUMBER?451.37

BORROWER    DUE DATE
  31          5     17
  82          5      4
  17          6      1
ALL COPIES BORROWED

DONE

RUN
BOOKS

TYPE CATALOG NUMBER?85.96

BORROWER    DUE DATE
  17          6      1
COPY AVAILABLE

DONE

RUN
BOOKS

TYPE CATALOG NUMBER?212.64

BOOK NOT IN LIBRARY

DONE
```

specifying the number of copies of that title owned by the library. Since each record in the catalog consists of positive numbers, the two consecutive negative numbers in the DATA statement at line 1999 unambiguously mark the end of the catalog. Because of the double operand in the READ statement at line 140, the pair of negative numbers, rather than just one, simplifies the coding necessary to pass to the part of the program which examines the second file.

The second file, which runs from line 2010 to line 2999, is a list of all the borrowed books. Each record consists of four numbers. The first is the decimal classification number for the book. The second is the borrower's identification code. The third and fourth numbers specify the month and day that the book is due to be returned. The four negative numbers in line 2999 mark the end of the second file. They prevent the computer from stumbling into an OUT OF DATA error.

Both the catalog of titles and the borrowed book list are dynamic files, that is, they are constantly changing. Whenever a book is added to the collection, the librarian transmits a DATA statement. If it is a new title, the librarian chooses an unused line number between 1010 and 1999. If it is an additional copy of an existing title, then the librarian replaces the appropriate line with a line that contains the updated number of copies. Whenever a book is borrowed, renewed, or returned, the librarian creates, alters, or deletes the appropriate DATA statement numbered between 2010 and 2999.

The main use of the program occurs when a library member wants to borrow a book. The librarian then supplies the classification number as input to BOOKS at line 120. Lines 130 to 190 search the catalog of titles for that classification number. If it is not in the catalog, then line 170 prints the message "book not in library." If the classification number is located, then the computer uses lines 200 to 220 to skip to the end of the catalog and the beginning of the list of borrowed books.

Lines 230 to 350 print a list of the borrowers who presently have copies and the dates that each is due. They also add up the total number of borrowed copies. Line 270 compares the total number of borrowed copies to the number of copies in the collection and either transfers to line 300 to tell the librarian that all copies are borrowed or lets the computer proceed to line 280 to say that a copy is available.

The library system described here is quite incomplete. There is no way to list all titles by the same author or to give statistical data to the librarian. The information is stored in a generally haphazard way. And there is no protection against inadvertent errors the librarian might commit in updating the records. Some possible improvements are suggested in the problems at the end of this section.

a citation index

A second library science problem is concerned with cross-referencing research papers published in journals. It is possible to tell what previous work a paper depends upon by looking at its bibliography. But a scholar also wants to know where a paper has led. For example, if in 1978 he is examining a paper published in the year 1971, he may want to know who has used the paper's results in the seven years since the paper appeared. The growing list of manuscripts which refer back to a given paper is called its forward bibliography. A published collection of forward bibliographies is called a citation index.

Whenever a research paper is published, it is assigned a classification number. No two papers are ever assigned the same number, although part of the number helps to identify the subject matter precisely. In the computer system there is a filed record consisting of a finite sequence of numbers of all the papers in its bibliography.

variable-length records

Unlike the records in the program BOOKS, the bibliographies for the citation index problem are of variable length. Given that all of the classification numbers are positive, some negative number might be used as an end-of-record indicator. Another way to handle records of variable length is to make the second number of each record equal to the number of items in the record.

Whenever a new paper in the field of interest is published, the librarian places its bibliography on the data stack. At any time, the librarian may obtain a forward bibliography by running the program and supplying the classification number of that program as input. The computer then prints a list of the classification numbers of every paper that mentions the specified paper in its bibliography.

Actually writing a model program for a citation-indexing project is left as a problem at the end of this section.

building a school

Another problem amenable to computer solution by table look-up techniques occurs in a small town where the children need a new school building. The people have enough money for lumber and

table 2 *skills of various volunteers*

volunteer	1	2	3	4	5	6	7	8	9	10	11	12	13	14	15	16	17	18	19	20	21
skills	C	M	C	E	C	C	P	M	C	P	E	C	C	W	E	E	P	E	C	C	C
	E	P		W	P			W	E				M				W	P	M	W	E	M
	W								M												

C = carpentry, M = masonry, P = plumbing, E = electrical work, W = metal work.

other materials but not enough for construction. At a town meeting, 33 citizens volunteer their labor.

An architect devises a plan which requires 30 different workers with an assortment of special skills, including at least 6 carpenters, 4 masons, 4 plumbers, 3 electrical workers, 3 metal workers, and 10 general helpers. Only 21 of the volunteers have any of the special skills but some have more than one. Table 2 describes the situation. If the volunteers can be assigned to fit the plan, then there will be 1 extra skilled worker and 3 extra general helpers.

A relatively efficient way to solve the problem is to first assign each volunteer with only one skill, then the volunteers with two skills, never exceeding the minimum number of skilled workers in each category, and finally, to assign the most versatile workers. The actual programming solution is left as a problem.

problems

1 Modify the program NOTICE to make it use less space on the data stack by reducing the record length from 6 to 2 items. To do this, encode the record in Table 1 as

8.412, 10010

and adjust other records accordingly. The modification requires a few extra program lines to obtain $R[1], \ldots, R[6]$.

2 Write a program that provides information for a baseball announcer. Each record should consist of a code number identifying a player, his number of times at bat, his batting average, and his number of home runs. The program should include a subroutine that prints a list of players with a batting average greater than a number to be specified as input by the announcer.

3 Write a subroutine for the program in Problem 2 that prints a list of players who have hit more home runs than some number to be specified as input by the announcer. Make the program capable of printing either a list of high-average hitters or great home-run hitters.

4 Append to the program BOOKS a subprogram with lines numbered between 3000 and 3999 which accepts a month and day as input and prints out a list of all overdue books, that is, books due prior to the month and day supplied as input. Even though the year a book is due is not stored on the borrowed book list portion of the data stack, a list of overdue books from late December may be obtained by supplying the numbers 12 and 32. The command RUN-3000 may be used to invoke this subprogram.

5 Append to the program BOOKS a subprogram to be used to catch errors whenever the librarian adds a record or changes a record in the first part of the data stack by making sure that each record in the book catalog consists of a file number and a number of copies. This subprogram's lines should be numbered between 4000 and 4999 and it should be invoked by the command RUN-4000.

6 Append to the program BOOKS a subprogram that assures that no book in the catalog is listed twice. This subprogram should be executed after the subprogram of Problem 5.

7 Write a model program for the citation-indexing project described in this section.

8 Write a program that solves the job assignment problem for constructing a school according to the plan described in the text of this section.

9 A physician needs a file of medical records of his patients. Let each record consist of a confidential patient identification code plus a collection of numbers that represent the patient's past diseases, for example, 1 = anemia, 2 = bronchitis, 3 = influenza, etc. When the physician's technical assistant supplies a patient's code number, a program should print the (variable length) history of the patient's previous ailments. Write the program.

10 Write a program to aid an attorney in retrieving information on legal precedents. Each (variable length) record should consist of a code number identifying a class of violations (e.g., jaywalking, overtime parking, etc.) and a sublist of numbers corresponding to some important legal precedents for cases involving such offenses. When the attorney's technical assistant supplies the violation code, the program should produce the list of precedents.

2 | *sorting and merging*

It is often necessary or desirable to rearrange stored data. Two of the most common rearrangement procedures are sorting and merging. The notion of sorting is familiar to everyday life. The index of a book, for example, is sorted into alphabetical order. A person may sort returned canceled checks from the bank into numerical order. The operation of combining two or more sorted files of similar items into a single sorted file is called merging. For example, alphabetically arranged lists of names of voters registered in individual precincts might be merged into a master list for an entire city.

utility subroutines

This section describes the utility subroutines SORT and MERGE. In a BASIC system, a utility subroutine may be stored under its name on the disk as if it were a program. But SORT and MERGE are not independent programs. Neither is designed to do anything useful when run by itself. In fact, both will terminate in error messages. The utility subroutines SORT and MERGE are specifically written so that they may be appended to a main program which requires a sorting or merging subroutine. The language BASIC includes a system command APPEND (described below) that renders this possible.

bubble SORT

The utility subroutine SORT employs the method known as "bubbling". The idea is that first the largest number in the list

```
LIST
SORT

1000   REM BUBBLE SORT ** UTILITY SUBROUTINE **
1010   REM FILE A FOR BOTH INPUT AND OUTPUT
1020   REM MAIN PROGRAM SUPPLIES L = LENGTH(A)
1030   FOR N=1 TO L-1
1040   REM BUBBLE INTO NTH POSITION * 1050-1110
1050   FOR I=1 TO L-N
1060   REM EXCHANGE IF A[I] > A[I+1] * 1070-1100
1070   IF A[I] <= A[I+1] THEN 1110
1080   LET Q=A[I+1]
1090   LET A[I+1]=A[I]
1100   LET A[I]=Q
1110   NEXT I
1120   NEXT N
1130   RETURN
```

bubbles to the top, that is, to the position with the largest subscript. Then the second largest number bubbles into the position with the second largest subscript, and so on.

Line 1000 provides the critical information that SORT is a utility subroutine. It is assumed that SORT will be appended to a main program which supplies a subscripted variable A, a DIM statement for A, and a number L indicating that the first L elements of A are to be sorted into ascending order.

testing a utility subroutine

It is intended that the main program to which SORT is appended will use the sorted output file. However, it must be first assured that SORT works correctly, and a special program SRTTST has been

```
LIST
SRTTST

100   REM GENERATE DUMMY INPUT TO TEST SORT
110   DIM A[100]
120   PRINT "TYPE LENGTH OF INPUT TEST FILE";
130   INPUT L
140   PRINT
150   PRINT "INPUT FILE"
160   FOR I=1 TO L
170   LET A[I]=INT(1000*RND(I))
180   PRINT A[I];
190   NEXT I
200   PRINT
210   PRINT
220   GOSUB 1000
230   PRINT "OUTPUT FILE"
240   FOR I=1 TO L
250   PRINT A[I];
260   NEXT I
270   PRINT
280   STOP
290   REM APPEND-SORT

APPEND-SORT
9999 END

RUN
SRTTST

TYPE LENGTH OF INPUT TEST FILE?29

INPUT FILE
 315   790   809   299   239   671   867   170   149   568   273   640
 343   873   886    15   372   136   953   507   318   578   270   422
   9   925   997   504   354

OUTPUT FILE
   9    15   136   149   170   239   270   273   299   315   318   343
 354   372   422   504   507   568   578   640   671   790   809   867
 873   886   925   953   997

DONE
```

written for this purpose. The program SRTTST is designed to test the utility subroutine SORT. It creates an unsorted file of numbers of whatever length the programmer designates and supplies that file as input to SORT. It prints out both the unsorted input file and the sorted output file.

appending subprograms

If the program SRTTST is in the scratch area and if the utility subprogram SORT has been saved in the disk storage area, then it is possible to test the subprogram SORT, as shown in the printout.

Every line number of SRTTST is lower than every line number of SORT. It is permitted, therefore, to issue the system command

APPEND-SORT

which brings SORT into the scratch area simultaneously with SRTTST. Since the highest numbered line then in the scratch area is not an END statement, an END statement is placed at line 9999 to enable the joint program to be executed when the systems command RUN is given. See Appendix A for the CALL/360 alternative to APPEND.

merging

There is an obvious way to merge two sorted files. If there were two lines of persons standing in order of ascending height, a combined line would be started by comparing the shortest person from one line with the shortest person from the other. The shorter of these would become first in the combined output line. Then the shortest person remaining in one input line would be compared with the shortest remaining person in the other input line, and the smaller of these would move to the rear of the output line. This procedure would continue until one input line ran out, at which time the remaining persons in the other input line would proceed in order to the rear of the output line. The flowchart in Figure 1 depicts the analogous method for merging two lists of numbers called C and D into an output file E.

The flowchart in Figure 1 indicates the subservient nature of the merging operation. A block labeled "supply input files C and D"

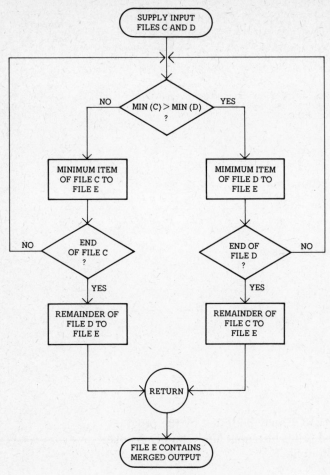

Figure 1   Flowchart of the program MERGE.

replaces the circular starting block used for independent procedures. Whereas a flowchart for a main program has one or more circular stop blocks, the flowchart in Figure 1 has a circular return block followed by a block explaining that after the procedure is executed file E contains the merged output.

The utility subprogram MERGE implements the procedure of the flowchart in Figure 1. The main program must supply the input files C and D, their DIM statements, and the numbers Y and Z of elements of C and D that are to be merged. The main program must also declare the dimension of the output file E.

```
LIST
MERGE

2000    REM ** UTILITY SUBROUTINE **
2010    REM MERGE FILES  C  AND  D  INTO FILE  E
2020    REM I,J,K INDEX C,D,E.  Y,Z = SIZES OF C,D
2030    LET I=1
2040    LET J=1
2050    LET K=1
2060    REM * IS NEXT ITEM FROM FILE C OR FROM FILE D ??
2070    IF C[I]>D[J] THEN 2150
2080    REM * ADD AN ITEM FROM FILE C
2090    LET E[K]=C[I]
2100    LET I=I+1
2110    LET K=K+1
2120    REM * ?? END OF FILE C ??
2130    IF I>Y THEN 2220
2140    GOTO 2060
2150    REM * ADD AN ITEM FROM FILE D
2160    LET E[K]=D[J]
2170    LET J=J+1
2180    LET K=K+1
2190    REM * ?? END OF FILE D ??
2200    IF J>Z THEN 2290
2210    GOTO 2060
2220    REM * ADD ON REMAINDER OF FILE D
2230    LET E[K]=D[J]
2240    LET J=J+1
2250    LET K=K+1
2260    REM * ?? END OF FILE D ??
2270    IF J>Z THEN 2360
2280    GOTO 2220
2290    REM * ADD ON REMAINDER OF FILE C
2300    LET E[K]=C[I]
2310    LET I=I+1
2320    LET K=K+1
2330    REM * ?? END OF FILE C ??
2340    IF I>Y THEN 2360
2350    GOTO 2290
2360    RETURN
2370    END
```

The utility subroutine MERGE may be tested by the program
MRGTST which creates and prints test input files C and D, invokes
MERGE, and prints the output file E.

```
LIST
MRGTST

100    REM GENERATE DUMMY INPUT TO TEST MERGE
110    DIM C[100],D[100],E[200]
120    DEF FNA(X)=5*X+INT(5*RND(X))
130    PRINT "TYPE LENGTHS OF FILES C & D"
140    INPUT Y,Z
150    PRINT
160    PRINT "FILE C"
170    FOR I=1 TO Y
180    LET C[I]=FNA(I)
190    PRINT C[I];
200    NEXT I
210    PRINT
220    PRINT
230    PRINT "FILE D"
240    FOR J=1 TO Z
250    LET D[J]=FNA(J)
260    PRINT D[J];
270    NEXT J
280    PRINT
290    PRINT
```

```
300   GOSUB 2000
310   REM PRINT TEST OUTPUT
320   PRINT "FILE E"
330   FOR K=1 TO Y+Z
340   PRINT E[K];
350   NEXT K
360   PRINT
370   STOP
380   REM APPEND-MERGE

APPEND-MERGE
9999 END

RUN
MRGTST

TYPE LENGTHS OF FILES C & D
?11,6

FILE C
 9     12    16    23    25    33    36    40    45    54    55

FILE D
 6     11    18    20    27    33

FILE E
 6      9    11    12    16    18    20    23    25    27    33    33
36     40    45    54    55

DONE
```

extracting, renumbering, and appending

The subprogram SORT could be directly appended to SRTTST
because every line of SORT is numbered above every line of
SRTTST. Similarly, MERGE could be directly appended to
MRGTST. Sometimes, however, a programmer might wish to
combine parts of several programs along with some lines supplied
one at a time from the keyboard into a new program. Possibly the
ranges of line numbers overlap somewhat. Fortunately, the BASIC
systems commands yield a lot of editing flexibility.

As an illustration, suppose that a program called CRZQLT (not
shown here) is to be created from some lines supplied one at a
time from the keyboard plus a subroutine in lines 500 to 760,
spaced about 10 apart, of a saved program named PR3.1 and the
data stack of a saved program named PR3.2, occupying lines 1000
to 1399 with spacing about 10 apart. The subroutine from PR3.1 is
to occupy lines numbered between 800 and 990 in CRZQLT,
while the data stack of PR3.2 is to occupy lines numbered between
2000 and 2999 in CRZQLT.

One way to begin is to extract the subroutine from PR3.1,
renumber its lines, and save them under a dummy name, say, CP1.
Then extract the data stack of PR3.2, renumber its lines, and save
them under another dummy name, say, CP2. The following systems
commands accomplish this job.

```
GET-PR3.1
DELETE-1,499
DELETE-761,9999
RENUMBER-800,5
NAME-CP1
SAVE
GET-PR3.2
DELETE-1,999
DELETE-1400,9999
RENUMBER-2000
NAME-CP2
SAVE
```

After clearing the scratch area and supplying the name CRZQLT, the programmer transmits lines numbered below 800 and appends CP1. Then lines numbered between 1000 and 1999 are transmitted from the keyboard, and CP2 is appended. The program CRZQLT is completed by the addition of any lines numbered above 2999. Unless they have further use, both CP1 and CP2 may be destroyed.

problems

1 Write a program that sorts numerical records of length 2 according to ascending order of the first of the two entries. Use this program to sort the records in the catalog of books, lines 1000 to 1999 of the program BOOKS. The first three records in the sorted output should be

85.96, 4
99.28, 4
113.35, 2

2 Write a program that sorts records of length 4 according to ascending order of their first and second entries. If the records in the borrowed-book list, lines 2000 to 2999 of the program BOOKS, are supplies to this sort, the output should be

85.96, 17, 6, 1
451.37, 17, 6, 1
451.37, 31, 5, 17
451.37, 82, 5, 4
515.42, 45, 4, 30
742.81, 117, 6, 8
1041.7, 31, 6, 5
2342.1, 54, 6, 3

3 Write a program that sorts records of length 4 according to ascending order of their third and fourth entries. Use this program to sort records in the borrowed-book list of BOOKS according to month and day due.

4   Write a program that sorts records of variable length according to ascending order of their first entries. Test the program.

5   Write a program that merges records of length 2, previously sorted according to ascending order of the first entry. Test the program.

6   Write a program that merges records of length 4, previously sorted according to ascending order of their first and second entries. Test the program.

7   Write a program that merges variable-length records which have been previously sorted according to ascending order of their first entries.

3 | *locating errors*

A novice programmer might hope that he could learn to write programs that run correctly on the very first trial. Such a hope is akin to wishing that one might never again make a "slip of the tongue" in speech. Rather than worry about never committing minor errors, an experienced programmer carefully develops the skill called "debugging", that is, removing the "bugs" (errors) in programs. Proofreading is a preliminary part of debugging. The real work comes in designing test data that will reveal "hidden" errors and in making minor modifications in the program (temporarily) to help isolate errors.

major errors

From a pragmatic viewpoint, a program contains a major error if it requires a lot of revision to do the job for which it is intended. Such errors may result from faulty analysis of the problem. For example, a program concerned with budgeting might assume that every kind of item to be purchased has a fixed cost when, actually, the costs vary. This sort of error often arises from a programmer's impatience to begin writing code. A program which fails to meet the needs of the situation at hand can be a total waste that is not mitigated by the programmer's proficiency at coding.

Experience teaches a programmer to plan carefully. The most essential step in planning is a thorough understanding of the problem. Once this is attained, the programmer may concentrate on solving the problem in general terms, possibly by a prose description of the solution but more probably by a flowchart. If the program is being designed to satisfy the needs of someone other than the programmer himself, perhaps an employer or a project leader, then both a prose description and a flowchart may be helpful.

If the problem is correctly analyzed within its own discipline, external to programming, and if a careful flowchart is prepared before any coding begins, then the program is likely to contain only minor errors, which can be detected by the techniques described here.

hand simulation

One debugging device is *hand simulation,* in which the programmer pretends that he is the computer and executes part of the program. If he were to simulate the entire program, that might yield some additional information about errors, but simulation is a tedious process. A drastically careful simulation technique is to subdivide a piece of scrap paper into three regions, one for values of variables, one for the data stack, and one for the return-address stack. Naturally, either of the stacks is omitted from the scrap paper if it does not occur in the program. The programmer lists the names of those variables in his program which seem to be related to the trouble across the top of the variable region on the scrap paper. Then he begins simulating execution.

The program ERROR has been written with a deliberate mistake that causes infinite looping. Its purported purpose is to decide if a number N is supplied as input occurs anywhere in the infinite sequence

1, 3, 6, 10, 15, 21, 28, . . .

in which the kth member of the sequence is the sum of the integers between 1 and k inclusive. The variable S successively assumes each number in the sequence as its value until either S = N (the number N is in the sequence) or else S > N (the sequence does not include the number N).

Since 212, which is supplied as input, is a relatively small number, the programmer correctly guesses after a short while of waiting in vain for output that there is an error. He begins simulating the program as shown in Table 3.

There is no need to reserve space either for a return-address stack or for a data stack. The programmer lists the names of the variables N, S, and I across the top of his piece of scrap paper. Down the left-hand margin he begins with line 100. All three variables remain unassigned, so the variable spaces in the row corresponding to

```
LIST
ERROR

100    REM IS N IN THE SEQUENCE 1,3,6,10,15,...
110    PRINT "ENTER A NUMBER"
120    INPUT N
125    PRINT
130    LET S=0
140    LET I=1
150    LET S=S+1
160    IF S=N THEN 200
170    IF S>N THEN 220
180    LET I=I+1
190    GOTO 130
200    PRINT I;"TH  ELEMENT OF SEQUENCE"
210    STOP
220    PRINT "NOT AN ELEMENT OF SEQUENCE"
999    END

RUN
ERROR

ENTER A NUMBER
?212




STOP
```

line 100 are left blank. At line 110, all three variables are still
unassigned. At line 120, the variables S and I remain unassigned.
If the program worked properly, then the variable I would assume
the successive integer values 1, 2, 3, . . . , while the variable S would

table 3 *partial simulation of the program*

line	N	S	I
100			
110			
120	212		
125	212		
130	212	0	
140	212	0	1
150	212	1	1
160	212	1	1
170	212	1	1
180	212	1	2
190	212	1	2
130	212	0	2

assume the values of integers in the sequence 1, 3, 6, 10, 15, ...

However, line 130 resets the value of S to 0, as shown at the bottom of Table 3. The programmer then realizes that line 190 of error should transfer not to line 130 but to line 150 and makes the correction

```
190   GOTO 150
```

If a program uses subroutines, then hand simulation also includes keeping a list of line numbers in the return-address stack region of the scrap paper. The list is initially empty. Whenever a GOSUB statement is executed, the programmer writes down the line number of the next statement in sequence after the GOSUB. Whenever a RETURN statement is executed, the simulated execution transfers to the statement with the most recently written line number (excluding the crossed-out line numbers) and crosses that number out.

If a program uses READ statements, then hand simulation includes writing numbers for the data stack in the appropriate region of the scratch paper and keeping track of the position of the data pointer.

Often a programmer does not bother to simulate an entire program. He may suspect that the error is located in some particular subroutine or loop or other group of instructions and simulate only that portion. Once a simulation verifies the correctness of a subroutine or loop, the programmer may regard its total execution as a single step in the simulation of a larger part of the program that invokes that subroutine or uses that loop.

tracing

If a small amount of hand simulation does not reveal the error or errors in a program, a technique called tracing can enable the computer to print out much of the information that is given in a chart like Table 3. It is assumed that the programmer has left gaps between line numbers of consecutive statements. The programmer temporarily inserts some extra PRINT statements, as shown for the program ERROR.

The remarks at lines 10 and 11 give the places where tracing statements have been inserted to ease their deletion after the error is found. If a line does not contain a transfer statement, then it is traced as shown at lines 131, 141, 151, and 181 by making the next line a PRINT statement whose operand consists of the traced line

```
LIST
ERROR

10   REM TRACING STATEMENTS AT LINES
11   REM 131,141,151,159,169,181,189
100  REM IS N IN THE SEQUENCE 1,3,6,10,15,...
110  PRINT "ENTER A NUMBER"
120  INPUT N
125  PRINT
130  LET S=0
131  PRINT 130,N;S
140  LET I=1
141  PRINT 140,N;S;I
150  LET S=S+1
151  PRINT 150,N;S;I
159  PRINT 160,N;S;I
160  IF S=N THEN 200
169  PRINT 170,N;S;I
170  IF S>N THEN 220
180  LET I=I+1
181  PRINT 180,N;S;I
189  PRINT 190,N;S;I
190  GOTO 130
200  PRINT I;"TH   ELEMENT OF SEQUENCE"
210  STOP
220  PRINT "NOT AN ELEMENT OF SEQUENCE"
999  END
```

number and the important variables. Observe that line 131 cannot trace the variable I because when it is first executed the value of I is unassigned. If a line does contain a transfer statement, then it is traced as shown at lines 159, 169, and 189 by making the previous line a PRINT statement.

It is not necessary to trace every line because the initial run of ERROR with a trace shows that lines 200, 210, 220, and 999 are never executed. It is usually sufficient to trace only statements

```
RUN
ERROR

ENTER A NUMBER
?212

130          212   0
140          212   0     1
150          212   1     1
160          212   1     1
170          212   1     1
180          212   1     2
190          212   1     2
130          212   0
140          212   0     1
150          212   1     1
160          212   1     1
170          212   1     1
180          212   1     2
190          212   1     2
130          212   0
140          212   0     1
150
```

programmer pushes BREAK key to halt execution

STOP

that change the value of a variable and transfer statements. Often a clever programmer gets by with only one or two strategically located extra PRINT statements.

systematic sample runs

Before a program is applied to the actual problem for which it is intended, it is a good idea to test it in some simpler situations. Hopefully, the programmer can design elementary tests that require a program to employ all of its capabilities.

For example, the program MERGE of the previous section is actually intended to merge "gigantic" files of numbers. The test given in that section examines its facility at merging small files. A single test is not really sufficient. Perhaps the only reason that the one given was successful depended on the fact that file C is longer than file D. A careful programmer would also test the case in which file D is longer than file C, because otherwise certain instructions might not be tested. The reader will observe from scanning the program MERGE that whenever file C ends in a larger number than file D, lines 2220 to 2280 are unused.

In a group project, it is better for someone other than the original programmer to test a program, since the original programmer is more likely to have prejudices that some parts of his program are "certain to be correct".

4 | *documentation*

It is often necessary for a programmer to communicate information about his work, either to another programmer or to someone who knows little about programming. The written information that a programmer creates is called documentation. Some programmers even prepare documentation for their own use, to make it easier to return to a program after time spent concentrating on something else. The amount of documentation and its exact nature vary according to the problem and the prospective readers.

abstract

The first part of the documentation is an abstract describing the purpose of the program. Preferably, the abstract is short. It should be understandable to someone who cannot program. The following abstract is for the program BOOKS, which appears in the first section of this chapter.

ABSTRACT   The program BOOKS assists the librarian for a small collection of publications. When the librarian supplies the decimal classification number for a title, the program produces a list of the identification codes for all borrowers who have copies of the requested volume and the date that each copy is due to be returned. The program then prints a message indicating whether or not there remains a copy on the shelf.

Observe that the abstract does not mention data stacks, loops, or other technical details of programming.

operational details

The documentation should include a description of how to use the program that does not compel the reader either to refer to the listing or even to know much about programming. Presumably the reader of this part of the documentation does know how to operate a teletypewriter. The complete operation of the program BOOKS involves changing the data stack when a book is added to the collection, changing the data stack whenever a book is borrowed, renewed, or returned, and running the program to obtain information about the availability of a requested title. All of these operations should be described in the documentation. For a program that only computes some numbers this part of the documentation is very simple. A printout of a sample run may be included here so that the user knows what output to expect.

flowchart

A clean copy of a flowchart whose description blocks do not depend on the programming language is extremely valuable. Such a flowchart can be understood by a programmer whose training may be in other languages than the one in which the program is coded.

listing

The documentation of a program always includes a clean listing. Explanation of the details is preferably given by remarks within the program. The importance of documentation by REM statements within a program cannot be overemphasized. Since a user or a programmer at a teletypewriter may not have immediate access to any other form of documentation of a given program, there should be sufficient explanation of program usage and coding techniques in the REM statements. Duplication of information given elsewhere is hardly wasteful, since it saves time that a programmer might spend in seeking such external information.

suggested reading

Knuth, Donald E. *The Art of Computer Programming: Volume 1, Fundamental Algorithms.* Addison-Wesley, Reading, Mass., 1968.

4

character strings

SOME PROGRAMMING applications are concerned with words rather
than numbers. Many BASIC systems have the facility to handle
both. This chapter investigates some of the uses of the verbal
capability of BASIC, including teaching programs, cryptography,
and literary text analysis. The verbal techniques described here
would certainly be helpful in certain applications of other chapters,
but they are deliberately avoided because a large number of
BASIC systems cannot manipulate words. The reading of this
chapter is recommended even to a programmer whose system does
not have the string-variable facility.

1 | conversational flavor

This section introduces most of the necessary terminology and some
special BASIC statements for handling character strings and string
variables. The main application here is to computer-assisted
instruction.

character strings

A *character string* (often called, simply, a *string*) is a formal name
for a sequence of teletypewriter symbols enclosed by quotation
marks. Strings have already occurred as operands of PRINT
statements.

The *length* of a string means the number of symbols between the quotation marks, counting the space characters (blanks) as symbols. Thus,

"ABCD"	has length 4
" ;Q] "	has length 5
""	has length 0
" "	has length 2

Most versions of BASIC limit the length of a string to 72 characters. The null string, which contains no characters and has length 0, should not be confused with a string consisting of one or more consecutive blanks. The distinction is analogous to the difference between the number 0 or a handful of zeroes and the absence of any number at all. A pragmatic distinction of importance to a programmer is that to print a null string, the teletypewriter carriage need not move, whereas to print a blank, the carriage moves one space to the right.

The quotation mark (") may not be a character in any string, but an apostrophe (') may be used to suggest enquotation, as in the example

```
285  PRINT " 'LOGIC PREVAILS,' SAID THE COMPUTER. "
```

It is not possible to print a quotation that includes a backspace character ($\leftarrow$), because when it is typed it simply erases the preceding character, as explained in Chapter 1.

string variables

There is a special kind of variable in BASIC whose value may be a string. The notation for such a variable (called a *string variable*) is a single letter (A, B, C, . . . , Z) followed by a dollar sign ($). A DIM statement is used to declare the maximum length of any string that a string variable will assume as its value during a program. Thus, the declaration

```
75  DIM Q$[37]
```

enables the string variable Q$ to represent any string whose length is less than or equal to 37. The computer reserves space in the part of the scratch area which contains present values of variables. The program HELLO illustrates how a string variable may be used to give a computer program a friendly, conversational flavor.

Line 100 of the program HELLO declares the maximum length

```
LIST
HELLO

100   DIM N$[30]
110   PRINT "TYPE YOUR NAME AND PUSH THE 'RETURN' BUTTON"
120   INPUT N$
130   PRINT
140   PRINT
150   PRINT "HELLO, ";N$
999   END

RUN
HELLO

TYPE YOUR NAME AND PUSH THE 'RETURN' BUTTON
?JESSICA


HELLO, JESSICA

DONE
```

of the string variable N$ to be 30. Line 110 tells the computer to
print a message. The computer begins the execution of line 120 by
printing a question mark. The teletypewriter operator follows the
instructions given in the printed message and transmits her name.
The computer then assigns to the string variable N$ the string
"JESSICA", which is of length 7. The teletypewriter carriage skips
two lines because of the PRINT statements in program lines 130
and 140. At line 150, the computer prints its greeting message.
Line 999 terminates the program.

string input

The reader might notice that Jessica was not required to type
quotation marks around her name. Since N$ is a string variable, the
computer knows to assume that the quotation marks are there.
This minor sacrifice of rigid grammar makes it possible to design
programs that will interest small children. It is permitted to type
quotation marks around string input.

string LET

The LET statement may also be used to assign the value of a string
variable, as shown in the following two lines.

```
110   LET C$="SHAZAM"
140   LET R$=B$
```

The right side of the equality symbol in a string LET statement
must be either a properly enquoted sequence of symbols or a string
variable. Instructions such as

```
310  LET F$=7.3
320  LET P$=H
```

result in error messages, because 7.3 is a number, not to be confused with the string "7.3", and the unenquoted letter H in a LET statement is a numeric variable, not the string variable H$ or the string "H". The language BASIC abhors such violations of grammar because the alternative is to allow ambiguity. If the reader feels that the computer is unnecessarily touchy about this point, he might consider the difference between a lion (a carnivorous animal) and the word "lion" (the noncarnivorous name of a carnivorous animal). The distinction is quite important.

string read

Items on the data stack may be strings, as well as numbers. If strings are mixed in with numbers, it is imperative that the program keep track of the type of item, string or number, indicated by the data pointer. The program NUMSTR shows what it means to keep track of the data type.

```
LIST
NUMSTR

90   REM ILLUSTRATE MIXTURE OF STRING AND NUMERIC DATA
100   DIM A$[3],B[2]
110   DATA 1,"ABC",2
120   DATA "DE ",3
130   READ B[1],A$,B[2]
140   PRINT B[1];A$,B[2]
150   READ A$,J
160   PRINT A$,J
999   END


RUN
NUMSTR

 1      ABC        2
DE                 3

DONE
```

The data stack of the program NUMSTR has five items. The first, third, and fifth are numbers. The second and fourth are strings. Only a number may be read into a numeric variable, and only a string may be read into a string variable. Any violation of this rule causes the running of the program to terminate in an error message.

conversational teaching programs

A conversational flavor often increases the effectiveness of a teaching program. The program ADD** is a conversational version of the program ADD*, which is listed in Chapter 2.

```
LIST
ADD**

10   REM   TEACH ADDITION
11   DIM A$[10]
12   PRINT "I AM A COMPUTER. WHAT'S YOUR NAME. "
13   INPUT A$
19   PRINT "NICE TO MEET YOU, ";A$;". PLEASE ";
20   PRINT "CHOOSE A NUMBER FROM 1 TO 300. ";
30   INPUT N
31   PRINT
32   PRINT
40   FOR J=1 TO N
50   LET K=RND(J)
60   NEXT J
70   LET J=0
80   IF J<2 THEN 100
84   PRINT "GOODBYE NOW, ";A$;". TAKE CARE."
90   STOP
100  LET J=J+1
110  LET I=1
120  LET X=INT(11*RND(I))
130  LET Y=INT(11*RND(I))
139  PRINT "PLEASE TELL ME, ";A$;", ";
140  PRINT "HOW MUCH IS ";X;"AND    ";Y;
150  INPUT Z
160  IF X+Y=Z THEN 210
170  IF I=3 THEN 240
180  LET I=I+1
189  PRINT "NO, ";A$;", THAT'S ";
190  PRINT "WRONG. TRY AGAIN.   ";
200  GOTO 150
210  PRINT "RIGHT. VERY GOOD."
220  PRINT
230  GOTO 80
240  PRINT "STILL WRONG. THE ANSWER IS   ";X+Y
241  PRINT "HAVE COURAGE, ";A$;". ";
242  PRINT "MAYBE YOU'LL DO BETTER NEXT TIME."
250  PRINT
260  GOTO 80
999  END


RUN
ADD**

I AM A COMPUTER. WHAT'S YOUR NAME.
?AARON
NICE TO MEET YOU, AARON. PLEASE CHOOSE A NUMBER FROM 1 TO 300. ?157


PLEASE TELL ME, AARON, HOW MUCH IS  5     AND    6    ?9
NO, AARON, THAT'S WRONG. TRY AGAIN.  ?13
NO, AARON, THAT'S WRONG. TRY AGAIN.  ?10
STILL WRONG. THE ANSWER IS    11
HAVE COURAGE, AARON. MAYBE YOU'LL DO BETTER NEXT TIME.

                          •
                          •
                          •
           18 more problems
                          •
                          •
                          •

PLEASE TELL ME, AARON, HOW MUCH IS  7     AND     10    ?17
RIGHT. VERY GOOD.

GOODBYE NOW, AARON. TAKE CARE.

DONE
```

string comparison

The language BASIC permits the programmer to compare two
strings in an IF statement. For example, the following statements
might be included in a program.

```
121  IF B$="YES" THEN 440
179  IF "AAA" <= N$ THEN 812
```

Either both sides of the relation in an IF statement have numeric
type or else both sides have string type.

Strings are compared one character at a time, from left to right,
according to the order specified in Table 1, which is called the
ASCII (American Standard Code for Information Interchange)
ordering. This ordering extends the usual alphabetic order to
include other keyboard characters. Thus, one alphabetic string is
less than (<) another alphabetic string if it would precede the

table 1   ASCII *ordering of teletypewriter*
symbols

(lowest)

bell	0	@	P
space	1	A	Q
!	2	B	R
#	3	C	S
$	4	D	T
%	5	E	U
&	6	F	V
'	7	G	W
(	8	H	X
)	9	I	Y
*	:	J	Z
+	;	K	[
,	<	L	]
—	=	M	\
.	>	N	↑
/	?	O	

(highest)

other in a dictionary. For instance,

"FOUR" < "THREE" < "TWO" < "Z"

A programmer may need a little experience to correctly apply
the ASCII ordering to some of the more exotic strings. The null
string (" ") precedes all others because it has no characters at all.
The string " Z" precedes the string "A" because its first character is
a blank, which comes before the letter "A" in the ASCII ordering.

problems

1 Write a program that demands a password as input, checks it
against a string on the data stack, prints the word "HELLO" if
they agree, and prints the word "GOODBYE" if they are unequal.
(An alternative to printing "GOODBYE" is to enter an infinitely
repeating loop which prints the bell character, simulating a burglar
alarm for failure to provide the correct password.)

2 Write a program that sorts four strings supplied as input into
ascending order.

3 Write a program that converts a positive BASIC integer less
than 10000 into its binary representation by printing one string
character at a time, starting from the left. For example, if the
integer 50 is supplied as input, the computer should print the output
110010.

4 Write a conversational program that monitors a game of
matchsticks (see the problems at the end of Section 1 of Chapter 2)
between two (human) players. The program should accept the
players' names as initial input and address them by their names
throughout the game.

5 Write a program, similar to the program NOTICE in Chapter 3,
that prints a mailing list of names as well as office numbers.

6 Write an information-retrieval program for a baseball
announcer, like the program called for in Problem 2 at the end of
Section 1 of Chapter 3, except use the players' names instead of
code numbers.

7 Write an information-retrieval program that stores the names
and birthdays of each of a group of persons on the data stack and
prints the name of every person whose birthday is in a month
supplied as input.

8 Write a program that accepts a person's birthday as input and
prints the name of the appropriate astrological sign.

2 | *cryptography*

The encoding and decoding of messages is called *cryptography.*
The techniques considered here are elementary, and the input and
output is restricted to single BASIC strings, instead of allowing
arbitrarily long messages.

notation for a character in a string

Many BASIC systems allow the programmer access to each
character of a string. Generally, the notation for the Ith character
of the string A$ is either A$[I] or A$[I, I]. The latter notation is
adopted here, for reasons which become apparent in the following
section. Thus, if

A$ = "JOSHUA"

then

A$[1, 1] = "J"
A$[2, 2] = "O"
A$[3, 3] = "S"
A$[4, 4] = "H"
A$[5, 5] = "U"
A$[6, 6] = "A"

The reader may determine by experimentation how the character
access feature, if any, on his system works. It is not present in
CALL/360.

notation for the length of a string

The language BASIC includes a built-in function LEN which has as
its value the length of any string supplied as argument. For
example, if

A$ = "NEVERMORE"

then

LEN(A$) = 9

Also

LEN(" ") = 0   and   LEN("A B") = 3

The function LEN ignores the declared dimension of a string
variable. Its value depends only on the particular string represented
at the time of application.

substitution encoding

One coding device which is popular with puzzle fans is substitution.
The first step for encoding messages with this device is to write a
table of substitutions, as shown in Table 2. Every letter of
the input message is replaced by its substitute, which is the
letter appearing below it in the table. The encoded message
is called a *cryptogram*. The program SUBST prepares cryptograms according to Table 2.

table 2   *a substitution table for coding*

letter	A B C D E F G H I J K L M N O P Q R S T U V W X Y Z
substitute	T F H X Q J E M U P I D C K V B A O L R Z W G N S Y

```
LIST
SUBST

100    REM ** SUBSTITUTION CODING
110    DIM A$[26],C$[26],M$[72]
200    REM ** ENCODING
210    READ A$,C$
220    PRINT "ENTER MESSAGE"
230    INPUT M$
240    FOR I=1 TO LEN(M$)
250    GOSUB 400
260    NEXT I
270    PRINT
280    PRINT M$
290    STOP
400    REM ** SUBR ** TRANSFORM M$[I,I]
410    REM INDEX J
420    FOR J=1 TO 26
430    IF M$[I,I]=A$[J,J] THEN 470
440    NEXT J
450    REM PRESERVE BLANKS
460    GOTO 480
470    LET M$[I,I]=C$[J,J]
480    RETURN
980    DATA "ABCDEFGHIJKLMNOPQRSTUVWXYZ"
990    DATA "TFHXQJEMUPIDCKVBAOLRZWGNSY"
999    END


RUN
SUBST

ENTER MESSAGE
?THE BLUE BOAT SAILS AT SUNSET

RMQ FDZQ FVTR LTUDL TR LZKLQR

DONE
```

The string variable M$ is used both for input and for output. The
loop in lines 240 to 260 relays one letter of the message at a time to

the subroutine in lines 400 to 480 which replaces it according to Table 2, which is coded as data in lines 980 and 990.

Sometimes a programmer's main concerns are machine storage space and program execution time. In these instances, he might omit REM statements and he might not isolate a subroutine which is only invoked at one line of the main program. That is, line 250 might be removed, and the lines of the subroutine might be renumbered and inserted between lines 240 and 260.

Usually, the main concern with a BASIC program is getting it to run successfully, not necessarily most efficiently. Therefore, a higher premium is placed upon clarity than upon brevity.

There is another noteworthy feature of SUBST. The substitution table can be changed merely by replacing line 990. A programmer should design his coding so that modifications can be easily made.

substitution decoding

A person who knows the substitution table may decode a cryptogram by replacing each of its letters by the one appearing above it in the table. The program SUBST was written with forethought to allow its modification into a program that decodes as well as encodes. This additional facility is achieved by appending the following lines.

```
120   PRINT "FOR ENCODING TYPE '0'; FOR DECODING TYPE '1'."
130   INPUT N
140   IF N=0 THEN 200
150   REM ** DECODING
160   READ C$,A$
170   GOTO 220

RUN
SUBST

FOR ENCODING TYPE '0'; FOR DECODING TYPE '1'.
? 1
ENTER MESSAGE
?RMQ FDZQ FVTR LTUDL TR LZKLQR

THE BLUE BOAT SAILS AT SUNSET

DONE
```

Many newspapers have a daily cryptogram because they make such enjoyable puzzles. Of course, the newspaper reader does not know the substitution table. He works it out by trial and error, using knowledge of English text.

For example, a one-letter word must be either "A" or "I". A three-letter word is likely to be "THE", particularly, if it begins a

sentence. And one letter of any two-letter word must be a vowel.
Furthermore, certain letters such as "E" and "R" occur far more
often than other letters, such as "Q" and "Z".

There are 26! (about 4×10^{26}) different possible substitution
tables, but the clues mentioned above and others make cryptograms
easy enough to solve that they are not often used to code
confidential information.

increment coding

One special kind of substitution procedure is incrementing. First an
integer i between 1 and 25 (inclusive) is chosen. Then the
substitution table is formed by writing the $(1 + i)$th letter of the
alphabet below the letter "A", the $(2 + i)$th letter below the letter
"B", and so on. In general, the $(n + i)$th letter of the alphabet is
written immediately below the nth letter, provided that $n + i \leqslant 26$.
If $n + i > 26$, then the $(n + i - 26)$th letter is written below the
nth letter. For instance, if the increment number $i = 18$ is chosen,
the result is Table 3.

An increment cryptogram makes a poor puzzle if it is known that
the encoding was by increment substitutions. As soon as the solver
guesses one letter, he can decode the entire message easily.
However, a clever trick leads to a new encoding procedure that
disguises messages in a way that is far more difficult to unravel than
a cryptogram.

keyword encoding

The trick, really just a generalization of simple increment coding, is
to use several different increments, for example, 18, 1, 22, 5, and 14.
These five incremental values are the sequence numbers of the
letters "R", "A", "V", "E", and "N" in the alphabet. The word
"RAVEN" is considered a *keyword*. The encoding scheme is to
increment the letters which are 1st, 6th, 11th, . . . of the message
by 18, to increment the letters of the message which are 2nd, 7th,
12th, . . . by 1, and so on. Table 4 shows the encoding of a message

table 3   *an increment-substitution table*

letter	A B C D E F G H I J K L M N O P Q R S T U V W X Y Z
substitute	S T U V W X Y Z A B C D E F G H I J K L M N O P Q R

table 4 *encoding a message with the keyword* RAVEN

message letters	T H E	M E S S A G E	A R R I V E D	S A F E L Y
sequence numbers	20 8 5	13 5 19 19 1 7 5	1 18 18 9 22 5 4	19 1 6 5 12 25
increment	18 1 22	5 14 18 1 22 5 14	18 1 22 5 14 18 1	22 5 14 18 1 22
encoded numbers	12 9 1	18 19 11 20 23 12 19	19 19 14 14 10 23 5	15 6 20 23 13 21
encoded letters	L I A	R S K T W L S	S S N N J W E	O F T W M U

using the keyword "RAVEN". The first row of the chart is the original message and the last row is the encoded message.

The program KEYWRD encodes using the keyword "RAVEN". The string variable A$ is assigned the string

"ABCDEFGHIJKLMNOPQRSTUVWXYZ"

and the string variable M$ is used for both input and output. The main loop converts a letter in steps corresponding to the rows of Table 4, which are clearly indicated by pairs of REM statements with asterisks. Lines 200 to 250 convert a letter of the message into its sequence number in the alphabet, as in the second row of Table 4. Lines 260 to 350 obtain the correct increment number, as given in the third row of Table 4. Lines 360 to 400 determined the alphabetic sequence number of the encoded letter, as in the fourth row. And line 410 produces the encoded letter as in the fifth row. To change the keyword, one need replace only lines 970 and 980.

Line 240 might appear somewhat mysterious. It is executed only if the FOR–NEXT loop in lines 210 to 230 determines that a character of the input message is not a letter of the alphabet, in which case the same character (e.g., a blank) is used in the output message.

```
LIST
KEYWRD

100  REM ***** KEYWORD *****
110  DIM A$[26],M$[72]
120  LET Q=1
150  LET A$="ABCDEFGHIJKLMNOPQRSTUVWXYZ"
160  PRINT "TYPE MESSAGE"
170  INPUT M$
180  REM ***** MAIN LOOP *****
190  FOR I=1 TO LEN(M$)
200  REM * FIND SEQ NUMBER  J  OF LETTER  M$[I,I]  *
210  FOR J=1 TO 26
```

```
220    IF M$[I,I]=A$[J,J] THEN 250
230    NEXT J
240    GOTO 420
250    REM *
260    REM ** FIND INCREMENT NUMBER  S   FOR  M$[I,I]   **
270    READ S
310    LET Q=Q+1
320    IF Q <= 5 THEN 350
330    LET Q=1
340    RESTORE
350    REM **
360    REM *** FIND ENCODING NUMBER  E   FOR  M$[I,I]   ***
370    LET E=J+S
380    IF E <= 26 THEN 400
390    LET E=E-26
400    REM ***
410    LET M$[I,I]=A$[E,E]
420    NEXT I
430    REM ***** END OF MAIN LOOP *****
440    PRINT
450    PRINT M$
460    STOP
970    REM KEYWORD IS "RAVEN"
980    DATA 18,1,22,5,14
999    END


RUN
KEYWRD

TYPE MESSAGE
?THE MESSAGE ARRIVED SAFELY

LIA RSKTWLS SSNNJWE OFTWMU

DONE
```

An ingenious way to test the program KEYWRD is to supply as
input the message

```
ZZZZZ ZZZZZ ZZZZZ
```

If the program is correct, the output should be

```
RAVEN RAVEN RAVEN
```

keyword decoding

Perhaps the most obvious way to decode a message encoded by a
keyword is to subtract off the increments from the sequence
numbers of the letters in the encoded message. The decoding
procedure would look like Table 4 turned upside down. In each
column of the chart, subtract the increment from the encoded
number. If the difference is less than 1, then add 26.

table 5   *decoding a message with a complementary keyword*

encoded letters	L I A	R S K T W L S	S S N N J W E	O F T W M U
encoded numbers	12 9 1	18 19 11 20 23 12 19	19 19 14 14 10 23 5	15 6 20 23 13 21
comple-mentary increment	8 25 4	21 12 8 25 4 21 12	8 25 4 21 12 8 25	4 21 12 8 25 4
decoded numbers	20 8 5	13 5 19 19 1 7 5	1 18 18 9 22 5 4	19 1 6 5 12 25
decoded letters	T H E	M E S S A G E	A R R I V E D	S A F E L Y

Modifying the program KEYWRD so that it can also decode would require a lot of instructions if the subtraction scheme is used. An easier programming solution is to add *complementary increments,* where the *complement* of an integer n between 1 and 25 is taken to be $26 - n$. Thus, the complements of the numbers 18, 1, 22, 5, and 14 are 8, 25, 4, 21, and 12. Table 5 shows the decoding of the encoded message.

If the sum of an encoded number and the complementary increment is greater than 26, then subtract 26 to obtain the decoded number. Proof that the method of complementary increments always works is left as an exercise for the reader.

Appending the following instructions to KEYWRD will give it decoding facility via the method of complementary increments.

```
130   PRINT "FOR ENCODING TYPE '0'; FOR DECODING TYPE '1'."
140   INPUT N
280   IF N=0 THEN 310
290   REM   COMPLEMENTARY INCREMENT FOR DECODING
300   LET S=26-S

RUN
KEYWRD

FOR ENCODING TYPE '0'; FOR DECODING TYPE '1'.
? 1
TYPE MESSAGE
?LIA RSKTWLS SSNNJWE OFTWMU

THE MESSAGE ARRIVED SAFELY

DONE
```

If the keyword is not known, then decoding a message is quite difficult. It is a big help to know at least the length of the keyword.

problems

1   Modify the program SUBST so that the spaces between words of the encoded message are suppressed. (The decoding procedure will not replace them, of course.)

2   Modify the program SUBST so that it inserts nonsense words at random between words of the encoded message. Use the following scheme. After each word is encoded, obtain a random number between 0 and 1. If it is less than ⅓ go directly to the encoding of the next word. Otherwise, generate a random number between 1 and 26 and interpret it as the first letter of a nonsense word. As usual, 1 is interpreted as "A", 2 as "B", and so on. Obtain another random number between 0 and 1. If it is less than ⅓ leave the nonsense word at one letter and go on to encoding the next word of the actual message. Otherwise, extend the nonsense word by another random letter, and so on.

3   Modify the program SUBST further along the direction indicated in Problem 2 by making it insert a random number of nonsense words between words of the encoded message.

4   Modify the program KEYWRD so that the usual spacing is suppressed, and instead, the letters of the output message are grouped into fives. For example, the encoded message in the text would be written out as LIARS KTWLS SSNNT WEOFT WMU.

5   Modify the program KEYWRD so that it inputs arbitrarily many lines of message.

6   Modify the program KEYWRD so that it inputs arbitrarily many lines of message and a continuous text as keyword. The idea is to alternately input lines of message and keyword text from, for example, a newspaper.

7   A coding scheme which is completely different from the substitution and keyword methods is permutation. Group the letters of the input message into fives (or larger groups, if desired). Pick a reordering of the numbers from 1 to 5, say, 4, 1, 5, 3, 2. Then permute each group of letters according to the reordering of the numbers. According to the sequence 4, 1, 5, 3, 2, the first letter in each group becomes second, because 1 is the second number in the sequence. The second letter becomes fifth, because 2 is the fifth number in the sequence. Likewise the third letter becomes fourth, the fourth letter becomes first, and the fifth letter becomes third. The message A THREE DOLLAR BILL IS PHONY is first grouped as ATHRE EDOLL ARBIL LISPH ONY and then permuted into

RAEHT LELOD LALBR PLESI OYN. Notice that special handling
of the last group is required if it is not a full five. Write a program
that encodes messages according to this scheme.

3 | *text analysis*

The programs of this section abstract some of the simpler
techniques of text analysis. They are concerned with the occurrence
of letters and words, which is important to manuscript identification
and to cryptography.

substrings

A consecutive sequence of characters within a string is called a
substring. For the sake of completeness, the null string is regarded
as a substring of every string, and any string is considered to be a
substring of itself. Thus, the string "THEN" has the following
substrings.

"" (null string)	length 0
"T", "H", "E", "N"	length 1
"TH", "HE", "EN"	length 2
"THE", "HEN"	length 3
"THEN"	length 4

Some BASIC systems permit the programmer to have direct access
to arbitrary substrings. In such a system, if B$ is any string variable,
then the notation B$[I, J] means the substring of B$ beginning
with the Ith character and running up through the Jth character.
Thus, if B$ = "ALEXANDER", then B$[4, 8] = "XANDE", and
B$[2, 2] = "L". In general B$[I, I] means the Ith letter.

Ordinarily B$[I, J] has no meaning if $I > J$. However, in the
special case that $I = J + 1$ at the time of evaluation of I and J, the
computer takes B$[I, J] to be the null string. This convention is a
great convenience in the design of certain loops.

frequency tabulation for a letter

The program COUNT tabulates the number of occurrences of the
letter "A" in a line of text. The string variable M$ accepts the
message as input at line 130. Line 150 sets the initial value of the
numeric variable S at zero. The FOR–NEXT loop in lines 160 to
190 scans the letters of the message and adds 1 to the value of S
each time it encounters the letter "A".

```
LIST
COUNT

100   REM COUNT THE NUMBER OF OCCURRENCES OF 'A'
110   DIM M$[72]
120   PRINT "TYPE MESSAGE"
130   INPUT M$
140   PRINT
150   LET S=0
160   FOR I=1 TO LEN(M$)
170   IF M$[I,I] <> "A" THEN 190
180   LET S=S+1
190   NEXT I
200   PRINT " 'A' OCCURS ";S;" TIMES"
210   END

RUN
COUNT

TYPE MESSAGE
?THIS PROGRAM ASSISTS IN TEXT ANALYSIS

 'A' OCCURS  4     TIMES

DONE
```

The program MOST determines which letter in a line of text occurs
most often. If the largest number of occurrences is shared by two or
more letters, the program MOST prints only the one which is

```
LIST
MOST

100   REM DETERMINE WHICH LETTER OCCURS MOST OFTEN
110   DIM M$[72],Z$[26]
120   REM B$ STORES MOST FREQUENT LETTER
130   DIM B$[1]
140   PRINT "TYPE MESSAGE"
150   INPUT M$
160   PRINT
170   READ Z$
180   DATA "ABCDEFGHIJKLMNOPQRSTUVWXYZ"
190   REM X COUNTS NUMBER OF OCCURRENCES OF MOST FREQUENT LETTER
200   LET X=0
210   FOR J=1 TO 26
220   REM ** LET Y = NUMBER OF OCCURRENCES OF Z$[J,J] IN M$
230   LET Y=0
240   FOR I=1 TO LEN(M$)
250   IF M$[I,I] <> Z$[J,J] THEN 270
260   LET Y=Y+1
270   NEXT I
280   REM **
290   IF X >= Y THEN 320
300   LET B$=Z$[J,J]
310   LET X=Y
320   NEXT J
330   PRINT B$;"   OCCURS ";X;" TIMES"
340   END

RUN
MOST

TYPE MESSAGE
?THIS PROGRAM ALSO ASSISTS IN TEXT ANALYSIS

S   OCCURS  8     TIMES

DONE
```

earliest in the alphabet. The most frequent letter, subject to the restriction just mentioned, and its number of occurrences are printed out. The flowchart in Figures 1 and 2 illustrates the logic of the program MOST.

occurrence of a word

Literature scholars are often concerned with the occurrence of certain critical words, phrases, and concepts. Attorneys also have this interest. Finding a word or a phrase is not much more difficult than finding a letter. The task of isolating a concept, however, is

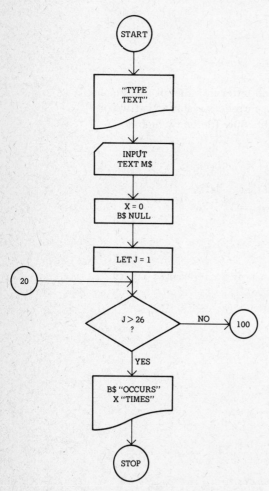

Figure 1   Flowchart of the program MOST, part 1.

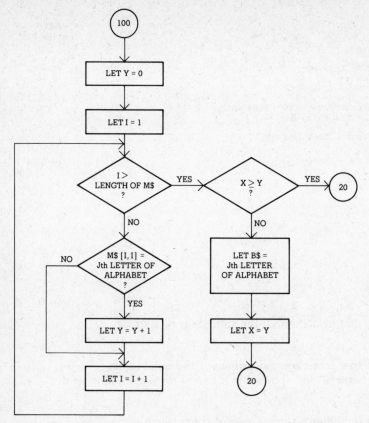

Figure 2   Flowchart of the program MOST, *part 2.*

extremely hard, and will not be considered here. The program THE
scans a single line of text without punctuation to determine if it
contains the word "THE".

For simplicity, the text supplied as input is without punctuation
characters. Therefore, any word, except possibly the first and last
words, is preceded and followed by a blank. The only difficulty is in
distinguishing an occurrence of the word "THE" from a substring
whose value is "THE" but which is contained in a larger word, such
as "WHETHER". This problem is resolved by looking for the
blanks before and after a substring "THE" of the line of text, as
shown in the FOR–NEXT loop in lines 140 to 160. Line 130
determines if "THE" is the first word of the text and line 170 looks
to see if "THE" is the last word.

```
LIST
THE

100   DIM M$[72]
110   PRINT "ENTER MESSAGE"
120   INPUT M$
130   IF M$[1,4]="THE " THEN 200
140   FOR I=1 TO LEN(M$)-4
150   IF M$[I,I+4]=" THE " THEN 200
160   NEXT I
170   IF M$[LEN(M$)-3,LEN(M$)]=" THE" THEN 200
180   PRINT "NO OCCURRENCES OF 'THE'"
190   STOP
200   PRINT "AT LEAST ONE OCCURRENCE OF 'THE'"
999   END


RUN
THE

ENTER MESSAGE
?WHO KNOWS WHETHER IT IS TUESDAY
NO OCCURRENCES OF 'THE'

DONE
```

problems

1   Write a program that prints out all the substrings of a string supplied as input.

2   Write a program that tabulates and prints out the number of occurrences of each letter of the alphabet in a line of text supplied as input.

3   Write a program that counts the number of occurrences of the word "THE" in a line of text supplied as input.

4   Write a program that accepts a string as input and which prints out the same string centered on the print line, so that there is at most one more blank at the right of the string than at the left.

5   Write a program that rearranges the words of a string supplied as input so that they are in alphabetical order.

6   Write a program that counts the number of different substrings of a string of length 4. For example, the string "ABAB" has one substring of length 0, two of length 1 ("A" and "B"), two of length 2 ("AB" and "BA"), two of length 3, and one of length 4 for a total of eight different substrings.

7   Write a program that prints out the substrings of a string in alphabetical order.

8   Write a program that computes the average length of a word in a line of text supplied as input. Let the line of text consist of words and single blanks separating them, but no punctuation marks. The average word length is a statistic actually used to determine authorship of a manuscript.

9 Write a program that examines a line of text and determines the ratio of letters in the first half of the alphabet to letters in the second half.

suggested reading

Sedelow, Sally Y. "The Computer in the Humanities and Fine Arts", *Computing Surveys* **2,** No. 2, 89–110 (June, 1970).

mathematical methods

THIS CHAPTER begins with a description of some techniques from the branch of mathematics called numerical analysis. What motivates this discussion is that an exact solution to a problem might be difficult or impossible to attain, and that even if it can be attained, it may be much more convenient for a computer to calculate an approximation. The methods presented are combing to find maxima and minima of functions, binary chopping to locate roots, and polygonal approximations to determine area. No calculus or other advanced mathematics is required.

The last three sections are relatively independent of each other and of what precedes them in the chapter. One explains a program that draws the graph of a function on the printout paper. Another introduces some built-in BASIC functions not yet described. The last section presents some special BASIC instructions for convenience in handling matrices.

1 | finding maxima and minima by combing

Suppose that a function $f(x)$ is defined on a finite interval $[a, b]$ and that it is desirable to know at what point or points the function exhibits a specific property. A naive way to determine this information within a small margin of error is to search the interval with a fine-tooth comb, precisely one whose teeth are no farther apart than the allowed margin. This section is concerned with programming a computer to perform such a search. The combing

115

finding
maxima
and
minima
by combing
section 1

method is a starting point for approximation techniques. It has application to a wide variety of problems. A more efficient but less elementary approach is developed in Section 2.

extreme values of a function

Suppose that $f(x)$ is a function which takes values at every number in the interval $[a, b]$. Also, suppose that c is a number in the interval $[a, b]$ such that $f(c)$ is greater than or equal to the value of the function at any other number in the interval. Under these circumstances, it is said that the function $f(x)$ has a *maximum at the number c* in the interval $[a, b]$.

Similarly, it is said that the function $f(x)$ has a *minimum at the number d* in the interval $[a, b]$ if $f(d)$ is less than or equal to the function value at any other number in the interval.

Collectively, the maximum value $f(c)$ and the minimum value $f(d)$ are called *extreme values* of the function $f(x)$ and the numbers c and d are called *extrema* in the interval $[a, b]$. It is quite possible for a function to achieve either or both of the extreme values more than once.

The precise determination of extrema and extreme values of differentiable functions is a standard topic in calculus. The approximation method given here applies to a wider class of functions and requires no knowledge of calculus.

the program MAXMIN

The program MAXMIN obtains approximate extreme values for whatever function FNA(X) is defined at line 110 on whatever interval has its endpoints designated at line 130. Line 150 assigns the value FNA(A) to the variable L as a first attempt at a minimum. Line 160 starts the variable U at the value FNA(A) as a first attempt at a maximum. Lines 155 and 165 initialize the variables M and V at the endpoint A where the first trial minimum and maximum occur.

```
LIST
MAXMIN

100   REM FIND APPROXIMATE MIN AND MAX OF FNA ON INTERVAL [A,B]
110   DEF FNA(X)=X↑3-6*X↑2+11*X-6
120   REM ENDPOINTS
130   DATA .75,2
140   READ A,B
150   LET L=FNA(A)
155   LET M=A
160   LET U=FNA(A)
165   LET V=A
```

```
170    REM INCREMENT
180    DATA .001
190    READ H
200    FOR X=A TO B STEP H
210    IF FNA(X) >= L THEN 230
215    LET M=X
220    LET L=FNA(X)
230    IF FNA(X) <= U THEN 250
235    LET V=X
240    LET U=FNA(X)
250    NEXT X
260    PRINT "MIN VALUE ";L;" OCCURS AT X = ";M
270    PRINT "MAX VALUE ";U;" OCCURS AT X = ";V
999    END


RUN
MAXMIN

MIN VALUE -.703125    OCCURS AT X =  .75
MAX VALUE  .384899    OCCURS AT X =  1.42298

DONE
```

FOR–NEXT *with* STEP

The program MAXMIN uses a new kind of FOR–NEXT loop in
lines 200 to 250. What is different is that as the variable X goes from
its lower limit A to its upper limit B, its value is not necessarily
increased by 1 during each iteration of the loop. Instead, the value
of X is incremented by the value of H, which is .001 in this case.
Any number or arithmetic expression may appear after the word
STEP in a FOR statement with STEP. If the step is positive, then
the loop terminates when the value of the FOR-variable exceeds the
value of the upper limit. The next section explains the possibility of
a negative step. A zero step results in an infinite loop.

Whenever line 210 determines that a function value is less than
the trial value of L, that function value becomes a new trial
minimum at line 220. Whenever line 230 discovers a function value
greater than the trial maximum U, line 240 assigns that function
value to U, replacing its old value. Correspondingly, the values of
the variables M and V are changed to indicate where the new trial
minimum and maximum values occur.

margin of error

For the program MAXMIN to work correctly, it is essential that the
changes in the function value should not occur too rapidly with
respect to the margin of error indicated at line 180. For any
continuous functions on a finite interval, it is always possible to
designate a small enough margin of error that the program
MAXMIN does work correctly, but deciding how small may be

117

**approxi-
mating
roots
by binary
chopping**
section 2

difficult. For polynomials of small degree and integer coefficients, the number .001 is sufficiently small.

problems

1   Find the minimum and maximum values of the polynomial function $f(x) = 4x^3 - 6x + 2$ on the interval $[-1, 7]$.

2   Find the minimum and maximum values of the polynomial function $f(x) = 7x^8 - 12x^5 - x^3 + 3$ on the interval $[-2, 1]$.

3   Write a program that uses a fine-tooth comb to search for roots of a function, that is, numbers on which the function has the value 0. Describe the hazards of this method.

4   Determine, approximately, where the function $(x^3 - x)/(x^2 + x + 1)$ has its minimum and maximum on the interval $[0, 1]$.

5   Find the minimum and the maximum of the polynomial $x^3 - 6x^2 + 8x + 1$ on the interval $[0, 4]$.

6   Find the minimum and the maximum of the polynomial $x^3 - 6x^2 + 8x + 1$ on the interval $[-1, 5]$.

2 | approximating roots by binary chopping

The usual approach to determining roots of a polynomial is by a combination of factoring and applying the quadratic formula to second-degree factors. However, when the roots are irrational, factoring may be difficult. In fact there is no general method for factoring a polynomial of degree five or higher. Finding the roots of certain functions other than polynomials may be even more difficult in practice. This section focuses on a numerical technique called *binary chopping* for calculating arbitrarily good approximate roots.

an initial approximation

Suppose that the value of a continuous function goes from negative to positive or from positive to negative in an interval. Then the graph of the function begins on one side of the x-axis and crosses to the other. Evidently, somewhere in that interval the graph of the function must cross the x-axis, as illustrated in Figure 1. The x-coordinate of a point of intersection between the graph of the function and the x-axis is a number on which the function value is 0, that is, a root of the function.

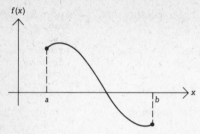

Figure 1   *The graph of a function that crosses the x-axis.*

For example, the polynomial $x^5 - 3x^2 + 1$ has the value 1 when $x = 0$, since

$$0^5 - 3 \times 0^2 + 1 = 0 - 0 + 1 = 1$$

and it has the value -1 when $x = 1$, since

$$1^5 - 3 \times 1^2 + 1 = 1 - 3 + 1 = -1$$

It follows that somewhere in the interval $[0, 1]$ there is a number on which the polynomial has the value 0. The initial approximation to a root by the binary-chopping method is the midpoint of an interval in which the function value changes sign, in this case the midpoint .5 of the interval $[0, 1]$.

The midpoint of an interval is no farther than half the interval length from any point in the interval. Thus, if a continuous function changes sign in an interval, the interval midpoint is no farther than half the interval length from a root of the function. In particular, the midpoint .5 of the interval $[0, 1]$ is within distance ½ of a root of the polynomial $x^5 - 3x^2 + 1$.

improving the approximation

If it so happens that the midpoint of the first interval is a root of the function, then the binary-chopping process is terminated, since an exact solution has been found. Otherwise, the function value at the interval midpoint is either positive or negative. A second interval is now to be considered and its endpoints are the midpoint of the first interval and the endpoint of the first interval where the function has opposite sign from its value at the midpoint.

The value of the polynomial $x^5 - 3x^2 + 1$ at the midpoint .5 of the interval $[0, 1]$ is $(.5)^5 - 3(.5)^2 + 1$, (i.e., .28125), which is positive. Since the polynomial value at the endpoint 0 is 1, a positive number, and the polynomial value at the endpoint 1 is -1, a

119

approxi-
mating
roots
by binary
chopping
section 2

negative number, the second interval for this example is [.5, 1] at whose endpoints the function values have opposite sign, rather than [0, .5], at whose endpoints the function values have the same sign.

Since the function value changes sign on the second interval, the function has a root in the second interval. In particular, the polynomial $x^5 - 3x^2 + 1$ has a root in the interval [.5, 1]. It is conceivable, of course, that there is also some even (nonzero) number of roots of the function somewhere in the interval between the midpoint and the endpoint on which the function value has the same sign as on the midpoint. However, the binary-chopping process is aimed at detecting one root at a time, not all of them simultaneously.

The second interval has half the length of the first, so the maximum distance its midpoint could be from a root is half the maximum possible distance that the midpoint of the first interval could be from a root. In particular, the midpoint .75 of the interval [.5, 1] is within distance $\frac{1}{4}$ of a root of the polynomial $x^5 - 3x^2 + 1$. The binary-chopping method takes the midpoint of the second interval as its second approximation to a root.

Another iteration of these steps yields a third approximation. Since the value of the polynomial $x^5 - 3x^2 + 1$ at $x = .75$ is about $-.450195$ (i.e., negative), the third interval for this example is [.5, .75]. Its midpoint .625, the third approximation, lies no farther than distance $\frac{1}{8}$ from a root.

As illustrated in Figure 2, the length of the interval under observation shrinks by a factor of one-half with each successive binary chop. Precisely, each time the interval is chopped in half, the approximation improves by one binary digit. Hence, it is possible to determine a number within an arbitrarily small distance of a root.

The program ROOT applies the binary-chopping process to whatever function is given in the DEF statement at line 110. The

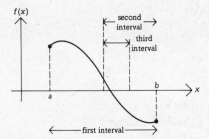

Figure 2   Shrinking intervals for the binary-chopping method of approximating roots.

allowable error tolerance for the final approximation is obtained
during program execution by the INPUT statement at line 130.

```
LIST
ROOT

100   REM   FIND APPROX ROOT OF FNA BY BINARY CHOPPING
110   DEF FNA(X)=X↑5-3*X↑2+1
120   PRINT "HOW CLOSE AN APPROXIMATION";
130   INPUT E
140   PRINT "SUPPLY INITIAL INTERVAL ENDPOINTS";
150   INPUT A,B
160   PRINT
170   PRINT
180   PRINT "LOWER          UPPER                        FN VALUE"
190   PRINT "ENDPT          ENDPT          MIDPT         AT MIDPT"
200   REM   APPROXIMATION: X = MIDPT OF INTERVAL [A,B]
210   LET X=(B+A)/2
220   PRINT A,B,X,FNA(X)
230   REM   STOP IF CLOSE ENOUGH APPROXIMATION
240   IF FNA(X)=0 THEN 260
250   IF X-A>E THEN 290
260   PRINT
270   PRINT "APPROX ROOT:",X
280   STOP
290   REM   SHRINK INTERVAL, FNA MUST STILL CROSS X-AXIS
300   IF SGN(FNA(A))=SGN(FNA(X)) THEN 330
310   LET B=X
320   GOTO 200
330   LET A=X
340   GOTO 200
999   END


RUN
ROOT

HOW CLOSE AN APPROXIMATION?.001
SUPPLY INITIAL INTERVAL ENDPOINTS?0,1


LOWER           UPPER
ENDPT           ENDPT          MIDPT          FN VALUE
                                              AT MIDPT
0               1              .5             .28125
.5              1              .75            -.450195
.5              .75            .625           -7.65076E-02
.5              .625           .5625          .107095
.5625           .625           .59375         1.61763E-02
.59375          .625           .609375        -2.99859E-02
.59375          .609375        .601563        -6.85453E-03
.59375          .601563        .597656        4.67408E-03
.597656         .601563        .599609        -1.08695E-03
.597656         .599609        .598633        1.79434E-03

APPROX ROOT:    .598633

DONE
```

endpoints for initial interval

The INPUT statement at line 150 obtains the programmer's choice
of endpoints for the initial interval. For a fixed function, different
designations of endpoints on successive runs of ROOT will result
in the computer's discovery of different roots. For example, the
polynomial $x^5 - 3x^2 + 1$ has a root somewhere in the interval

121

approxi-
mating
roots
by binary
chopping
section 2

$[-1, 0]$, because its value varies continuously from the negative number -3 to the positive number 1. It has another root somewhere in the interval $[1, 2]$ because its value varies continuously from the negative number -1 to the positive number 21 on that interval.

It is not necessarily easy to determine endpoints for the initial interval of a binary chopping process. For a "tricky" function, some inventiveness may be needed to find two numbers on which the function has opposite signs. One general approach is to seek maxima and minima, as discussed in the previous section, or to use calculus.

It is wholly unwise to ignore the possibility that a particular function has no roots. The value of the polynomial function $x^4 + x^2 + 7$ is always positive, and therefore it has no roots. Other functions may be strictly negative. Obviously, one necessary condition for the existence of a root is that the maximum and minimum of the function must not both be positive or both be negative.

improvement on binary chopping

The binary-chopping process for determining roots has an appealing simplicity and it works on any continuous function. However, there are important special classes of continuous functions for which other methods are better, in the sense that one wishes to minimize the number of iterations needed to get close to a root. Most of these other methods rely on calculus or on higher mathematics. One alternative method which does not use calculus, the so-called secant method, is described in Problem 4 at the end of this section.

maxima and minima by binary chopping

For a continuous function on a finite interval, a binary-chopping approach yields approximate maximum and minimum function values much more rapidly than combing, provided that some care is exercised in deciding what interval to chop. Roughly, the idea is that instead of being concerned with where the function is negative and where it is positive, as in the root-seeking procedure, the extreme value-seeking method is concerned with where the function is increasing and where it is decreasing.

There are some special cases in which detecting the maximum of a function $f(x)$ on an interval $[a, b]$ is particularly simple. One of these is when $f(x)$ increases in value from the initial endpoint a until some interior point c and then decreases until the terminal endpoint b. Figure 3 illustrates this case. It is then possible to directly apply a binary-chopping approach. Similarly, binary

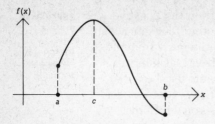

Figure 3   *The graph of a function $f(x)$ on the interval $[a, b]$ which
increases from a to c and then decreases from c to b.*

chopping detects the minimum of a function that decreases up to
some point and then increases.

local maxima and minima

In general, functions may switch back and forth between increasing
and decreasing more than once in an interval. Where it goes from
increasing to decreasing, the graph has a "peak" and it is said that
the function has a *local maximum*. Where it goes from decreasing
to increasing, the graph has a "valley", and it is said that the
function has a *local minimum*. Figure 4 shows the graph of a
function with more than one local maximum and more than one
local minimum.

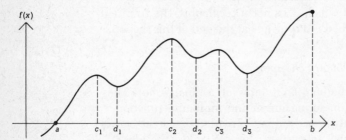

Figure 4   *The graph of a function with local maxima at c_1, c_2, and c_3
and local minima at d_1, d_2, and d_3.*

Figure 4 also illustrates the fact that the maximum or minimum
of a continuous function on an interval may occur at either endpoint
as well as at a turning point between increasing and decreasing, in
the general case. The maximum of the function illustrated occurs at
the endpoint b, not at any of the local maxima c_1, c_2, or c_3. The
minimum occurs at the endpoint a, not at any of the local minima
d_1, d_2, or d_3.

Some of the problems below are concerned with the determination of maxima and minima. It is the responsibility of the programmer to determine whether to use binary chopping or some modification. Do not use combing.

problems

1 Determine the cube root of the number 7 to four decimal places by applying the program ROOT to the polynomial $x^3 - 7$.

2 Find a root of the function $x^7 - 5x^2 + 1$ within .001 error tolerance.

3 Use the program ROOT to find the x-coordinate in the interval [0, 1] of a point where the graph of the function $f(x) = \sqrt{2x}$ meets the graph of the function $g(x) = 1/x$. Allow .001 error. Hint: This problem is equivalent to finding a root of the function $h(x) = \sqrt{2x} - 1/x$.

4 The secant method of approximating a root of a continuous function $f(x)$ also begins with a choice of an interval $[a, b]$ in which $f(a)$ and $f(b)$ have opposite signs. Whereas the binary-chopping process takes the midpoint of an interval as its approximation, the secant method chooses an approximation proportionally closer to whichever endpoint has its function value closer to 0. Precisely, the secant method approximation is

$$x = a + (b - a)\,\frac{|f(a)|}{|f(a)| + |f(b)|}$$

Like the binary chopping process the secant method successively shrinks the interval under observation. The endpoints of the next interval are the approximation x, as above, and the endpoint of the current interval where the function has opposite sign from its value at x.

The appropriate change in the program ROOT is to replace lines 210 and 250 by

```
210   LET X=A+(B-A)*ABS(FNA(A))/(ABS(FNA(A))+ABS(FNA(B)))
250   IF B-A>E THEN 290
```

Apply this modified version of ROOT to the polynomial $x^5 - 3x^2 + 1$ and observe how much faster it obtains the desired approximation than the sample run of the original ROOT program in the text.

5 Does the polynomial $5x^4 - 3x^3 + 4x^2 + 1$ have any roots?

6 Is the square root of 11 plus the cube root of 2 less than 4.58?

7 The function $x^3 - 9x^2 + 20x - 5$ has a maximum value in the interval $[0, 4]$. Find where it occurs, within .001 error allowance.

8 The function $x^3 - 9x^2 + 10 - 5$ has a minimum value in the interval $[4, 5]$. Find where it occurs, within .001 error allowance.

9 Determine where, approximately, the function $(x^3 - x)/(x^2 + x + 1)$ has its maximum on the interval $[-1, 0]$.

10 Where on the interval $[-1, 1]$ does the function $x^3 - 3x^2 + 4x - 2$ have its maximum and minimum?

11 Find the minimum and maximum of the function $(x - 2)(x - 3)(x - 4)$ on the interval $[2, 4]$.

12 Does the function $x^4 + 3x + 2.1$ have any roots? Find its minimum. If it is positive, then there are no roots.

13 Does the function $x^4 + 3x^3 + 2.1$ have any roots?

3 | *area*

This section describes a method for computing an approximation to the area of a planar region, part or all of whose boundary is curved. The idea is to approximate the region by a family of nonoverlapping simple plane figures, like triangles, rectangles, and trapezoids, whose areas are easy to compute, and to sum the areas of those simple figures.

area of rectangles, triangles, and trapezoids

In elementary plane geometry, formulas for the area of triangles and trapezoids are derived from the basic definition that the area of a rectangle is the product of its height and its base. The area of a triangle is one-half the product of its height and its base. A *trapezoid* is a four-sided plane figure, two of whose sides are parallel, as shown at the bottom of Figure 5. The area of a trapezoid is the product of the average length of the parallel sides and the distance between them.

area of a polygon

A *polygon* is a planar region whose boundary is connected and consists of a finite number of straight line segments joined end to end. Rectangles, triangles, and trapezoids are examples of polygons.

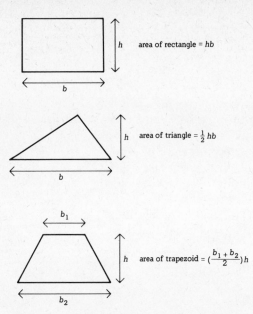

Figure 5   Some plane figures and their areas.

Other examples are illustrated in Figure 6. A general method for calculating the exact area of any polygon is to subdivide the polygon into triangles and to add the areas of the triangles.

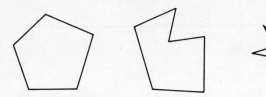

Figure 6   Some polygons.

area of a region with curved boundary

Whereas a polygon can be exactly filled with triangles of appropriate sizes, a region with curved boundary cannot. Nevertheless, a lower bound for the area of such a region may be obtained by packing it nearly full of nonoverlapping polygons and summing their areas. The more completely full the region is packed, the closer this lower bound comes to the actual area. Similarly, an upper bound for the area of such a region may be obtained by covering it with nonoverlapping polygons and adding up their areas. If the covering polygons do not extend too far outside the region then a good upper bound is obtained.

area between a curve and the x-axis

The packing and covering method for approximating area will now be applied to the problem of calculating the area between a curve representing the values of a continuous function $f(x)$ and the x-axis over a finite interval. For certain functions, techniques of integral calculus will give an exact answer. The method given here gives only an approximate answer, but it applies to a larger class of functions and requires no table of symbolic integrals.

Figures 7 and 8 illustrate ways of packing and covering the region between the curve representing the polynomial function

$$x^3 - 6x^2 + 11x$$

and the x-axis over the interval [0, 4] with rectangles.

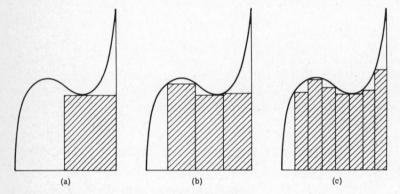

| (a) | (b) | (c) |

Figure 7   Improving inner approximations.

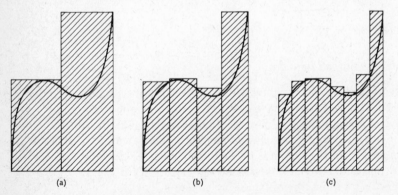

| (a) | (b) | (c) |

Figure 8   Improving outer approximations.

The interval [0, 4] is divided into subintervals. For a given subdivision, the family of inner rectangles is chosen so that the base of each rectangle is a subinterval and the height is the minimum function value over that subinterval. The family of outer rectangles is chosen so that the base of each rectangle is also a subinterval, but the height is the maximum function value. It is known that for any continuous function (e.g., a polynomial function) on an interval, a sufficiently fine subdivision yields inner and outer sums whose difference is arbitrarily small.

The difference between the actual area and the inner sum is less than or equal to the difference between the outer and inner sums. It follows that for a sufficiently fine subdivision, the inner sum is an approximation to the area. Similarly, the outer sum taken over a sufficiently fine subdivision is a good approximation to the area.

intermediate sums

Actual calculations of area often use families of rectangles that neither pack nor cover the region. For a given function on an interval and a fixed subdivision of that interval, suppose that a family of rectangles is chosen so that the base of each is one of the subintervals and the height lies between the minimum and maximum function values on that subinterval, and suppose that there is one rectangle for each subinterval. Then the area of the rectangle over any subinterval lies between the areas of the lower and the upper rectangles for that subinterval. It follows that the sum of the areas of this intermediate family lies between the lower sum and the upper sum. If both the lower sum and the upper sum are satisfactory approximations to the area of the region, then so is any intermediate sum.

the program AREA

The program AREA calculates an approximation to the area lying between the x-axis and the curve representing whatever function is defined at line 110 over whatever interval is designated at line 130. It uses an intermediate sum to circumvent the problem of calculating minimum and maximum function values on each subinterval, thereby economizing on time. The variable S accumulates the total area of the intermediate family.

```
LIST
AREA

100   REM AREA BETWEEN CURVE AND X-AXIS
110   DEF FNA(X)=X↑3-6*X↑2+11*X
120   REM ENDPOINTS OF INTERVAL
130   DATA 0,4
140   READ A,B
150   REM SUBINTERVAL WIDTH
160   DATA .01
170   READ H
200   LET S=0
210   FOR X=A TO B-H STEP H
220   LET S=S+H*FNA(X+H*RND(1))
230   NEXT X
240   PRINT "AREA = ";S
999   END


RUN
AREA

AREA =   23.8816

DONE
```

error estimate

Choosing random function values in each subinterval allows the program AREA to arrive at a quick answer. But the program does not reveal how good or bad an approximation it is to the actual area.

There is little problem in estimating the error in an area approximation if the function $f(x)$ under observation is increasing (or merely nondecreasing) on the interval of interest. Then the minimum function value on each subinterval occurs at the initial endpoint, which is where to obtain the height of the inner rectangle for that subinterval. Similarly, the height of the outer rectangle is the function value of the terminal endpoint of the subinterval, because that is where the maximum of an increasing function occurs. Therefore it is easy to compute inner and outer sums for increasing functions. Likewise, it is easy to compute inner and outer sums for decreasing functions. In either case the difference between the outer and inner sums is an upper bound for the error in an approximation to the area by any intermediate sum.

By finding the local maxima and minima of a function, a programmer can chop the interval of interest into several smaller intervals on each of which the function is either increasing or decreasing. This yields a general method for estimating the error, even for functions whose graphs alternately rise and fall several times on the interval of interest.

The program AREA* computes an approximation to the area between a rising curve and the x-axis and an upper bound for the possible error, that is, the difference between the upper and lower sums. If the possible error is too large, then a finer subdivision of

```
LIST
AREA*

100    REM AREA BETWEEN RISING CURVE AND X-AXIS
110    DEF FNA(X)=X↑3
120    REM ENDPOINTS OF INTERVAL
130    DATA 0,1
140    READ A,B
150    REM ERROR TOLERANCE
160    DATA .01
170    READ E
180    REM SET INITIAL LOWER, MIDPT, UPPER SUMS TO ZERO
190    LET H=1
200    PRINT "SUBINTERVAL"
210    PRINT "WIDTH","LOWER SUM","MIDPOINT SUM","UPPER SUM"
220    REM SET INITIAL LOWER, MIDPT, UPPER SUMS TO ZERO
230    LET L=0
240    LET M=0
250    LET U=0
260    REM COMPUTE LOWER, MIDPOINT, UPPER SUMS
270    FOR X=A TO B-H STEP H
280    LET L=L+H*FNA(X)
290    LET M=M+H*FNA(X+H/2)
300    LET U=U+H*FNA(X+H)
310    NEXT X
320    PRINT H,L,M,U
330    IF U-L<E THEN 360
340    LET H=H/2
350    GOTO 220
360    PRINT
370    PRINT "AREA = ";M
380    END

RUN
AREA*

SUBINTERVAL
WIDTH              LOWER SUM        MIDPOINT SUM     UPPER SUM
 1                 0                .125             1
 .5                .0625            .21875           .5625
 .25               .140625          .242187          .390625
 .125              .191406          .248047          .316406
 .0625             .219727          .249512          .282227
 .03125            .234619          .249878          .265869
 .015625           .242249          .24997           .257874
 7.81250E-03       .246109          .249992          .253922

AREA =   .249992

DONE
```

the interval of interest is taken and a new approximation is
obtained.

The program AREA* uses a double loop in lines 220 to 350. The
inner loop in lines 270 to 310 computes the lower sum, the midpoint
sum, and the upper sum using the uniform subinterval width H.
The midpoint sum is calculated by using the function value at the
subinterval midpoint as the height of the rectangle for that
subinterval. If the difference between the upper and lower sums is
less than the maximum error tolerance specified in line 160, then
line 330 transfers out of the loop. Otherwise, line 340 cuts the
subinterval width in half, and line 350 transfers back to recalculate
the approximate area.

realistic error tolerance

If the error tolerance specified at line 160 is too small, then the program AREA* might lead the computer into an overwhelming number of calculations. The programmer is cautioned to avoid demanding an unnecessarily precise approximation. If the need for accuracy is great, then it is important for the programmer to learn an approximation method which converges rapidly. The trapezoidal approximation, explained below, is better than the midpoint approximation in most cases, but books on numerical analysis contain even better methods.

trapezoidal approximation

A special kind of intermediate sum is usually depicted as a sum of the areas of trapezoids rather than rectangles. On each subinterval, a continuous function must assume the average of its values at the initial and terminal endpoints. The appropriate rectangle for the subinterval would have its height equal to this average. However, a trapezoid of equal area serves as well. The fourth side should be a slanted line segment lying close to the curve, as illustrated in Figure 9.

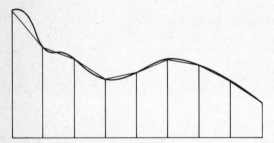

Figure 9   Trapezoidal approximation to area.

Writing a program that makes a trapezoidal approximation to area is left as a problem.

problems

1   Calculate a good approximation to the area between the curve representing the function $x^4 + x^3 + x^2$ and the *x*-axis over the interval $[2, 3]$.

2   The function $f(x) = \sqrt{1 - x^2}$ describes a semicircle of radius 1 in the upper half plane. Since the area of a circle is the product of π and the square of the radius, the area of this semicircle is $\pi/2$. Use this information and the program AREA to compute an approximation to the value of π.

3 Find the area between the curve representing the function $f(x) = (x + 1)/(x + 2)$ and the x-axis over the interval $[1, 2]$.

4 Find the area between the curve representing the function $f(x) = 1/x$ and the x-axis over the interval $[1, 10]$.

5 Modify the program AREA to find a number e such that the area between the curve $f(x) = 1/x$ and the x-axis over the interval $[1, e]$ is 1.

6 Modify the program AREA* so that it works correctly on functions that alternately rise and fall possibly several times on the interval of interest. One way to do this is to predetermine the places where local maxima and minima occur and to store this information as data.

7 Write a program that approximates area according to the trapezoidal method.

8 Write a program that compares successive approximations by intermediate sums using function values taken at random points in the subintervals to successive approximations by the trapezoidal rule.

9 Make some modifications to AREA* that will increase its efficiency (at the possible expense of clarity to the reader).

4 | *plotting a graph*

The program GRAPH plots the graph of a function supplied at line 110 over an interval designated at line 130. In the printout shown here the function is $x^3 - 6x^2 + 11x - 6$ and the interval is $[.5, 3.5]$. The data supplied in line 160 are essential to proper operation as explained below.

```
LIST
GRAPH

100   REM PLOT THE GRAPH OF FNA OVER INTERVAL [A,B]
110   DEF FNA(X)=X↑3-6*X↑2+11*X-6
120   REM ENDPOINTS
130   DATA .5,3.5
140   READ A,B
150   REM LOWER AND UPPER FUNCTION VALUE BOUNDS
160   DATA -2,2
170   READ L,U
180   REM HORIZONTAL AND VERTICAL SCALE FACTORS
190   LET H=(B-A)/64
195   LET V=(5*H)/3
```

```
200   FOR Y=U TO L STEP -V
210   FOR X=A TO B STEP H
220   IF ABS(FNA(X)-Y) <= V/2 IHEN 250
230   PRINT " ";
240   GOTO 260
250   PRINT ".";
260   NEXT X
270   PRINT
280   NEXT Y
290   PRINT
300   PRINT
999   END

RUN
GRAPH
```

DONE

horizontal x-axis

The standard practice in plotting graphs is to indicate the argument values by the horizontal coordinate (i.e., distance units along the x-axis) and the function values by the vertical coordinate (i.e., distance units along the y-axis). Since the width of the printout paper is finite and the teletypewriter cannot squeeze characters arbitrarily close together, a single run of the program GRAPH can display the function values only over a finite interval indicated by the DATA statement in line 130.

The interval [.5, 3.5] is particularly interesting because the function assumes the value 0 there three times, at $X = 1$, $X = 2$, and $X = 3$. Furthermore, a turning point where the function stops increasing and starts decreasing occurs for some argument between 1 and 2, and another turning point, where the function stops decreasing and starts increasing again occurs between 2 and 3. A programmer who also wanted a display for arguments between 3.5 and 6.5 would only have to change line 130 and rerun the program. The printout could be placed to the right of the one shown here to obtain a continuous display.

scale factors

The teletypewriter prints ten characters to the inch in the horizontal direction (i.e., along a print line) and six lines to the inch in the vertical direction, so that the distance between two consecutive dots in the horizontal direction is only $\frac{3}{5}$ the distance between two dots in the same column on consecutive print lines. The program GRAPH uses 64 horizontal print columns to represent the three units between the endpoints .5 and 3.5. The distance between two consecutive dots on a print line corresponds therefore to a distance of $\frac{3}{64}$ ($= .046875$) units, the horizontal scale factor. To avoid distortion the correct distance between two consecutive print lines (the vertical scale factor) is $\frac{5}{3}$ the horizontal scale factor, that is, $\frac{5}{64}$ ($= .078125$). The scale factors are computed by lines 190 and 195.

FOR–NEXT *with negative step*

The plotting procedure used in the program GRAPH is somewhat bizarre. The usual pencil and paper way is to plot the function value over the lower argument endpoint and then function values over successively larger arguments. The teletypewriter carriage does not move up and down a page. What it must do is to find all arguments with the highest function value on the interval, print dots for them on the top line, then all arguments with the next highest function value, printing dots for them on the next line, and so on. The outer FOR-variable in the double FOR–NEXT loop in lines 200 to 280 corresponds, therefore, to the vertical coordinate.

The step in the FOR statement at line 200 is negative (i.e., −.078125). In such cases, the upper limit precedes the word TO and the lower limit follows. The computer begins the loop by assigning the upper limit (in this case, 2) to the FOR-variable Y. After each iteration, the value of the FOR-variable decreases by the value of the negative step. When it drops below the lower limit (in this case, −2), the loop terminates.

choosing lower and upper function bounds

The lower bound given as data in line 160 should actually be less than or equal to the minimum of the function defined in line 110 over the interval indicated by data in line 130. Similarly, the upper bound in line 160 should be greater than or equal to the maximum of the function on that interval. Naturally no dots are printed until the value of the FOR-variable Y drops from the upper bound 2 to the actual maximum 1.875.

problems

1 The printout of the run of GRAPH makes a portion of the graph over the subinterval [1, 2] look flat. Display the function values over this subinterval more accurately by altering the data in the program.

2 Plot the graph of the function $FNA(X) = (X + ABS(X))/2$ over the interval $[-2, 2]$.

3 Plot the graph of the function
$FNA(X) = X - (X \uparrow 3)/6 + (X \uparrow 5)/120$ over the interval $[-3, 3]$.

4 Write a graph-plotting program that indicates argument values in the vertical direction on the paper, so that the printout should be viewed sideways. Apply this program to the function given in the previous problem.

5 | other built-in functions

Earlier sections of these notes have introduced and used the five general purpose built-in functions RND, INT, ABS, SGN, and SQR. Most versions of BASIC also include another six built-in functions, which are of particular interest in engineering, science, and mathematics.

trigonometric functions

Given any angle X expressed in radians, SIN(X), COS(X), and TAN(X) are its sine, its cosine, and its tangent. Conforming to standard mathematical practice these trigonometric functions are defined for arguments which are negative or greater than 2π as well as arguments between 0 and 2π.

If a programmer prefers to express angle measure in degrees he may define trigonometric functions accordingly. Since 1 degree equals $\pi/180$ radians, it follows that X degrees equals approximately $3.14159 \cdot X/180$ radians. Thus, the sine of an angle of X degrees may be obtained in the language BASIC as SIN(3.14159 * X/180). If a programmer includes the line

```
50   DEF FNS(X)=SIN(3.14159*X/180)
```

in a program, his program will evaluate every occurrence of FNS(X) as the sine of X, taking X as an angle expressed in degrees.

The program TRIG is concerned with a right triangle whose hypotenuse is of length C and whose other two sides are of lengths

```
LIST
TRIG

40    REM FNS(X DEGREES)=SIN(X)
50    DEF FNS(X)=SIN(3.14159*X/180)
60    REM FNC(X DEGREES)=COS(X)
70    DEF FNC(X)=COS(3.14159*X/180)
100   PRINT "TYPE LENGTH OF HYPOTENUSE";
110   INPUT C
120   PRINT "TYPE ANGLE BETWEEN HYPOTENUSE AND SIDE A";
130   INPUT Q
140   PRINT
150   LET A=C*FNC(Q)
160   LET B=C*FNS(Q)
200   PRINT "THE LENGTH OF SIDE A IS ";A
210   PRINT "THE LENGTH OF SIDE B IS ";B
220   PRINT "THE AREA OF THE TRIANGLE IS ";A*B/2
999   END


RUN
TRIG

TYPE LENGTH OF HYPOTENUSE?12
TYPE ANGLE BETWEEN HYPOTENUSE AND SIDE A?30

THE LENGTH OF SIDE A IS   10.3923
THE LENGTH OF SIDE B IS   6.
THE AREA OF THE TRIANGLE IS   31.1769

DONE
```

A and B. When TRIG runs, the programmer must supply the length of the hypotenuse and the number of degrees in the angle between the hypotenuse and the side of length A as input. The program TRIG will print the lengths A and B of the sides and the area of the triangle.

To obtain the other three trigonometric functions, the programmer must use the relations

$$\text{cotangent}\ (x) = \frac{1}{\text{tangent}\ (x)}$$

$$\text{secant}\ (x) = \frac{1}{\text{cosine}\ (x)}$$

$$\text{cosecant}\ (x) = \frac{1}{\text{sine}\ (x)}$$

because they are not built into BASIC.

The arctangent function is built into BASIC. Given any real number Y, ATN(Y) is an angle between 0 and π radians whose tangent is the number Y. The other inverse trigonometric functions are not predefined functions of BASIC. One of the problems at the end of this section is to use the DEF statement to define the functions arcsine and arccosine.

exponential function

The exponential function EXP (not to be confused with the exponentiation operator ↑) assigns to its argument X the sum of the infinite expression

$$1 + \frac{X}{1!} + \frac{X^2}{2!} + \frac{X^3}{3!} + \cdots$$

where the exclamation point denotes the factorial function, which was discussed earlier. The letter *e* is the usual mathematical symbol for the number EXP(1), whose value is approximately 2.71828. It is known that for any number X, the value of EXP(X) is exactly the same as the result of taking the number *e* to the power X. Therefore, EXP(X) is always positive.

logarithm function

For any positive number N, LOG(N) is the unique number X such that EXP(X) = N ($e^X = N$). That is, LOG(N) is the logarithm of N to the base *e*, the so-called natural logarithm. It it known that, for a number N greater than 1, LOG(N) is the area between the curve which graphically represents the function $1/x$ and the x-axis over the interval [1, N].

If the predefined function LOG is applied to a nonpositive argument during the execution of a program, then the run will be terminated and the computer will print an execution error message, such as

```
LOG OF NEGATIVE ARGUMENT IN LINE 380
```

problems

1 Write a DEF statement that defines FNC(X) to be the cosecant of the angle X expressed in degrees.

2 It is known from elementary methods that

$$\arcsin(x) = \arctan\left(\frac{x}{\sqrt{1-x^2}}\right)$$

and

$$\arccos(x) = \arctan\left(\frac{\sqrt{1-x^2}}{x}\right)$$

Write a DEF statement so that FNY(X) is evaluated as arcsin(X). Write another DEF statement so that FNZ(X) is evaluated as arccos(X).

3 Write a DEF statement that defines FNT(X) to be the function 2^X.

4 Write a DEF statement that defines FNL(X) as the logarithm of X to the base 10.

5 Find a root of the function $f(x) = \sin x - x + x^3/6$ in the interval [0, 2].

6 Find a root of the function $f(x) = \sin x - \cos x$ in the interval [0, 1].

7 Find a local maximum of the function $\sin x$ in the interval [0, 2].

6 | matrix operations

In this section, the word "vector" means a subscripted variable with one subscript and the word "matrix" means a subscripted variable with two subscripts. It is common to think of a vector as a

row of elements and a matrix as a rectangular array of elements such
that all elements with the same first subscripts are in the same row
and all elements with the same second subscript are in the same
column. The language BASIC includes some instructions which
simplify the coding of programs involving vectors and matrices each
of which starts with the word MAT. This section gives a concise
explanation of these instructions. For further discussion of the
operations performed and an introduction to their applications the
reader should consult an elementary text on linear algebra. The
statements MAT READ and MAT PRINT are explained in Section 5
of Chapter 2.

MAT ZER *and* MAT CON

If C is any matrix or vector, then the instruction

```
120   MAT C=ZER
```

sets every element of C to 0, and the instruction

```
160   MAT C=CON
```

sets every element of C to 1.

```
LIST
MAT1

100   REM ** MAT ZER & MAT CON
110   DIM C[2,3]
120   MAT C=ZER
130   MAT   PRINT C;
140   PRINT
150   PRINT
160   MAT C=CON
170   MAT   PRINT C;
999   END


RUN
MAT1

 0      0      0

 0      0      0


 1      1      1

 1      1      1


DONE
```

copy matrix and scalar product

If A and B are matrices or vectors of the same size, then the instruction

160   MAT B=A   (copy a matrix)

copies the elements of A into B, and the instruction

200   MAT B=(R)*A   (scalar multiplication)

where R is any arithmetic expression, sets each element B[I, J] (or B[I]) to the product of the value of R and the value of A[I, J] (or A[I]).

```
LIST
MAT2

100    REM ** COPY MATRIX & SCALAR PRODUCT
110    DIM A[2,3],B[2,3]
120    MAT   READ A
130    MAT   PRINT A;
140    PRINT
150    PRINT
160    MAT B=A
170    MAT   PRINT B;
180    PRINT
190    PRINT
200    MAT B=(11-2↑3)*A
210    MAT   PRINT B;
980    DATA 1,0,-2,0,12,31
999    END


RUN
MAT2

  1      0     -2

  0     12     31


  1      0     -2

  0     12     31


  3      0     -6

  0     36     93


DONE
```

matrix sum and matrix difference

If A, B, and C are matrices or vectors of the same size, then the instruction

```
200  MAT C=A+B
```
     (matrix sum)

assigns to each element C[I, J] (or to C[I]) the value of the sum A[I, J] + B[I, J] (or the sum A[I] + B[I]) and the instruction

```
240  MAT C=A-B
```
     (matrix difference)

sets each element C[I, J] (or C[I]) to the value of the difference A[I, J] − B[I, J] (or A[I] − B[I]).

```
LIST
MAT3

100   REM ** MATRIX SUM & MATRIX DIFFERENCE
110   DIM A[4],B[4],C[4]
120   MAT   READ A
130   MAT   PRINT A;
140   PRINT
150   PRINT
160   MAT   READ B
170   MAT   PRINT B;
180   PRINT
190   PRINT
200   MAT C=A+B
210   MAT   PRINT C;
220   PRINT
230   PRINT
240   MAT C=A-B
250   MAT   PRINT C;
980   DATA 1,0,-2,0,12,31
990   DATA 5,-2,1,0,3,1
999   END


RUN
MAT3

 1      0     -2      0


 12     31     5     -2


 13     31     3     -2


-11    -31    -7      2

DONE
```

matrix product

If A is an M × N matrix, if B is an N × P matrix, and if C is an
M × P matrix, then the instruction

```
200  MAT C=A*B
```
(matrix product)

sets each element C[I, J] to the value of the sum

$$A[I, 1] * B[1, J] + A[I, 2] * B[2, J] + \cdots + A[I, N] * B[N, J]$$

Most versions of BASIC do not permit the same matrix to be named
on both sides of the equality symbol in a MAT multiplication
instruction.

```
LIST
MAT4

100    REM ** MATRIX PRODUCT
110    DIM A[2,3],B[3,4],C[2,4]
120    MAT   READ A
130    MAT   PRINT A;
140    PRINT
150    PRINT
160    MAT   READ B
170    MAT   PRINT B;
180    PRINT
190    PRINT
200    MAT C=A*B
210    MAT   PRINT C;
970    DATA 0,3,-1,2,0,7
980    DATA 1,0,-2,0,12,31
990    DATA 5,-2,1,0,3,1
999    END


RUN
MAT4

   0      3     -1

   2      0      7



   1      0     -2      0

  12     31      5     -2

   1      0      3      1



  35     93     12     -7

   9      0     17      7

DONE
```

matrix identity

If Q is a square matrix, then the instruction

```
120   MAT Q=IDN
```

sets Q to an identity matrix, that is, a matrix whose elements on the
main diagonal all have the value 1 and whose other elements all
have the value 0.

```
LIST
MAT5

100   REM ** MAT IDN
110   DIM Q[3,3]
120   MAT Q=IDN
130   MAT  PRINT Q;
999   END


RUN
MAT5

 1     0     0

 0     1     0

 0     0     1


DONE
```

matrix transpose

If A is an M × N matrix and B is an N × M matrix, then the
instruction

```
160   MAT B=TRN(A)
```
   (transpose)

assigns to each element B[I, J] the value of the element A[J, I].
Most versions of BASIC do not permit a square matrix to be named
on both sides of the equality symbol in a MAT TRN instruction.

```
LIST
MAT6

100   REM ** TRANSPOSE
110   DIM A[2,3],B[3,2]
120   MAT   READ A
130   MAT  PRINT A;
140   PRINT
150   PRINT
160   MAT B=TRN(A)
170   MAT  PRINT B;
980   DATA 2.14,3.7,8.2,-4.03,2.1,.02
999   END
```

```
RUN
MAT6

  2.14        3.7        8.2

 -4.03        2.1        .02


  2.14       -4.03

  3.7         2.1

  8.2         .02

DONE
```

matrix inverse

If A and B are square matrices of the same size, then the instruction

```
160   MAT B=INV(A)
```
(matrix inverse)

assigns values to the elements of B so that B is the inverse of the
matrix A. If the matrix A is noninvertible, then the computer prints
an error message such as

```
NON-INVERTIBLE MATRIX IN LINE 287
```

The program MAT 7 inverts a matrix of integers. The actual inverse
of the given matrix is also a matrix of integers, but a round-off error
causes the second element of the first row to be computed as
$-5.36442 \text{ E} -07$ instead of 0.

```
LIST
MAT7

100   REM ** INVERT SQUARE MATRIX
110   DIM A[3,3],B[3,3]
120   MAT   READ A
130   MAT   PRINT A;
140   PRINT
150   PRINT
160   MAT B=INV(A)
170   MAT   PRINT B
980   DATA -2,6,-3,7,-13,7,-1,4,-2
999   END


RUN
MAT7

-2      6     -3
```

```
  7    -13    7
 -1     4    -2
```

```
-2.              -5.36442E-07    3.

 7.               1.            -7.

15                2             -16
```

DONE

redimensioning

In order to promote efficient use of memory space, many BASIC
systems permit the dimensions of a matrix to be redefined during
the execution of a program, as shown in the program MAT 8.

```
LIST
MAT8

100   REM ** REDIMENSIONING
110   DIM M[2,11]
120   MAT M=ZER
130   MAT  PRINT M;
140   PRINT
145   PRINT
150   MAT  READ M[3,2]
160   MAT  PRINT M;
170   PRINT
175   PRINT
180   MAT M=IDN[M[2,1],M[2,1]]
190   MAT  PRINT M;
990   DATA 7,13,4,0,-2,11
999   END


RUN
MAT8

 0    0    0    0    0    0    0    0    0    0    0

 0    0    0    0    0    0    0    0    0    0    0


 7    13

 4     0

-2    11


 1    0    0    0

 0    1    0    0

 0    0    1    0

 0    0    0    1


DONE
```

Line 110 gives M the original dimension 2 × 11. The computer reserves 22 locations for the elements of M. The matrix M may be redimensioned to any shape that requires no more than the original 22 locations. For example, line 150 changes the shape of M to 3 × 2. And when line 180 is executed, the value of M[2, 1] is 4 so M is redimensioned to 4 × 4. The most commonly used instructions in redimensioning are MAT READ, MAT INPUT, MAT CON, and MAT IDN. Some systems also permit other MAT instructions to redimension matrices.

problems

1   Write a program that applies the function $f(x) = x^2 - 4x + 3$ to a 3 × 3 matrix M supplied as input. That is, compute

M * M − (4) * M + (3) * I

where I denotes the 3 × 3 identity matrix.

2   Write a program that experimentally checks the matrix equation

TRN(B) * TRN(A) = TRN(A * B)

3   Write a program that prints the product of the inverse of the matrix A (given below) and a 3 × 1 matrix Y supplied as input.

matrix A		
−1	−2	3
0	−1	3
2	4	−5

4   Let A be any N × M matrix. Let X be a 1 × N matrix of all 1's and let Y be an M × 1 matrix of all 1's. The value of the single element of the product X * A * Y is the sum of the entries of A. Write a program that uses this fact to sum the elements of a 3 × 4 matrix supplied as input.

suggested reading

Acton, Forman. *Numerical Methods That Work.* Harper & Row, New York, 1969.

simulation

THE HIGH speed of a digital computer enables it to make calculations that would take a person much longer to complete. In some cases, such as the weekly payroll of a large corporation, the computer is performing almost the same calculations that a human clerk would do, only faster and, hopefully, more accurately. In other cases, problems are solved by programs using methods which, because of the large amount of computation, would not be feasible without the aid of a computer. One of these methods involves the *simulation* of some dynamic situation by keeping track of the progress of all pertinent characteristics of the situation as it might actually occur.

This chapter illustrates how simulation techniques can be used to solve problems in population growth, ecology, gambling, political science, baseball, and archaeology. Some of the problems discussed can be solved with conventional mathematical methods, but they illustrate methods which are applicable to difficult problems, such as the ones discussed in the sections on archaeology and baseball.

1 | *deterministic and Monte Carlo simulation*

In Sections 2 and 3 of this chapter it will be shown how simple simulation programs can solve the following two problems.

1 The population of the state of Idaho in 1960 was 667191. If the annual growth rate is .4 percent, what was its population in 1970? What will its population be in 1980?

2 In a fair dice game, what percentage of the rolls should come up 7 or 11?

There is a fundamental difference between the two problems. If the information given in the first problem is correct, the exact population of Idaho in any future year can be calculated. The simulation of the growth of the population in Idaho is *deterministic;* there is no element of chance. (This does not mean that the population of Idaho in the future can be predicted with certainty, only that the exact population that would result from a .4 percent annual growth rate can be calculated.)

In the dice problem, however, the result of throwing the dice is uncertain. For this reason, a simulation of the throw of dice is called *nondeterministic.* Even if the outcome of any particular occurrence of an uncertain or random event cannot be predicted, it is possible to make some statements about what will happen if the event is repeated many times. A typical nondeterministic simulation consists of simulating a random event many times, recording certain information about the sequence of events. A nondeterministic simulation is often called a Monte Carlo simulation, due to the uncertainty of many of the events which take place there.

abstracting relevant information

For each of these situations, only a small portion of the information which would completely describe the event is needed to answer the particular question by simulation. The computer program records only the relevant information. For the first problem, the only pertinent information is the population of Idaho each year. Such details as the number of births, deaths, and emigrations are not essential and are ignored. To simulate the dice game, the only necessary information is the value of the dice after each roll, the number of times the dice are rolled, and the number of times 7 or 11 is rolled.

2 | deterministic models of population and water pollution

The program IDAHO solves the population growth problem presented in Section 1. In the program the variable P represents the population of Idaho and the variable Y represents the year. The value of P is printed when Y = 1970 and when Y = 1980.

The calculation of a population with a constant annual growth rate is mathematically equivalent to calculating the balance in a savings

```
LIST
IDAHO

10  LET P=667191.
20  FOR Y=1961 TO 1980
30  LET P=P+.004*P
40  IF INT(Y/10) <> Y/10 THEN 60
50  PRINT Y,P
60  NEXT Y
70  END

RUN
IDAHO

  1970          694364.
  1980          722644.

DONE
```

account which pays interest compounded annually (see Problem 8 at the end of this section). The population of Idaho in 1980 may also be calculated by the formula $P = 667191 * (1.004) \uparrow 20$.

Deterministic simulation provides a natural way to solve many problems and is often easier to understand than any other method. A deterministic simulation program which solves a problem about water pollution provides a second illustration of the technique.

a water quality problem

The residents of Mudville, located on the shore of Lake Sludge, notice that the quality of the water in their beautiful lake has deteriorated in recent years and they make a special study of the situation producing the following facts, shown in Figure 1.

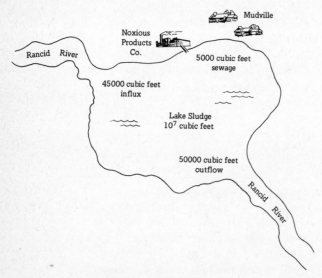

Figure 1   The environs of Mudville.

1 The volume of Lake Sludge is 10^7 cubic feet and is .5 percent polluted, that is, the lake contains .5 percent $\times 10^7 = .005 \times 10^7 = 5 \times 10^4 = 50000$ cubic feet of polluting materials.

2 The influx from Rancid River is 45000 cubic feet per day, which is .2 percent polluted.

3 The town of Mudville puts 5000 cubic feet of sewage, which consists of 10 percent pollutants, into the lake daily.

It is generally believed that it will be undesirable to live in Mudville if the lake ever becomes 1 percent polluted, which will eventually happen under present conditions, since the net inflow is more than 1 percent polluted.

a simulation of the water flow

A deterministic simulation which can calculate when the pollution level in the lake reaches 1 percent needs to record only one item of information, the amount of pollutants in Lake Sludge. That is the value of the variable P in the program POLUT. The initial value of P is the current quantity of pollutants in the lake, which is $.005 \times 10^7$ cubic feet. Each day, counted by the variable D, the value of P is increased by the quantity of pollutants coming from sewage and the influx of Rancid River. The value of P is then decreased by the amount of pollutant which flows out of the lake. This calculation is repeated until the percentage of pollutants in the lake, $P/10^7$, is more than 1 percent.

```
LIST
POLUT

10    LET P=.005*1.E+07
20    FOR D=1 TO 10000
30    LET P=P+.002*45000.+.1*5000
40    LET P=P-(P/1.E+07)*50000.
50    IF P/1.E+07>.01 THEN 70
60    NEXT D
65    PRINT "NO DANGER FOR AT LEAST 10000 DAYS"
66    STOP
70    PRINT "MUDVILLE IS DOOMED IN ";D;"DAYS"
80    END

RUN
POLUT

MUDVILLE IS DOOMED IN  271   DAYS

DONE
```

testing corrective actions

If the Noxious Products plant were closed and sewage treatment facilities built, the town could reduce the pollutant level of the sewage going into the lake to .1 percent. If the septic tanks along

Rancid River were replaced by a sewer system, the pollutant level of the river would drop to .03 percent. If these actions could be implemented immediately, how long would it be before the pollution level of the lake dropped to .1 percent?

The program CLENUP is similar to the program POLUT. The pollutant levels of the water sources have been changed and the simulation is stopped when $P < .001 \times 10^7$.

```
LIST
CLENUP

10   LET P=.005*1.E+07
20   FOR D=1 TO 10000
30   LET P=P+.0003*45000.+.001*5000
40   LET P=P-(P/1.E+07)*50000.
50   IF P/1.E+07<.001 THEN 70
60   NEXT D
65   PRINT "POLLUTANT LEVEL NOT BELOW .1% AFTER 10000 DAYS
66   STOP
70   PRINT "POLLUTANT LEVEL DOWN TO .1% AFTER";D;"DAYS"
80   END

RUN
CLENUP

POLLUTANT LEVEL DOWN TO .1% AFTER 398   DAYS

DONE
```

By simply changing the numbers in the program CLENUP, it is possible to predict the effect on the lake of any changes in the pollutant levels of the river or the town's sewage.

The simulation technique illustrated in the program CLENUP is being used to solve some very complex problems. In *American Scientist*, Walter Orr Roberts, president of the University Corporation for Atmospheric Research, discussed a simulation program to model the weather system of the entire world.[*]

Not only will the model, when built and tested, permit experiments to refine weather and climate forecasting research, but also we anticipate, as suggested above, that such a model will permit experiments in global weather modification—safely in the model, and not in nature. We should be able, for example, to level the Rockies or rotate the earth backwards and see what the impact is on weather. Or, more usefully and realistically, we hope to be able to simulate, for a few thousand dollars, cleaning up world air pollution, so that we may be able to evaluate the meteorological consequences of such a clean-up—giving us a handle to the value of so doing in the real world. This would be a very powerful decision-making aid.

[*] Walter Orr Roberts, "Man on a Changing Earth," *American Scientist* **59**, No. 1, 16–19 (Jan.–Feb., 1971).

151

determinis-
tic models
of popula-
tion and
water
pollution
section 2

problems

1 The population of the United States in 1960 was 179.323 million. By 1970 it had increased 11.7 percent to 200.264 million. If it increases by 11.7 percent each decade, what will the population of the United States be in 2000?, in 2050?

2 The town of Bettysburg had 10324 residents in 2073. Every year there is a new baby born for each 173 residents and one death for every 211 residents. Every year exactly 47 new residents move to town and 76 move away. Write a deterministic simulation that will determine the population in 2084.

3 Suppose the pollutant level of Rancid River is reduced to .03 percent, but the residents of Mudville are not willing to close the Noxious Products plant because most of them would lose their jobs. Therefore, the pollutant level in the town's sewage will be 1 percent, even after installation of a treatment facility. What will happen to the pollution level of the lake? Put a print statement in the simulation program that will display the pollution level of the lake every 30 days.

4 The individuals of certain species of birds may be any one of three genetic types: BB, Bb, or bb. Individuals of type BB and Bb have brown eyes and those of type bb have blue eyes. Each year during mating season, mating between the members of each pair of gene type produces a number of offspring which is equal to 10 percent of the minimum number of individuals in the two groups. To illustrate, if there are 31 million BB adults and 22 million bb adults, they will produce $.10 \times \min$ (31 million, 22 million) $= 2.2$ million offspring. The genotype of each offspring is determined by selecting at random one of the genes (B or b) from each parent. Each year, after the offspring are produced, 15 percent of the brown-eyed adults and 5 percent of the blue-eyed adults die. The new offspring become reproducing adults in 1 year.

If the current population is

type	population (millions)
BB	16.3
Bb	41.2
bb	75.6

what will be the population of each type in 30 years?

5 Change Problem 4 so that mating takes place only between individuals with the same color eyes.

6 Change Problem 4 so that mating takes place only between individuals with different colored eyes.

7 Assume that a metropolitan area can be divided into three regions: urban, exurban, and suburban. The following table shows the annual migration from each region to the other.

	urban	exurban	suburban
urban	—	.007	.003
exurban	.002	—	.006
suburban	.001	.003	—

For example, .003 or .3 percent of the urbanites move to the suburbs each year. In addition, each region has a 1.2 percent internal growth rate. If the present populations of the urban, exurban, and suburban regions are 2.3, 1.7, and 1.9 million, respectively, what will be the population of each region in 30 years?

8 A man and his wife plan to save money from their paychecks to make a down payment on a home. They intend to make monthly deposits in a savings account on which the bank pays monthly interest at the rate of $\frac{5}{12}$ of 1 percent. (The bank advertises a nominal annual rate of 5 percent, but it actually pays somewhat more, because the interest is compounded monthly.) How many months will they need to accumulate $8,000?

9 A house is bought for $30,000 with a down payment of $8,000. The $22,000 balance is borrowed at an interest rate of 7½ percent per annum. Payments are to be made monthly and out of each payment is deducted the interest due for 1 month. The remainder is applied to reduce the principal. How much, to the nearest dollar, should the payments be in order that the loan will be paid off in 30 years?

3 | *gambling*

The problem of determining the percentage of times the throw of two dice will result in 7 or 11 was posed in Section 1. One way to solve the dice problem by simulation is to actually roll a pair of dice 1000 times and record the number of times the result is 7 or 11.

It might be more interesting to obtain the results by observing a dice game in progress. An easier and faster way, however, is to have a computer simulate 1000 rolls of the dice.

The computer simulates a random event by producing a "random" number. For any argument the value of the BASIC function RND is a "random" number between 0 and 1, as described in Chapter 2. To simulate the roll of a single die, one of the numbers 1, 2, 3, 4, 5, or 6 should be generated. The value of $FNR(N)$ defined by statement 10 in the program DICE is an integer between 1 and N.

The number $RND(0)$ lies between 0 and 1 and the number $N * RND(0)$ lies between 0 and N, so that $INT(N * RND(0))$ is an integer in the range 0 to $N - 1$ and $FNR(N)$ is one of the integers 1, 2, 3, . . . , N. Thus, the value of $FNR(6)$ simulates the roll of one die and $FNR(52)$ simulates the drawing of a single card from a standard deck.

The program DICE estimates the percentage of rolls of two dice which yield a 7 or 11. The variable S records the number of *successes*, that is, the number of times the dice come up 7 or 11. The variable T counts the number of trials. The loop consisting of statements 40, 50, 60, and 70 simulates a single trial. If the trial is successful the value of D, representing the sum of the value on the two dice, will be 7 or 11 and the value of S will be increased by 1.

```
LIST
DICE

10   DEF FNR(N)=INT(N*RND(0))+1
20   LET S=0
30   FOR T=1 TO 1000
40   LET D=FNR(6)+FNR(6)
50   IF (D-7)*(D-11) <> 0 THEN 70
60   LET S=S+1
70   NEXT T
80   PRINT "THE PERCENTAGE OF ROLLS WHICH ARE 7 OR 11 IS";S/10
90   END

RUN
DICE

THE PERCENTAGE OF ROLLS WHICH ARE 7 OR 11 IS 20.6

DONE
```

Notice that it would be incorrect to replace statement 40 by

```
40   LET D=2*FNR(6)
```

This statement generates only one roll and doubles it, so that the result would always be even. Statement 40 in the program generates two random numbers, which may be the same, but more often will not be.

The program DICE simulates the event of rolling two dice 1000 times. The problem of deciding how many times to simulate the event in order to get a good approximation to the true value is a difficult one. Ten times is obviously not enough and 1 trillion simulations would require too much time on any computer. One way to approach this problem is to run the program 3 or 4 times with some fairly small number of simulations of the event. If the answers are all fairly close to each other, that is an indication that the number of simulations was sufficient. If the answers are quite different, then the number of simulations could be increased by a factor of ten if there is sufficient computer time available to execute the program. The dice program was run 4 more times with the following results:

22.5 percent   25.1 percent   21.8 percent   21.2 percent

The true answer is $\frac{6}{36} + \frac{2}{36} = \frac{8}{36} = \frac{2}{9} = 22.2$ percent. A method for calculating the true answer will be discussed in Section 4.

roulette

Roulette is a popular game in the gambling casinos. Many interesting questions about the game can be answered by simple simulation programs, which will be Monte Carlo simulations, due to the uncertainty of the result of spinning the roulette wheel.

When the roulette wheel is spun, a metal ball is allowed to drop onto the wheel and come to rest in one of 38 different positions on the wheel. The 38 positions are numbered 1 to 36, half colored red and half colored black, and 0 and 00 which are green, as shown in Figure 2. Before the wheel is spun, bets may be placed on "red", "black", "even", "odd", any individual number, or on several different combinations of numbers. Figure 2 shows what the betting table looks like, how bets are made, and the amount paid to the winners. A winner who bets on a combination that pays 6 to 1 is paid $6 for each $1 bet and the amount bet is also returned.

a comparison of two betting strategies

Suppose a gambler enters a Las Vegas casino with $1,000. He decides to play roulette, betting each time on red. He is considering two different betting strategies.

Strategy 1   Bet $1 each time.

Strategy 2   Bet $1 on the first spin and on any spin following a win. On any spin following a loss, bet $1 more than the total losses

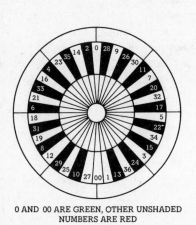

0 AND 00 ARE GREEN, OTHER UNSHADED
NUMBERS ARE RED

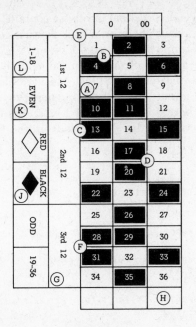

A	SINGLE NUMBERS	PAYS 35 TO 1
B	TWO NUMBERS ......(split)...........	PAYS 17 TO 1
C	THREE NUMBERS	PAYS 11 TO 1
D	FOUR NUMBERS	PAYS 8 TO 1
E	FIVE NUMBERS	PAYS 6 TO 1
F	SIX NUMBERS	PAYS 5 TO 1
G	DOZEN	PAYS 2 TO 1
H	COLUMN...........................	PAYS 2 TO 1
J	COLOR	PAYS EVEN
K	ODD OR EVEN......................	PAYS EVEN
L	HIGH OR LOW	PAYS EVEN

Figure 2   Roulette betting and payoffs.

since the last win, or whatever is left of the $1,000, whichever is smaller.

If each bet takes 1 minute, how much money should the gambler expect to have after 1 hour using one of these strategies?

the fixed-bet strategy

The program ROUL1 simulates a 1-hour gambling session in which the gambler bets $1 each minute on the red. The information which the program must record consists of only the amount of money in the gambler's possession and the number of bets that have been made. The value of FNR(38) simulates the spin of the roulette wheel. The DATA statement in line 54 contains each of the red positions. The result of the spin R is checked against these 18 red positions to determine if the gambler wins. The variable M represents the amount of money in the gambler's possession and statement 20 initializes M to $1,000. The variable T counts the trials, or the time in minutes, and the loop consisting of lines 40–70 simulates one bet. M is reduced by 1 when the bet is placed, and if he wins, he gets back the $1 that he won plus the $1 he bet.

```
LIST
ROUL1

5   REM     FIXED BET STRATEGY
10  DEF FNR(N)=INT(N*RND(O))+1
20  LET M=1000
30  FOR T=1 TO 60
40  REM  ***  PLACE BET  ***
41  LET M=M-1
49  RESTORE
50  REM  ***  SPIN WHEEL  ***
51  LET R=FNR(38)
52  FOR I=1 TO 18
53  READ N
54  DATA 1,3,5,7,9,12,14,16,18,19,21,23,25,27,30,32,34,36
55  IF R=N THEN 60
56  NEXT I
57  GOTO 70
60  REM  ***  PAY OFF  ***
61  LET M=M+2
70  NEXT T
80  PRINT "THE AMOUNT OF MONEY LEFT IS   $";M
90  END


RUN
ROUL1

THE AMOUNT OF MONEY LEFT IS $ 1004

DONE
```

The 1-hour gambling session is simulated only once by the program. The program would have to be run many times in order to get a good estimate of what the average win or loss would be. Of course, a loss should be expected since there are 20 losing positions and only 18 winning ones on the roulette wheel.

the strategy to recoup losses

The second gambling strategy is simulated by the program ROUL2. This program simulates the spin of a roulette wheel and the test for red in a more efficient manner. It does not really matter which positions on the wheel are red; the important fact is that 18 out of the 38 positions are red. Thus, over a long period, 18 out of 38 spins produce a red and 20 out of 38 result in black or green. The value of RND(0) is a number between 0 and 1 and over a long period the value of RND(0) will be less than 18/38 in about 18 out of each 38 cases. In ROUL2, a value of RND(0) less than 18/38 represents a spin of red. Statement 10 assigns 18/38 to the variable W and line 260 generates a random number and checks whether or not it is less than W. The program would be less efficient if line 260 were replaced by

```
260  IF RND(0) > 18/38 THEN 290
```

because the division of 18 by 38 would be performed each time line 260 is executed, rather than once at the beginning of the program.

The variable T counts the number of bets as in ROUL1. Statements 220–290 simulate one bet. The variable L records the amount lost on the previous bet; for the first bet, and after any bet that was won, $L = 0$. Statement 231 assigns the amount to be bet as $L + 1$ unless the gambler doesn't have that much money left. In that case all that he has is bet. Thus the amount bet should be $L + 1$ or M, whichever is smaller.

The program ROUL2 simulates any number of 60-minute betting sessions. The number of sessions, N, is typed in by the programmer. The variable K counts the number of sessions to be simulated and after each session, the amount of money remaining in the gambler's possession is added to a total S, so that the average amount left can be printed after all sessions have been simulated. Statement 20 sets S to 0 initially.

```
LIST
ROUL2

5   REM     VARIABLE BET STRATEGY
10    LET W=18/38
20    LET S=0
30    PRINT "HOW MANY TIMES SHOULD BETTING SESSION BE SIMULATED";
40    INPUT N
50    PRINT
60    PRINT "TRIAL    AMOUNT LEFT"
110   FOR K=1 TO N
120   LET M=1000
130   LET L=0
210   FOR T=1 TO 60
220   IF M=0 THEN 300
230   REM   *** BET IS PREVIOUS LOSS + 1
231   LET B=L+1 MIN M
240   LET M=M-B
250   LET L=L+B
260   IF RND(0)>W THEN 290
270   LET L=0
280   LET M=M+2*B
290   NEXT T
300   PRINT K;"     ";M
```

```
310   REM  ***  ADD AMOUNT LEFT TO TOTAL
311   LET S=S+M
320   NEXT K
330   PRINT
340   PRINT "THE AVERAGE AMOUNT LEFT IS $";S/N
390   END


RUN
ROUL2

HOW MANY TIMES SHOULD BETTING SESSION BE SIMULATED? 25

TRIAL    AMOUNT LEFT
  1        1026
  2        1032
  3        1021
  4        1024
  5        1026
  6        1034
  7        1027
  8        1027
  9        1024
 10        1028
 11        1036
 12        1029
 13         775
 14        1028
 15        1026
 16        1022
 17        1012
 18        1036
 19        1028
 20           0
 21        1031
 22        1028
 23           0
 24        1030
 25        1024

THE AVERAGE AMOUNT LEFT IS $ 934.96

DONE
```

As might be expected the gambler employing this strategy either wins a few dollars or goes broke almost every time.

problems

1 Write a program that will determine the percentage of times the sum of two dice will be 2, 3, or 12.

2 Two dice are rolled until a 4 or 7 comes up. What percentage of the time will the 4 be rolled before a 7 is rolled?

3 Use the function FNR of the program DICE to create a program which deals a five-card poker hand. Remember that the same card cannot occur twice in a hand.

4 A certain skier likes to have the snow 5 feet deep. He skis at a slope in New Hampshire where the snow begins falling as early as

August 24. From August 24 to July 4 the percentage of days with
snow is 25 percent. On a snowy day, there is always a deposit
of exactly 2 feet. On other days, 4 inches of snow melt away.
What percentage of skiing seasons will have a 5-foot accumulation
by September 12?

5 Modify the program ROUL2 so that after 60 minutes, the
gambler continues until he either has more than $1,000 or he goes
broke.

6 If $1 is bet each time, determine which of the following bets
results in the smallest average loss: single numbers, two numbers,
six numbers, column, odd, or even. See Figure 2 for the amount
won on each type of bet.

7 If two cards are drawn from a standard deck of playing cards,
what percentage of the time will the cards be an ace and a face
card (ten, jack, queen, or king). When simulating the draw of the
second card, remember that there are only 51 cards in the deck and
the same card cannot be drawn twice.

8 Suppose a gambler bets $1 on the following game. Two dice are
rolled. If the result is odd, the bettor loses. If the dice are even, a
card is drawn from a standard deck. If the card is 1 (an ace), 3,
5, 7, or 9, the bettor wins the value of the card, otherwise he loses.
What, on the average, will the bettor win (or lose) on this game?

9 A man on a vacation in Las Vegas strikes up a conversation at a
bar with the regular casino patron, Miss Lisa Bet. The man says he
would really like to return home and be able to tell his friends he
won money from the gambling casino, but he knows that all of the
games favor the house, so he is reluctant to play. Miss Bet makes
the following proposal: "Let me advise you while you are gambling.
You must be willing to risk losing up to $100. I am so confident that
you will win some money from the casino that I will pay you $200
if you do not win. If you do win money, you must pay me $100 for
my advice". The man agrees, figuring that if he wins, it will be
worth $100 (less what he wins) to say that he "beat the house"
and if he loses the $100, he will get $200 from Lisa and be $100
richer. Miss Bet takes the man to the roulette table and tells him to
bet $1 each time on the red. If his wins ever exceed his losses, he is
to stop. He also must stop if he loses $100.

    a What are the expected winnings for (1) the man, (2) Miss
Bet, and (3) the casino? (These three numbers must sum to 0.)

    b Find the answer to part (a) if the strategy used is to bet each
time on the red and always bet $1 more than the amount of
money lost (or all that remains of the $100).

10 Each January 1 in Smogsville the air pollution index is 100.
Smoggy days and clear days occur "randomly", the probability of

each being ½. On a smoggy day, the index goes up 10 points. On a clear day the index decreases by 10 percent of its value. Simulate 10 years of 365 days each to estimate the probability that the pollution index is greater than 105 on any given day.

4 | *queues and probability*

The next example is typical of many simulation programs which solve problems concerning queues (waiting lines). Queues are involved in such things as the study of highway traffic flow, scheduling of jobs in an industrial plant, and people waiting for service from a bank teller.

the bank teller

Suppose a bank teller can serve two patrons each minute. Suppose in any 1 minute, zero, one, two, or three new arrivals may get in the line and each number is as likely as any other number, that is, during about ¼ of the minutes of a typical day, none get in line, during ¼ of the minutes of the day, one gets in line, etc. The concise mathematical way of describing the way people arrive is to say that the *probability* of no arrivals is ¼, the probability of one arrival is ¼, etc., or in standard notation, $\Pr(0) = \Pr(1) = \Pr(2) = \Pr(3) = \frac{1}{4}$. How long, on the average, will a depositor have to wait in line?

This problem can be solved with a fairly simple Monte Carlo simulation program. The program must keep track of the number waiting in line, the total number that have been served, and the total time that has been spent waiting in line by all of the patrons. The uncertainty in the program is the number of people that arrive each minute.

In the program Q, the variable L represents the length of the queue, P is the total number served, A is the number of arrivals in any given minute, W is the total number of minutes waited by all patrons, and T counts the time in minutes since the opening of the bank. Lines 30–70 simulate 1 minute of the day. Statement 31 generates the number of new arrivals. This number is added to the length of the queue and to the total number served. Statements 51–53 simulate the servicing of two people in line, if there are that many. If the line contains only one or no patrons, that is how many are served. One way to calculate the total number of man-minutes spent in the line is to add the number of minutes spent in line by each person. However, it is easier to sum the number of people in the line each minute, which is done in statement 61. When the bank closes, the people in the queue are served (lines 80–84). Finally the results are printed. The entire simulation is repeated for five 6-hour days.

```
LIST
Q

1    FOR D=1 TO 5
10   REM   L IS THE LENGTH OF THE QUEUE
11   LET L=0
12   REM   P IS THE NUMBER OF PATRONS SERVED IN ONE DAY
13   LET P=0
14   REM   W IS THE TOTAL WAITING TIME
15   LET W=0
20   FOR T=1 TO 360
30   REM   **   GENERATE THE NUMBER OF ARRIVALS
31   LET A=INT(4*RND(0))
40   REM   **   ADD ARRIVALS TO TOTAL PATRONS AND TO QUEUE
41   LET P=P+A
42   LET L=L+A
50   REM   **   SERVE TWO CUSTOMERS
51   LET L=L-2
52   IF L >= 0 THEN 60
53   LET L=0
60   REM   **   ADD NUMBER IN LINE TO WAIT TIME
61   LET W=W+L
70   NEXT T
80   REM   **   SERVE PATRONS AFTER BANK CLOSES
81   FOR T=1 TO INT((L+1)/2)
82   LET L=L-2
83   IF L >= 0 THEN 85
84   LET L=0
85   LET W=W+L
86   NEXT T
90   PRINT
91   PRINT "DAY";D
92   PRINT "NUMBER SERVED";P
93   PRINT "AVERAGE WAITING TIME";W/P;"MINUTES"
98   NEXT D
99   END

RUN
Q


DAY 1
NUMBER SERVED 583
AVERAGE WAITING TIME .535163     MINUTES

DAY 2
NUMBER SERVED 537
AVERAGE WAITING TIME .348231     MINUTES

DAY 3
NUMBER SERVED 520
AVERAGE WAITING TIME .469231     MINUTES

DAY 4
NUMBER SERVED 501
AVERAGE WAITING TIME .411178     MINUTES

DAY 5
NUMBER SERVED 549
AVERAGE WAITING TIME .349727     MINUTES

DONE
```

random variables

The queuing example provides a framework within which to look a bit more carefully at some of the elementary principles of probability theory. Probability theory deals with *random events,* events whose outcome, in general, is uncertain. A *random variable* is a quantity whose value depends upon a random event. The number of arrivals in 1 minute, the number of patrons served in a day, and the average waiting time are all random variables associated with the bank teller queuing problem. The number of arrivals in 1 minute may be only one of the four possible numbers 0, 1, 2, or 3. The average waiting time could be any positive number. It will be easiest to discuss properties of random variables which can assume only a finite number of different values, but similar ideas also relate to other situations.

Suppose a random event is repeated over and over many times. Suppose X is a random variable associated with the event, and $v_1, v_2, \ldots, v_n$ represent the possible values that X may have. There are numbers $p_1, p_2, \ldots, p_n$, one for each possible value of X, which represent the percentage of times that X has the value $v_1, v_2, \ldots, v_n$. The numbers p_i are called *probabilities* and the notation $p_i = \Pr(X = v_1)$ is used, which reads "p_i is the probability that the random variable X has the value v_i". If, in the queuing problem, A represents the random variable whose value is the number of customers arriving in a given minute, then

$$\Pr(A = 0) = \Pr(A = 1) = \Pr(A = 2) = \Pr(A = 3) = .25$$

This information is displayed in Figure 3.

Sometimes $\Pr(X = v)$ is written more briefly as $\Pr(v)$, as was done earlier when describing the probabilities associated with the variable A.

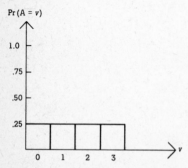

Figure 3   Probability distribution of the number of patrons arriving.

Notice that the sum of the probabilities of any random variable must be 1, and each probability must be a number between 0 and 1.

calculating probabilities

The probabilities associated with a random variable X can be calculated in many interesting cases. One of the ways to calculate probabilities is to count the number of different and *equally likely* ways that a certain random event can take place. Call that number N. Then, count how many of these events yield the particular value of interest, say, v, for the variable X. Call that S. The probability that $X = v$ is then S/N.

Example Two dice are rolled. Let D be the sum of the dots on the two dice. What is $Pr(D = 7)$? All of the possible rolls are listed in Table 1.

table 1 *the possible results when two dice are rolled*

die no. 1	die no. 2	D	D = 7?	die no. 1	die no. 2	D	D = 7?
1	1	2		4	1	5	
1	2	3		4	2	6	
1	3	4		4	3	7	√
1	4	5		4	4	8	
1	5	6		4	5	9	
1	6	7	√	4	6	10	
2	1	3		5	1	6	
2	2	4		5	2	7	√
2	3	5		5	3	8	
2	4	6		5	4	9	
2	5	7	√	5	5	10	
2	6	8		5	6	11	
3	1	4		6	1	7	√
3	2	5		6	2	8	
3	3	6		6	3	9	
3	4	7	√	6	4	10	
3	5	8		6	5	11	
3	6	9		6	6	12	

There are N = 36 equally likely results (if the dice are fair) and S = 6 cases result in a value of 7 for D. Thus $\Pr(D = 6) = \frac{6}{36} = \frac{1}{6}$. Other questions can also be answered about D from the table.

The probability of 7 or 11 is

$$\Pr(D = 7) + \Pr(D = 11) = \frac{6}{36} + \frac{2}{26} = \frac{8}{36} = \frac{2}{9}$$

The probability of a 2, 3, or 12 is

$$\Pr(D = 2) + \Pr(D = 3) + \Pr(D = 12) = \frac{1}{36} + \frac{2}{36} + \frac{1}{36}$$
$$= \frac{4}{36} = \frac{1}{9}$$

The probability distribution of D is shown in Figure 4.

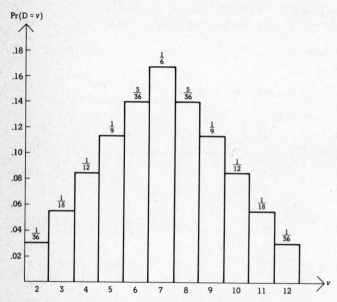

Figure 4   Probability distribution of the value of two dice.

Other interesting questions about the results of the dice can be answered by examining the table. The probability of rolling doubles is $\frac{6}{36} = \frac{1}{6}$. What is the probability of rolling 4 before rolling a 7? Here the last roll is the only one of interest, so N is now 3 + 6 = 9, the number of cases in which either a 4 or 7 is rolled. Three of the nine rolls result in a 4, hence the probability is $\frac{1}{3}$.

In many interesting cases, it is not feasible to actually list all of the possible results of a random event. For example, there are

$$\frac{52!}{13! \; 39!} = 635,013,559,600$$

different bridge hands, and fortunately there are methods for
calculating this number without actually listing all of the possible
hands. Chapters on permutations and combinations in certain
mathematics texts provide a basis for this skill.

generating random numbers with a given distribution

It is of interest to be able to generate numbers which have a given
probability distribution. Suppose it is known that the number A of
new customers arriving at the checkout stand in a supermarket in
any 1 minute has the distribution

v	$Pr(A = v)$
0	.273
1	.324
2	.116
3	.214
4	.073

A way to simulate arriving customers is to generate a single
random number R, between 0 and 1. If $0 \leqq R < .273$, then $A = 0$;
if $.273 \leqq R < .597 = .273 + .324$, then $A = 1$, etc. The following
BASIC statements generate a value for the variable A with a
distribution given by the table.

```
1   DIM P[5]
2   MAT  READ P
3   DATA .273,.324,.116,.214,.073

40  LET R=RND(0)
41  FOR I=1 TO 5
42  LET R=R-P[I]
43  IF R<0 THEN 45
44  NEXT I
45  LET A=I-1
```

Suppose the distribution is a little more complicated due to the
fact that the values of v are not simply 0, 1, 2, ... If the
distribution of A is to be

v	$Pr(A = v)$
0	.137
2	.562
5	.212
13	.089

then a new vector of v's can be added and the program changed to include the statements

```
1   DIM P[4],V[4]
2   MAT  READ P
3   DATA .137,.562,.212,.089
4   MAT  READ V
5   DATA 0,2,5,13


40  LET R=RND(0)
41  FOR I=1 TO 4
42  LET R=R-P[I]
43  IF R<0 THEN 45
44  NEXT I
45  LET A=V[I]
```

Using this example as a model, BASIC statements can be written which simulate any random variable which may assume a finite number of different values.

The queuing problem could be changed by specifying a different probability distribution for the random variable A. It could be made more complex by also specifying a probability distribution for a random variable S, the number of customers served each minute. This would reflect the fact that different patrons require different amounts of service time from the bank teller.

the uniform distribution

There are many interesting probability distributions for which the random variable may assume infinitely many different values. One of these is called the *uniform* distribution and it is this distribution which the random-number generator RND simulates. For a uniform distribution two numbers, a and b, a minimum and a maximum value, are specified. The random variable may assume any value between a and b and each number is as likely as any other. For the RND function, $a = 0$ and $b = 1$. Actually, the RND function can produce only finitely many different values, but the number of values is large, many thousands at least. Thus, the effect is as if it

could produce any number between 0 and 1. It has already been
shown how some distributions can be simulated using RND. As an
illustration of how RND can be used to simulate other random
variables, the following statement generates a random number U,
whose distribution is approximately that of a random variable
uniformly distributed between A and B.

```
69  LET U = (B-A)*RND(0) + A
```

Anyone who desires to be an expert in simulation must have a
good knowledge of probability theory. He can then be assured that
a simulator is easier than direct calculation, that the probability
distributions given are properly implemented, and that the answers
make sense. However, the examples in this chapter are intended
to show that the principles involved are not difficult and with a
little experience, the neophyte probabilist could use simulation to
solve some problems in the area of his own interest.

accuracy of data

There is one statement concerning simulations that is obvious, but
nevertheless needs to be emphasized. It is the old "garbage in,
garbage out" truism in a different guise. Any results of a simulation
will have meaning only if the assumptions about the distributions of
the random variables in the program are correct. In the queuing
example, average waiting times provided by the program are valid
only if the distribution of arrivals is accurate. Often these
distributions can be obtained by actual observation. Why not then
simply have the observer record waiting times and forget the
simulation? The answer is that once the distribution of arriving
customers is obtained, different types of service can be simulated by
the program based on the same data. For example, the effect of
having a second teller can be simulated, avoiding the expense and
inconvenience of actually performing the experiment.

There is another more subtle way in which meaningful answers
depend upon input data. The input data usually are measured data
(or even numbers whose values represent only intelligent guesses).
What if their values are wrong by 2 percent? In some cases this
kind of error may affect the answer by only a little bit. But there are
cases when a 2 percent error in the data would produce a 100
percent error in the results. This is true not only of simulation
programs, but of any programs which use input data whose values
are not known precisely. One way to check for this disastrous

possibility is to change the input data by 2 percent and rerun the program. If the results are quite different with a 2 percent change in some of the input data, a more careful study of the whole problem is indicated.

The final three sections of this chapter do not introduce any new principles concerned with simulation, but they do illustrate the application of simulation techniques to three quite different problems. The discussion of these examples should reinforce the idea that a little knowledge of basic mathematics is sometimes helpful in almost any discipline.

problems

1 Let D be the random variable whose value is the sum of the dots on two fair dice which are rolled.

   a What is the probability that $D > 7$?

   b What is the probability that D is even?

2 When a roulette wheel is spun, what is the probability that the result is

   a 00

   b 0 or 00

   c 1, 2, 3, 4, 5, or 6

   d in the first column (see Figure 2, Section 3)

   e odd

3 If two cards are drawn from a standard deck, what is the probability that one is an ace and one is a face card? (See Problem 7, Section 3.) To solve this problem, visualize (without writing them down) all of the possibilities. For each possible first card, there are 51 possibilities for the second card, so the list would have 52×51 entries.

4 Write a BASIC subroutine beginning with statement number 400 which will generate a random number R which is uniformly distributed between 0 and $\frac{1}{2}$ one-third of the time and uniformly distributed between $\frac{1}{2}$ and 1 two-thirds of the time.

5 Ten students are working at a teletype terminal connected to a central computer. Periodically the students request service of the computer by hitting the RETURN button which transmits a command to the computer. The computer processes the command and types a response. Let the random variable S represent the time for each student between receiving an answer from the computer and issuing the next command. Let C be the random variable which represents the time required by the computer to process each command. Suppose S and C have probability distributions

s	Pr(S = s)	c	Pr(C = c)
3	.02	1	.44
4	.03	2	.41
5	.02	3	.12
6	.01	6	.02
12	.02	7	.01
13	.05		
14	.16		
15	.11		
16	.05		
27	.13		
28	.29		
29	.11		

The computer processes the commands one at a time in the order received. If two commands are received in the same second, the one from the lowest numbered terminal is processed first. What is the average response time of the system, that is, what is the average time between issuing a command and receiving an answer?

6 At a particular restaurant, the number A of diners which arrive in any 5-minute period is given by the distribution

A	Pr(A)
0	.63
1	.11
2	.21
3	.01
4	.04

There are no new arrivals whenever there are 15 or more diners in the restaurant.

If the number of patrons is P when a new customer enters the restaurant, then the total time T needed to be served and to eat is given by the following table.

P	T
0	30
1	35
2	35
3	40
4	40
5	40
6	45
7	50
≥ 8	60

What is the average time a customer spends in the restaurant?

5 | *political polls*

An amateur political scientist has taken a poll of ten people to determine whether or not controversial Proposition A will pass. Of the ten people polled, six stated they would vote for Proposition A and four said they would vote against it. What is the probability that the proposition will pass?

There is only one uncertainty in this polling situation; the proportion P of the population in favor of the proposition. However, the problem is easier to solve if the number polled in favor of the proposition (six, in this case) is also treated as a random variable. A value for P is generated and then the poll of ten people can be simulated. All polls in which F, the number polled in favor of the proposition, is not six are ignored. The answer to the problem is then the average value of P for the limited sample of simulations in which $F = 6$. The probability that the proposition will pass is called a *conditional* probability because it depends on the given condition $F = 6$.

the POLL *program*

In the program POLL1, 1000 simulations are made. The variable N records the number of times that $F = 6$. All other simulations are ignored. Of the N simulations in which $F = 6$, the number of times the proposition would have passed ($P \geq .5$) is recorded as the value of S. The probability that the proposition will pass, given that $F = 6$, is then estimated by S/N.

In the program POLL1, the value of P is generated by taking the average value of two random numbers between 0 and 1. This tends to give P values near .5 more often than values near 0 and 1, in an attempt to reflect the fact that propositions on a ballot are rarely defeated or passed by, say, a ten-to-one vote split. A more accurate simulation could be obtained by studying actual voting figures and incorporating into the program a more accurate method of generating the value of P.

In order to see how the simulation is progressing, the program prints the values of P, F, S, and N after each 100 simulations.

```
LIST
POLL1

10   REM   N WILL BE THE NUMBER OF TIMES F=6
11   LET N=0
20   REM   S WILL BE THE NUMBER OF TIMES THE PROP. WILL PASS
21   LET S=0
30   FOR T=1 TO 1000
110  REM   GENERATE PERCENTAGE P OF POPULATION IN FAVOR
111  LET P=(RND(0)+RND(0))/2
120  LET F=0
130  REM   POLL 10 PEOPLE AND RECORD F, THE NUMBER IN FAVOR
131  FOR I=1 TO 10
140  IF RND(0)>P THEN 160
150  LET F=F+1
160  NEXT I
170  IF F <> 6 THEN 220
180  LET N=N+1
190  IF P<.5 THEN 220
210  LET S=S+1
220  IF INT(T/100) <> T/100 THEN 240
230  PRINT T,P;F;S;N
240  NEXT T
249  PRINT
250  PRINT "THE PROBABILITY THAT THE PROPOSITION WILL PASS IS";S/N
999  END


RUN
POLL1

100       .516437    4    8    13
200       .710702    8    18   28
300       .615762    7    32   47
400       .721787    8    42   62
500       .61661     6    51   77
600       .235714    1    59   87
700       .612243    3    68   101
800       .626995    9    72   106
900       .258424    2    83   119
1000      .832641    10   92   133

THE PROBABILITY THAT THE PROPOSITION WILL PASS IS .691729

DONE
```

another polling problem

The amateur political scientist next decides to take a poll of 100 people to decide if Proposition B will pass. He decides that if at least 55 people say they favor the proposition, he will risk his reputation and predict that the proposition will pass. What is the probability that the proposition will pass ($P \geq .5$), given that F, the number polled in favor, is at least 55?

The program POLL2, which solves this problem is very similar to POLL1. All simulations in which $F < 55$ are ignored and the total number of simulations made is only 100, because a smaller percentage will be eliminated. The values of P, F, S, and N are printed after each 10 simulations.

```
LIST
POLL2

10   REM  N WILL BE THE NUMBER OF TIMES F>50
11   LET N=0
20   REM  S WILL BE THE NUMBER OF TIMES THE PROP. WILL PASS
21   LET S=0
30   FOR T=1 TO 100
110  REM  GENERATE PERCENTAGE P OF POPULATION IN FAVOR
111  LET P=(RND(0)+RND(0))/2
120  LET F=0
130  REM  POLL 100 PEOPLE AND RECORD F, THE NUMBER IN FAVOR
131  FOR I=1 TO 100
140  IF RND(0)>P THEN 160
150  LET F=F+1
160  NEXT I
170  IF F<51 THEN 220
180  LET N=N+1
190  IF P<.5 THEN 220
210  LET S=S+1
220  IF INT(T/10) <> T/10 THEN 240
230  PRINT T,P;F;S;N
240  NEXT T
249  PRINT
250  PRINT "THE PROBABILITY THAT THE PROPOSITION WILL PASS IS";S/N
999  END


RUN
POLL2

10        .34177     34   4    4
20        .119891    12   6    6
30        .676807    70   11   11
40        .883863    93   16   16
50        .593436    61   24   24
60        .677757    67   30   32
70        .493505    49   34   36
80        .709695    60   38   40
90        .436332    36   40   42
100       .591363    67   44   47

THE PROBABILITY THAT THE PROPOSITION WILL PASS IS .93617

DONE
```

problems

1 Suppose that 55 percent of the voting population favors Proposition C. What percentage of the time will an unbiased poll of 101 people show more against than for the proposition? (This simulation would be used to validate or understand the polling process, not to predict the outcome of the voting.)

2 Two dice are rolled. Find, by simulation, the probability that the second dice is odd, given that the first one is even.

3 A poker hand is dealt. Find the probability that the hand contains at least one pair, given that it contains no face cards (ten, jack, queen, king) or aces.

4 Find the probability that more than 70 percent of the results will be heads if a fair coin is tossed 10 times; 100 times.

5 A gambler enters a casino with $1,000 and bets $1 on red at the roulette table each minute. What is the probability that he will have $1,000 or more after 1 hour?

6 A company manufactures light bulbs in lots of 100 bulbs. If D is the random variable representing the number of defective items in a lot, the probability distribution of D is given by

v	$Pr(D = v)$
0	.18
1	.27
2	.22
3	.16
4	.12
5	.04
6	.01

A lot is considered acceptable if $D \leq 2$. A test for quality is established in which five bulbs are tested in each lot. If any one of the five tested is defective, the bulbs are destroyed and the material recycled into the manufacturing process. If none of the five bulbs tested is defective, the lot is sold.

a What is the probability that an unacceptable $(D > 2)$ lot is sold?

b What is the probability that an acceptable lot is destroyed and recycled?

c What is the average number of defective bulbs in the lots which are sold?

6 | the archaeologist

An archaeologist is digging in an ancient town site that is 100 meters × 100 meters. From ancient writings it is known that there was a circular temple with a 10-meter radius at some unknown location within the site. The archaeologist decides to locate the temple by digging a series of trenches 10 meters long until one of them intersects the circular foundation of the temple. If the location and direction of the trenches are selected at random, how many trenches should the archaeologist expect to dig until he intersects the foundation of the temple?

In the Monte Carlo simulation program DIG, which solves this problem, the elements of uncertainty are the location of the trial trenches and the location of the temple. Although the temple is surely on the site, the archaeologist doesn't know precisely where it is, and so to him its location is uncertain.

The program DIG must keep track of the location of the temple, the location of the trial trenches, and the number of trial trenches.

One interesting thing about the archaeology problem is that some elementary knowledge of algebra, trigonometry, and analytic geometry is helpful to understand the simulation. These bits of mathematics will be explained when needed.

Suppose that the 100×100-meter town site is marked off in 1-meter squares (analytic geometry). Any point in the site can be specified by two coordinates, x and y, representing distance east and distance north, respectively, from the southwest corner. Some sample points are shown in Figure 5.

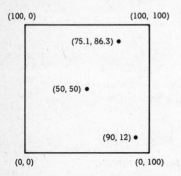

Figure 5   Designation of the points in the town site.

The location of the temple is conveniently represented by the coordinates of its center, variables X1 and Y1 in the program DIG. Since the radius of the temple is 10 meters, the values of X1 and Y1 must be between 10 and 90. The random number $80 * \text{RND}(0) + 10$ is between 10 and 90, because $0 \leq \text{RND}(0) < 1$

and $0 \leqq 80 * RND(0) < 80$, so that $10 \leqq 80 * RND(0) + 10 < 90$.
Thus the statements

```
30   REM   **   PLACE TEMPLE
40   LET  X1=80*RND(1)+10
50   LET  Y1=80*RND(1)+10
```

place the temple at some position inside the town site.

The choice of a scheme to generate numbers representing a
10-meter trench is not so straightforward. In the program DIG, a
trench is simulated by generating a point within the site and then
selecting a direction from the point. The other end of the trench is
then the point 10 meters from the first point in the direction
specified. It is possible that the second point is not inside the site.
If that is the case, then numbers representing another trial trench
are generated. Here a little knowledge of trigonometry is essential
and the built-in trigonometric functions SIN and COS can be used.
Let X2 and Y2 be the coordinates of the point selected for one end
of the trench. A direction can be represented by a number of
degrees from 0 to 360, but the BASIC trigonometric functions
expect the arguments to be given in radians ($360° = 2\pi$ radians),
so the direction is given by an angle A between 0 and $2\pi = 6.28319$
radians. The statements

```
110   REM   **   PLACE END OF TRENCH
120   LET  X2=100*RND(2)
130   LET  Y2=100*RND(2)
```

generate one endpoint of the trench and the statements

```
140   REM   **   SELECT DIRECTION OF TRENCH
150   LET  A=6.28319*RND(3)
```

generate the direction of the trench.

The cosine and sine of an angle are found by drawing a triangle
as shown in Figure 6. The cosine of A is then the width of the
triangle (w) divided by the length of the hypotenuse, which
will always be 10 in this problem. Thus $\cos(A) = w/10$, so
$w = 10 \cdot \cos(A)$. Similarly, $\sin(A) = h/10$ and $h = 10 \cdot \sin(A)$.
The other end of the trench is thus given by

```
181   LET  X=X2+10*C
185   LET  Y=Y2+10*S
```

where $C = COS(A)$ and $S = SIN(A)$. The values of $COS(A)$ and $SIN(A)$ are stored by the variables C and S because they will be needed again in the program.

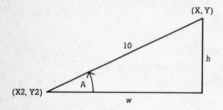

Figure 6   A triangle.

If this point is not within the site then another set of values for X2, Y2, and A is generated. The point (X, Y) is within the site if both values are between 0 and 100. Statements 182, 183, 186, and 187 make these checks.

Now the program must verify that the trench intersects the foundation of the temple. This calculation is a little easier to understand if the trench is dug as a sequence of ten circular holes, each 1 meter in diameter, as shown in Figure 7.

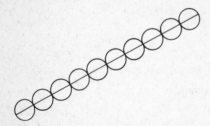

Figure 7   A "trench" consisting of ten circular holes.

One of the circular holes will intersect the foundation of the temple if the distance between the centers of the two circles is between 9.5 and 10.5 meters, because the radius of the temple is 10 meters and the radius of the hole is .5 meter. Let (X, Y) be the center of a hole. The theorem of Pythagoras states that the square of the hypotenuse of a right triangle is the sum of the squares of the sides. Thus the distance D between the centers of the circles is the square root of $(X1 - X) \uparrow 2 + (Y1 - Y) \uparrow 2$ (see Figure 8).

Using some rules of algebra, the circles intersect if and only if

$$9.5 \leq D \leq 10.5$$

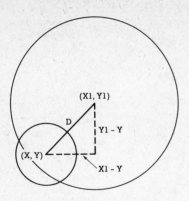

Figure 8   Two intersecting circles.

or

$$(10 - \tfrac{1}{2})^2 \leq D^2 \leq (10 + \tfrac{1}{2})^2$$

or

$$10^2 - 2(\tfrac{1}{2}) \cdot 10 + (\tfrac{1}{2})^2 \leq D^2 \leq 10^2 + 2(\tfrac{1}{2}) \cdot 10 + (\tfrac{1}{2})^2$$

or

$$-10 \leq D^2 - 100.25 \leq 10$$

or

$$|D^2 - 100.25| \leq 10$$

or

$$\text{ABS}((X1 - X) \uparrow 2 + (Y1 - Y) \uparrow 2 - 100.25) \leq 10$$

This condition is checked by statement 340.

Using the same formula that was used to calculate the location of the other end of the trench, statements 220 and 230 locate the center of the first hole and statements 360 and 370 compute the location of the next hole each time the FOR–NEXT loop for each hole is executed.

In the program DIG, the variable N records the total number of trial trenches needed by all of the simulations. The variable K counts the 100 simulations. The variable T records the number of trenches needed to find the temple. Its value is printed for each simulation.

The distribution of the 100 values of T printed during the simulation is shown in Figure 9.

```
LIST
DIG

10   LET N=0
20   FOR K=1 TO 100
30   REM  **  PLACE TEMPLE
40   LET X1=80*RND(1)+10
50   LET Y1=80*RND(1)+10
60   FOR T=1 TO 100
110  REM  **  PLACE END OF TRENCH
120  LET X2=100*RND(2)
130  LET Y2=100*RND(2)
140  REM  **  SELECT DIRECTION OF TRENCH
150  LET A=6.28319*RND(3)
160  LET C=COS(A)
170  LET S=SIN(A)
180  REM  **  CHECK IF OTHER END OF TRENCH IS IN SITE
181  LET X=X2+10*C
182  IF X<0 THEN 110
183  IF X>100 THEN 110
185  LET Y=Y2+10*S
186  IF Y<0 THEN 110
187  IF Y>100 THEN 110
210  REM  **  LOCATE CENTER OF FIRST HOLE
220  LET X=X2+.5*C
230  LET Y=Y2+.5*S
310  REM  **  DIG HOLES
320  FOR H=1 TO 10
330  REM  **  CHECK IF HOLE INTERSECTS FOUNDATION OF TEMPLE
340  IF ABS((X1-X)↑2+(Y1-Y)↑2-100.25) <= 10 THEN 430
350  REM  **  LOCATE CENTER OF NEXT HOLE
360  LET X=X+C
370  LET Y=Y+S
390  NEXT H
410  REM  **  TEMPLE NOT FOUND
420  NEXT T
430  REM  **  TEMPLE FOUND
431  LET N=N+T
440  PRINT T;
450  NEXT K
460  PRINT
470  PRINT
480  PRINT "THE AVERAGE NUMBER OF TRENCHES NEEDED IS";N/100
490  END
```

```
RUN
DIG

38   20    2   17   62   44    9   63   37   13   20   41
77    9   47   17    4    7   42   14   29    2   46   32
 6   11    5    1    9    1   46   10    1   13    6    6
10   24   18   25   10   15    3   18   14   23    1   74
14   64   29    2    5    3   20   55   24   12   20   52
15   21   58    4   21   52   15   11    3    6   15   11
40   36   26    1    7   24   38   22   13   31   13    4
20   23   31   14   12   18   26   73   20    3   32    8
12    4   37   37

THE AVERAGE NUMBER OF TRENCHES NEEDED IS 21.99

DONE
```

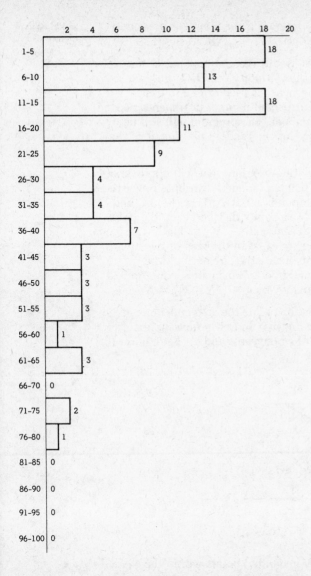

Figure 9   Distribution of the number of trenches needed.

problems

1   In the archaeology problem of this section, is there some
maximum number of trial trenches? That is, is there some number
m such that the archaeologist can be assured that he will have to
dig no more than m trenches to find the temple?

2 What happens in the DIG program if the temple is not found after digging 100 trial trenches?

3 An intelligent archaeologist would certainly not select the location of his trenches at random. Modify the DIG program so that a fixed sequence of trial trenches is used. Pick the trenches to be dug in such a way that the expected number of trenches needed to locate the temple will be minimal. The program will still be a Monte Carlo simulation because of the random placement of the temple.

4 Write a Monte Carlo simulation program that will approximate the value of π. Generate 1000 points randomly distributed over the unit square determined by the points $(0, 0)$, $(0, 1)$, $(1, 1)$, and $(1, 0)$. Calculate the number N of points that lie inside the circle inscribed within the square with center at $(\frac{1}{2}, \frac{1}{2})$ and radius $\frac{1}{2}$. Since the area of the circle is $A_c = \pi r^2 = \pi/4$ and the area of the square $A_s = 1$, the percentage of points inside the circle should be $A_c/A_s = \pi/4$. Thus $N/1000$ should be approximately equal to $\pi/4$ and π should be given approximately by $4 \times (N/1000) = N/250$.

5 Write a Monte Carlo simulation to find the area under any given curve $y = f(x)$ between $x = a$ and $x = b$. Let m be a number larger than $f(x)$ for any value of x between a and b. (See Figure 10.)

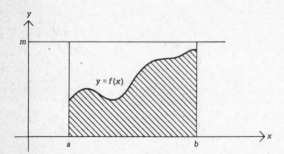

Figure 10   Area below curve $y = f(x)$.

The percentage of randomly generated points within the shaded area should be approximately equal to the area under the curve (shaded) divided by the area of the rectangle, which is $m \cdot (b - a)$. The point (x, y) is in the shaded area if $y \leqq f(x)$.

7 | baseball

What is the best batting order for a baseball team? It seems reasonable to put the player with the lowest batting average (usually the pitcher) last in order to minimize the number of times

he will bat. Coaches and managers traditionally put the best
extra-base hitter in the fourth position and concentrate the other
good hitters in the first half of the batting order. Are these tactics
really the best or is it possible to achieve better results by, say,
spreading the good hitters throughout the batting order?

computer-assisted decisions

The Monte Carlo simulation program named BASBAL described in
this section does not completely answer the question posed. It
simulates the offensive half of ten nine-inning games where the
batting performance for each of the nine players and a batting order
is specified. The program estimates the expected number of runs
scored using a particular batting order.

It would be impractical to let the computer try each possible
batting order to see which one yields the most runs because there
are $9! = 362880$ different batting orders and simulating several
games using each of them would take a lot of computer time. In
solving this problem, the computer and the coach make an excellent
team. The coach can begin by feeding the computer an intuitively
appealing batting order for his players. The computer simulates the
outcome of several games. The coach may rearrange the batting
order until he obtains one that appears to give a consistently high
average number of runs.

the program BASBAL

In order to make the simulation program short and easy to
understand, many aspects of the game have been simplified. For
example, errors are completely ignored; a runner can never be put
out on base and can never steal a base; if the batter hits a single, a
runner on second base always scores; and each batter may get only
a hit, a walk, or an out.

The batting statistics for each player are recorded in the DATA
statements 51–59. These numbers represent times at bat, hits,
doubles, triples, home runs, and walks. The batting average and
player's name are never used by the program and could be
eliminated along with statements 41 and 42 if the program is to be
run on a system which does not allow string variables.

A probability distribution based on each player's batting statistics
is stored in an array D. If P is a player number, then the probability
of player P getting a single, double, triple, home run, walk, and out
are computed and stored in $D[P, 1]$ through $D[P, 6]$. Since a walk

does not contribute to a player's batting average, the number of walks is not included in the "official" number of times at bat. Thus, for example, the probability of a double is the number of doubles divided by the number of times at bat plus the number of walks.

The batting order is given by O[1], . . . , O[9]. The first batter in the game is P = O[1], the second is O[2], and so forth. The variable T records the total score in all ten games, the variable G counts the games, and S counts the score in each game. N records the position in the batting order, P is the number of the player at bat, I counts the nine innings of each game, B[1], B[2], and B[3] record the number of runners (zero or one) on each base, and U counts the three outs in each inning. For each player at bat, a random number K from 1 to 6 is generated which represents a hit, walk, or out according to the distribution D. At line 190 a branch is made to one of the six statements listed, depending on the value of K.

The results of running the program for two different batting orders are shown.

The batting statistics used in this program are those of the 1969 World Champion New York Mets (Metropolitan Baseball Club, *Radio and TV Guide*, New York Mets Press, 1970).

```
LIST
BASBAL

10   DIM A[6],D[9,6],B[3],O[9],H[4]
20   REM  **  COMPUTE DISTRIBUTION D
30   FOR P=1 TO 9
40   MAT   READ A
41   DIM P$[20]
42   READ X,P$
50   REM   AB,H,2B,3B,HR,BB,AVE
51   DATA 483,164,25,4,12,64,.34,"JONES"
52   DATA 303,91,9,3,14,36,.3,"SHAMSKY"
53   DATA 362,101,14,7,3,36,.279,"BOSWELL"
54   DATA 565,153,23,4,26,59,.271,"AGEE"
55   DATA 365,92,12,3,6,32,.252,"GROTE"
56   DATA 395,98,11,6,0,54,.248,"HARRELSON"
57   DATA 340,81,10,2,10,40,.237,"KRANEPOOL/SWOBODA"
58   DATA 400,87,11,3,1,40,.218,"GARRETT"
59   DATA 421,46,6,0,1,12,.109,"PITCHERS"
60   LET Q=A[1]+A[6]
61   LET D[P,1]=(A[2]-A[3]-A[4]-A[5])/Q
62   LET D[P,2]=A[3]/Q
63   LET D[P,3]=A[4]/Q
64   LET D[P,4]=A[5]/Q
65   LET D[P,5]=A[6]/Q
66   LET D[P,6]=(A[1]-A[2])/Q
69   NEXT P
70   PRINT "TYPE BATTING ORDER"
71   MAT   INPUT O
72   PRINT
73   PRINT "GAME ";1;2;3;4;5;6;7;8;9;10
74   PRINT "SCORE";
```

```
80    REM  **  T IS TOTAL RUNS IN ALL GAMES
81    LET T=0
100   REM  **  PLAY TEN GAMES
101   FOR G=1 TO 10
110   REM  **  S IS GAME SCORE
111   LET S=0
120   REM  **  N INDICATES POSITION IN BATTING ORDER
121   LET N=1
130   REM  **  P IS PLAYER NUMBER
131   LET P=O[N]
140   REM  **  PLAY NINE INNINGS
141   FOR I=1 TO 9
150   REM  **  CLEAR THE BASES
151   MAT B=ZER
160   REM  **  U COUNTS THREE OUTS
161   FOR U=1 TO 3
170   LET Q=RND(O)
171   FOR K=1 TO 6
172   LET Q=Q-D[P,K]
173   IF Q<O THEN 181
174   NEXT K
175   STOP

180   REM  **  NEXT BATTER UP
181   LET N=N+1
182   IF N<10 THEN 185
183   LET N=1
185   LET P=O[N]
190   GOTO K OF 211,221,231,241,251,261
210   REM  **  SINGLE
211   LET S=S+B[3]+B[2]
212   LET B[3]=0
213   LET B[2]=B[1]
214   LET B[1]=1
215   GOTO 170
220   REM  **  DOUBLE
221   LET S=S+B[3]+B[2]+B[1]
222   LET B[3]=0
223   LET B[2]=1
224   LET B[1]=0
225   GOTO 170
230   REM  **  TRIPLE
231   LET S=S+B[3]+B[2]+B[1]
232   LET B[3]=1
233   LET B[2]=0
234   LET B[1]=0
235   GOTO 170
240   REM  **  HOME RUN
241   LET S=S+B[3]+B[2]+B[1]+1
242   MAT B=ZER
243   GOTO 170
250   REM  **  WALK
251   LET S=S+B[3]*B[2]*B[1]
252   LET B[3]=B[2]*B[1]
253   LET B[2]=B[1]
254   LET B[1]=1
255   GOTO 170
260   REM  **  OUT
261   NEXT U
270   NEXT I
280   PRINT S;
281   LET T=T+S
290   NEXT G
291   PRINT
292   PRINT "AVERAGE SCORE";T/10
293   PRINT "DO YOU WANT TO PLAY AGAIN (IF SO, TYPE 1)";
294   INPUT Q
295   PRINT
296   IF Q=1 THEN 70
299   STOP
999   END
```

```
RUN
BASBAL

TYPE BATTING ORDER
?1,2,3,4,5,6,7,8,9

GAME  1     2     3     4     5     6     7     8     9     10
SCORE 1     0     4     4     2     8     0     4     1     5
AVERAGE SCORE 2.9
DO YOU WANT TO PLAY AGAIN (IF SO, TYPE 1)?1

TYPE BATTING ORDER
?1,5,2,6,3,7,4,8,9

GAME  1     2     3     4     5     6     7     8     9     10
SCORE 1     0     7     2     3     5     5     1     6     1
AVERAGE SCORE 3.1
DO YOU WANT TO PLAY AGAIN (IF SO, TYPE 1)?0


DONE
```

problems

1 Simplified computer basketball is played between two equal teams whose success with possession of the ball is governed by the following mutually exclusive probabilities:

.15 chance of losing ball without taking a shot

.30 chance of shooting and making a basket

.40 chance of shooting and missing

.15 chance of being fouled in the act of shooting, in which case there are two foul shots, each scoring a point with probability .75

A team which shoots and misses has a .40 chance of getting the rebound. Write a program that prints a running score of the basketball game, allowing a total of 100 shots at baskets, not including foul shots.

2 A family is trying to determine the most economical nighttime setting for the thermostat in their house. The utility company estimates the cost, in cents, for each night at

$$\frac{(m-t)^2}{10} + \frac{(72-t)^2}{100}$$

where m is the mean nighttime temperature and t is the thermostat setting, both measured in degrees Fahrenheit. The mean nighttime temperature m varies uniformly between 20°F and 70°F during the year.

Write a program that will simulate the values of m for 1 year and calculate the utility cost for a given value of t. Use the program with various values of t to find the most economical setting.

This problem shows how maxima and minima (see Chapter 5)

can also be found by trial and error. The situation is complicated by the fact that the quantity to be minimized (cost) depends on a random variable (m).

8 | *generating random numbers*

In most programming languages there is a function or subroutine available, such as RND in BASIC, which generates "random" numbers. There is a method for generating "random" numbers which is not difficult to use and could be convenient if there is no random-number generator in the language or the one available is not satisfactory. Any random-number generator that is used extensively should be tested and some simple tests are described in Appendix B.

a random-number generator

To generate a sequence of numbers between 0 and 1, start with any such number, say, .01, multiply it by some integer, such as 31, add a third number, say, .97, and look only at the fractional part.

$$
\begin{array}{r}
.01 \\
\times \quad 31 \\
\hline
.31 \\
+ \quad .97 \\
\hline
1.28
\end{array}
$$

The first number generated is .28. To generate another number, multiply the previous one by 31, add .97 and ignore the integer part.

$$
\begin{array}{r}
.28 \\
\times \quad 31 \\
\hline
28 \\
84 \\
\hline
8.68 \\
+ \quad .97 \\
\hline
9.65
\end{array}
$$

In this case, .65 would be the second number generated.

This particular scheme will generate some of the 100 numbers .00, .01, .02, . . . , .99 in some mixed-up order and then repeat the sequence over and over. The method can be refined by using numbers with more than two digits. For random-number generators

that use this method, the numbers involved will typically have
from 5 to 15 digits, depending upon the computer being used.
Thousands or even millions of numbers can be generated before the
sequence begins to repeat itself.

The subroutine beginning at line 90 in the program RAND
generates numbers R using the method discussed. For the particular
choice of numbers used in this program, 50 numbers are generated
before the sequence begins to repeat. This is obviously not a good
random generator to use in a sophisticated simulation program, but
it does illustrate a method that is commonly used.

```
LIST
RAND

10    READ I,M,K
20    DATA 1,31,97
30    FOR N=1 TO 60
40    GOSUB 90
50    PRINT R,
60    NEXT N
70    STOP
90    LET I=I*M+K
91    LET I=I-INT(I/100)*100
92    LET R=I/100
93    RETURN
99    END


RUN
RAND
```

.28	.65	.12	.69	.36
.13	0	.97	.04	.21
.48	.85	.32	.89	.56
.33	.2	.17	.24	.41
.68	.05	.52	.09	.76
.53	.4	.37	.44	.61
.88	.25	.72	.29	.96
.73	.6	.57	.64	.81
.08	.45	.92	.49	.16
.93	.8	.77	.84	.01
.28	.65	.12	.69	.36
.13	0	.97	.04	.21

```
DONE
```

The choice of the "multiplier" M and "adder" K is important. In
an extreme example, if M were changed to 10 in the program
RAND, all numbers generated would end with 7, the last digit of K.

The following rules will ensure that all possible numbers will be generated before the sequence repeats.

1 The "multiplier" M should be 1 plus a multiple of 20, for example, 21, 41, 61, ...

2 The "adder" K should not be divisible by 2 or 5.

Most computers do arithmetic calculations using binary arithmetic, rather than the decimal system (see Chapter 9). The rules given above are also applicable if binary arithmetic is used.

problems

1 Rerun the program RAND using values of M and K that will cause 100 numbers to be generated before the sequence repeats itself.

2 Write a BASIC subroutine that will generate three-digit decimal numbers between 0 and 1.

3 Show that if the BASIC program RAND uses values M = 1 and K = 1, all 100 values will be generated before the sequence repeats itself. Would this be a good random-number generator to use in a simulation program?

suggested readings

Hull, Thomas E. *Introduction to Computing*. Prentice-Hall, Englewood Cliffs, N.J., 1966.

Hull, Thomas E., and Alan R. Dobell. "Random Number Generators", *Society of Industrial and Applied Mathematics Review* **4,** 230–254 (July, 1962).

Kemeny, John G., J. Laurie Snell, and Gerald L. Thompson. *Introduction to Finite Mathematics*. Prentice-Hall, Englewood Cliffs, N.J., 1956.

Roberts, Walter Orr. "Man on a Changing Earth", *American Scientist* **59,** No. 1, 16–19 (Jan.–Feb., 1971).

？

two puzzles

THE "LOGICAL complexity" of a program is a somewhat informal notion which is mainly related to the interaction between transfer statements of all sorts. Decisions and loops are thought to contribute more to the complexity than sequential processing. Puzzles are a rich source of easily stated problems that may require complicated approaches to their solutions. This chapter is concerned with the solution to two puzzles, emphasizing the necessity for efficiency. The second puzzle is geometric, and it allows consideration of certain difficulties which arise in trying to restate a problem given in a nonalgebraic context in an equivalent form suitable for solution by a computer.

1 | an algebraic puzzle

The technique of nesting FOR-loops is second nature to experienced BASIC programmers. However, in solving problems where many of the simultaneous combinations of FOR-variables should be skipped, some modifications of the raw form of the method might be necessary to achieve reasonable efficiency. This section is concerned with an algebraic puzzle that illustrates such a situation.

frowns and smiles

The problem here is to assign the ten decimal digits 0, 1, 2, 3, 4, 5, 6, 7, 8, 9 to the letters "F", "R", "Ø", "W", "N", "S", "M", "I", "L", "E" so that the equation

FRØWN (times) 7 = SMILE

is true. (In order to avoid confusion with the digit zero, the symbol Ø is sometimes used to denote the letter "oh".) Each of the ten letters must represent a different digit. For the purposes of this problem, a numeral may have a leading zero. The BASIC program developed here will find all possible solutions. There is no a priori reason, of course, to believe that there is even one solution.

a naïve approach

A naïve approach is to nest ten FOR–NEXT loops so that each of the variables F, R, Ø, W, N, S, M, I, L, E ranges through the numbers 0 to 9. After each assignment of the ten variables, the computer makes a test.

1 Has each of the variables been assigned a different digit?

A direct approach to test (1) requires 45 steps for an affirmative answer. First, the variable F is compared to each of the nine variables R, Ø, W, N, S, M, I, L, E. Then the variable R is compared to the eight variables Ø, W, N, S, M, I, L, E. (It need not be recompared to F.) Then Ø is compared to the remaining seven variables, and so on. The total number of comparisons is

$$9 + 8 + 7 + 6 + 5 + 4 + 3 + 2 + 1 = 45$$

If an affirmative answer to test (1) is obtained, the computer makes a second test.

2 Does the equation FRØWN (times) 7 = SMILE hold?

Answering question (2) involves the formation of two numbers

$$X = (10000 * F) + (1000 * R) + (100 * Ø) + (10 * W) + N$$

$$Y = (10000 * S) + (1000 * M) + (100 * I) + (10 * L) + E$$

and a comparison of the number 7 * X to the number Y.
 Under this naïve approach, the computer begins with the attempts

00000	00000	00000	00000
× 7	× 7	× 7	× 7
00000	00001	00002	00003

A hundred thousand attempts later, the computer is applying test (1) to the possibilities

00001	00001	00001	00001
× 7	× 7	× 7	× 7
00000	00001	00002	00003

After 123, 456, 789 attempts, an affirmative answer to test (1) is obtained for

01234
× 7
56789

which then fails to satisfy test (2).

Using this procedure, the computer applies test (1) and, if the result is positive, test (2) to 10 billion combinations of digits for the variables F, R, Ø, W, N, S, M, I, L, E in its search for all solutions. On a moderately fast time-sharing system, such a program would run for several months.

efficiency

Most of the other problems presented in this book involve so little computation that it hardly matters what programming solution is applied. However, this particular problem requires a much more efficient approach than the one just described.

Suppose that instead of assigning all possible values to each of the variables F, R, Ø, W, N, S, M, I, L, E, the program allows only the variables F, R, Ø, W, N, to range from 0 to 9. The program may then determine the number

$$X = (10000 * F) + (1000 * R) + (100 * Ø) + (10 * W) + N$$

and the number

$$Y = 7 * X$$

It is now possible to produce values of the variables S, M, I, L, E such that test (2) holds automatically by simply allowing them to be the digits of the number Y. The first few trials of this new approach are

00000	00001	00002	00003
× 7	× 7	× 7	× 7
00000	00007	00014	00021

After 1234 attempts in which the variables F, R, Ø, W, N alone fail test (1), the program obtains the trials

01234	01235	01236	01237
× 7	× 7	× 7	× 7
08638	08645	08652	08659

This second procedure requires fewer trials than the first by a factor of 100000. A fast time-sharing system would produce all solutions in a few minutes. A slow time-sharing system might need about an hour.

further efficiency

The values of the variables F, R, Ø, W, N, S, M, I, L, E are produced consecutively in a computer program that solves the puzzle. Once two of them are equal, the answer to test (1) cannot be affirmative, so it is useless to produce values for the remaining variables. Incorporating this principle into a program yields further efficiency. Instead of beginning at FRØWN = 00000, the program considers only combinations of values for the variables F, R, Ø, W, N that are mutually different. Once one of the ten possible values is chosen for F, there remain only nine values for R, then eight for Ø, seven for W, and six for N. The 100000 combinations attempted in the second procedure have been whittled down to 30240 ($10 \times 9 \times 8 \times 7 \times 6$). Under this new method, the first ten values of FRØWN are

01234	01235	01236	01237	01238
01239	01243	01245	01246	01247

Additional savings are obtained from the observation that if the value of FRØWN exceeds 14285, then the value of SMILE exceeds 100000. That is, its decimal numeral contains more than five digits, which is not permitted. Terminating the program at that point, instead of haplessly continuing with additional values of FRØWN, yields further time savings. Even a slow time-sharing system could print out all solutions to the puzzle within a few minutes.

The flowchart in Figures 1 and 2 depicts the method of solution just described. The program FROWN solves the puzzle according to that flowchart.

The subscripted variable B is employed to make the tests for distinct digits as easy as possible. Whenever one of the digits 0, 1, . . . , 9 is assigned, the value of an element of B is switched from 0 to 1. The element B[1] refers to the digit 0, B[2] refers to

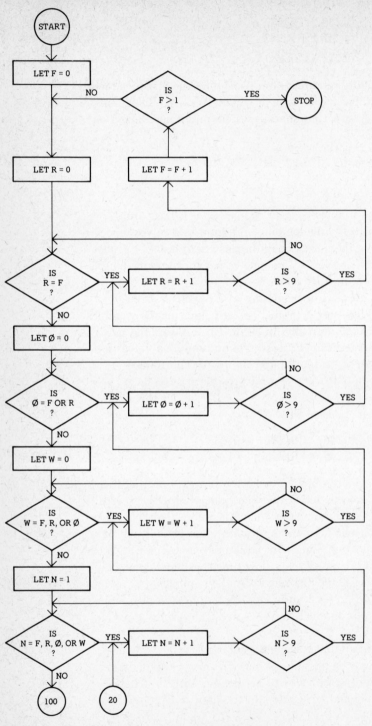

Figure 1   Flowchart of the program FROWN, part 1.

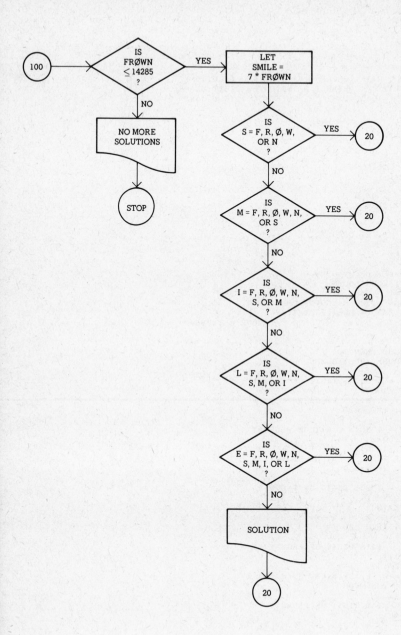

Figure 2   Flowchart of the program FROWN, part 2.

the digit 1, B[3] refers to the digit 2, and so on. It is too bad that most versions of BASIC do not permit the subscript 0 so that the correspondence would be more direct.

```
LIST
FROWN

100   REM ***  FROWN*7 = SMILE  *** FIND ALL SOLUTIONS
105   REM   SUBSCRIPTED VARIABLE B INDICATES DIGIT USAGE
107   REM   B[J+1] = 0 IF DIGIT J UNUSED, = 1 IF J USED
110   DIM B[10]
120   MAT B=ZER
200   FOR F=0 TO 1
210   LET B[F+1]=1
220   FOR R=0 TO 9
225   REM   IS R = F ?
230   IF B[R+1]=1 THEN 720
240   LET B[R+1]=1
250   FOR O=0 TO 9
255   REM   IS O = F OR R ?
260   IF B[O+1]=1 THEN 700
270   LET B[O+1]=1
280   FOR W=0 TO 9
285   REM   IS W = F, R, OR O ?
290   IF B[W+1]=1 THEN 680
300   LET B[W+1]=1
310   FOR N=1 TO 9
315   REM   IS N = F, R, O, OR W ?
320   IF B[N+1]=1 THEN 660
330   LET B[N+1]=1
340   LET X=10000*F+1000*R+100*O+10*W+1*N
345   REM   SMILE HAS AT MOST 5 DIGITS
347   REM   14285*7 = 99995 < 100000 < 100002 = 14286*7
350   LET Y=X*7
360   LET Z=Y
370   IF X <= 14285 THEN 400
380   PRINT "NO MORE SOLUTIONS"
390   STOP
395   REM   LET S = 10000'S DIGIT OF FROWN*7
400   LET S=INT(Z/10000)
405   REM   IS S = F, R, O, W, OR N ?
410   IF B[S+1]=1 THEN 650
420   LET B[S+1]=1
425   REM   LET M = 1000'S DIGIT OF FROWN*7
430   LET Z=Z-10000*S
440   LET M=INT(Z/1000)
445   REM   IS M = F, R, O, W, N, OR S ?
450   IF B[M+1]=1 THEN 640
460   LET B[M+1]=1
465   REM   LET I = 100'S DIGIT OF FROWN*7
470   LET Z=Z-1000*M
480   LET I=INT(Z/100)
485   REM   IS I = F, R, O, W, N, S, OR M ?
490   IF B[I+1]=1 THEN 630
500   LET B[I+1]=1
505   REM   LET L = 10'S DIGIT OF FROWN*7
510   LET Z=Z-100*I
520   LET L=INT(Z/10)
525   REM   IS L = F, R, O, W, N, S, M, OR I ?
530   IF B[L+1]=1 THEN 620
540   LET B[L+1]=1
545   REM   LET E = 1'S DIGIT OF FROWN*7
550   LET E=Z-10*L
555   REM   IS E = F, R, O, W, N, S, M, I, OR L ?
560   IF B[E+1]=1 THEN 610
565   PRINT
570   PRINT "FROWN = ";X
580   PRINT "SMILE = ";Y
```

```
590   REM CONTINUE FINDING SOLUTIONS
600   REM  RESET USAGE VARIABLE B
610   LET B[L+1]=0
620   LET B[I+1]=0
630   LET B[M+1]=0
640   LET B[S+1]=0
650   LET B[N+1]=0
660   NEXT N
670   LET B[W+1]=0
680   NEXT W
690   LET B[O+1]=0
700   NEXT O
710   LET B[R+1]=0
720   NEXT R
730   LET B[F+1]=0
740   NEXT F
999   END
```

The following instructions are included when FROWN is run in order to trace the progress of the variables F and R.

```
204   PRINT
205   PRINT F
235   PRINT R;
```

```
RUN
FROWN


0
1       2
FROWN =   2394
SMILE =   16758

FROWN =   2637
SMILE =   18459
3       4
FROWN =   4527
SMILE =   31689
5
FROWN =   5274
SMILE =   36918.

FROWN =   5418
SMILE =   37926.

FROWN =   5976
SMILE =   41832.
6       7
FROWN =   7614
SMILE =   53298.
8       9
1
0    2     3     4
FROWN =   14076
SMILE =   98532.
NO MORE SOLUTIONS

DONE
```

The language BASIC suppresses leading zeroes when it prints numerals, so the value of F is 0 in all but the last solution.

problems

1 Assign the ten decimal digits to the letters "F", "Ø", "R", "T", "Y", "E", "N", "S", "I", and "X" so that the sum below holds.

FØRTY
  TEN
+TEN
――――
SIXTY

2 Determine whether the equation

FØUR * FØUR = SIXTEEN

has a solution.

3 Find a solution to the following simultaneous equations. (The letters "A", "B", "C", "D", "E", "F", "G", and "H" represent distinct digits.)

ABCDEF * C = CDEFAB
ABCDEF * G = BCDEFA
ABCDEF * B = EFABCD
ABCDEF * E = FABCDE
ABCDEF * H = DEFABC
ABCDEF * A = ABCDEF

4 Find mutually distinct positive integers A, B, C, and D, each less than 15, such that

$$A^3 + B^3 = C^3 + D^3$$

5 A positive integer is called irreducible if it is either the number 1 or a prime number. A famous unsolved problem is to prove or disprove the conjecture of Goldbach that every positive even integer is the sum of two irreducible odd numbers. Write a program that verifies the Goldbach conjecture for even numbers less than 1000.

6 A triangle is a right triangle if and only if the square of the length of the longest side is equal to the sum of the squares of the lengths of the other two sides. Write a program that picks from ten positive numbers supplied as input all the different subsets of three numbers that could be the lengths of the sides of a right triangle.

7 In line 370 of the program FROWN, why would it be sufficient to compare X to 14098?

2 | the colored cubes puzzle

A well-known puzzle, illustrated in Figure 3, consists of four cubes.
Each of the six sides of each cube is colored one of four colors: blue,
green, red, or white. The problem is to arrange the four blocks in a
row so that no two faces in front, on top, in back, or on the bottom
are the same color.

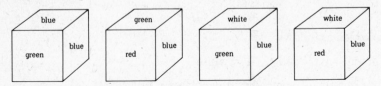

Figure 3   The colored cubes puzzle.

translating the setting

Perhaps the reader's initial reaction to the colored cubes puzzle is
that it is the most abstract example in this book. The combinatorial
geometry used in its solution is probably the most sophisticated
mathematics appearing here. Yet, in its relationship to the computer,
this problem is much closer to everyday life than most of the more
concrete examples. The big resemblance of the colored cubes puzzle
to problems like urban development or ecology is that it is not
immediately obvious how to write the program that provides the
solution. The computer is no better equipped to move the colored
cubes about in space than it is to build a hospital or to preserve a
species of wildlife. Nor is it well equipped to discuss these problems
in their native form. What is required is a translation of the problem
as it appears to human beings into an equivalent problem that has
meaning to a computer. Translating the setting is often the most
difficult part of the solution.

To solve the colored cubes puzzle, it will first be reformulated as
a problem about a 4 × 6 matrix. Each row of the matrix will
represent a single block. The components of the row will represent
sides of the block, and the values of the components will designate
colors. Certain rearrangements of the components correspond to
rotations of the cube.

starting position

The blocks are first placed in a row as shown in Figure 3. The order
and the position of individual blocks is entirely arbitrary. Table 1
extends the coloring of the sides shown in Figure 3.

table 1 *initial position of the blocks*

	left	right	front	back	top	bottom
block 1	white	blue	green	green	blue	red
block 2	white	blue	red	red	green	red
block 3	red	blue	green	white	white	red
block 4	white	blue	red	green	white	green

The colors are encoded as follows.

$1 = \text{blue}$ $2 = \text{green}$ $3 = \text{red}$ $4 = \text{white}$

Table 2 is the matrix obtained by encoding the colors in Table 1. The computer will obtain a solution, if one exists, by working with Table 2.

table 2 *matrix representing table 1*

$$
\begin{bmatrix}
4 & 1 & 2 & 2 & 1 & 3 \\
4 & 1 & 3 & 3 & 2 & 3 \\
3 & 1 & 2 & 4 & 4 & 3 \\
4 & 1 & 3 & 2 & 4 & 2
\end{bmatrix}
$$

positions of a cube

A cube has six faces. Since each cube in this puzzle is colored with only four colors, on any one cube there is at least one pair of faces that has the same color. The mistake of referring, for example, to "the green side of the fourth cube", should be avoided. If a particular face is placed on the left side of a block, the opposite face automatically goes to the right, and any of the remaining four faces may be at the top. Designating a left face and a top face automatically fix all of the other faces. Thus, each cube has 24 (six times four) possible positions.

arrangements of a row

In general, if six items are to be placed in a row, then there are six ways to choose a first item. Five remain to choose a second item, four for the third, and so on. It follows that if the six items are distinct, then there are 720 ($6 \times 5 \times 4 \times 3 \times 2 \times 1$) ways to place them in a row. If some pair of items is indistinguishable, this total is reduced.

Since a row of six items has more possible arrangements than a cube has possible positions, it is clear that not every rearrangement of the numbers in a row of Table 2 can correspond to a position of the corresponding cube. This is theoretically demonstrated by observing that the interchange of the first and second components of a row of Table 2 corresponds to a rotation of the cube that exchanges the left and right faces without moving any of the other faces. Naturally, such a rotation is impossible.

What is needed is a careful analysis of which 24 rearrangements of a row correspond to actual rotations of a cube.

quarter-turn on the left–right axis

It is possible to rotate a cube, without changing the left and right faces, so that

1 the bottom face moves to the front
2 the back face moves to the bottom
3 the top face moves to the back
4 the front face moves to the top

This is called a *quarter-turn on the left–right axis* (see Figure 4). According to the key at the top of Table 1, this corresponds to the following row rearrangement.

1 component 3 is replaced by component 6
2 component 6 is replaced by component 4
3 component 4 is replaced by component 5
4 component 5 is replaced by (original) component 3

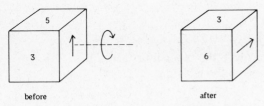

Figure 4   Quarter-turn on the left–right axis.

Successive quarter-turns on the left–right axis move a cube through each of its four possible positions for a fixed left face. What is still needed is a method to place each of the faces at the left.

interchanging left and right faces

If the original right face can be moved to the left, then successive quarter-turns on the left–right axis can achieve four additional positions for the block, bringing the total to eight. The geometry of the cube requires that if the right face replaces the left, then the left face replaces the right. This interchange is obtained here by using the top and bottom faces on an axis and giving the block a half-turn. This method evidently interchanges the front and back faces also, so that

1 the right face moves to the left side
2 the left face moves to the right side
3 the back face moves to the front side
4 the front face moves to the back side

This procedure is called a *reversal* of the left–right axis.

This reversal of the left–right axis (see Figure 5) is equivalent to the following row rearrangement.

1 component 1 is replaced by component 2
2 component 2 is replaced by (former) component 1
3 component 3 is replaced by component 4
4 component 4 is replaced by (former) component 3

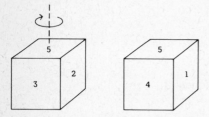

Figure 5   Reversal of the left–right axis.

What is still needed is some way to place the other four faces (besides the original left and right faces) to the left side.

moving the original front face to the left side

The original front face of the cube can be moved to the left side by restoring the original position and then giving the block a quarter-turn on its top–bottom axis, so that

1   the original front face moves to the left
2   the original right face moves to the front
3   the original back face moves to the right
4   the original left face moves to the back

In the corresponding rearrangement of row elements,

1   component 1 is replaced by component 3
2   component 3 is replaced by component 2
3   component 2 is replaced by component 4
4   component 4 is replaced by component 1

Interchanging the left and right faces now brings the original back face to the left side. It follows that quarter-turns on the left axis, plus reversal of left–right axis, plus quarter-turns on the top–bottom axis are sufficient techniques to obtain 16 of the possible 24 positions of a cube.

moving the original top face to the left side

If the cube is restored to its original position, then the original top face may be moved to the left side by executing a quarter-turn on the front–back axis. Thus,

1   the top face moves to the left
2   the right face moves to the top
3   the bottom face moves to the right
4   the left face moves to the bottom

Equivalently, for row rearrangements,

1   component 1 is replaced by component 5
2   component 5 is replaced by component 2
3   component 2 is replaced by component 6
4   component 6 is replaced by component 1

The remaining positions of the cube can now be obtained by applying quarter-turns on the left–right axis and reversal of the left–right axis.

summary: obtaining all positions of a cube

In the program **CUBES**, which solves the colored cubes puzzle, the faces of a cube will be placed at the left in the following order.

1   original left face
2   original right face
3   original front face
4   original back face
5   original top face
6   original bottom face

For each possible left side, the cube will be rotated through four quarter-turns on the left–right axis.

efficiency achieved through geometry

Since there is no advantage in interchanging any two blocks (or, equivalently, interchanging two rows of the matrix representing the blocks), and since each block may assume 24 positions (obtained by rotations), there appear to be 331776 (i.e., 24^4) possible arrangements of the blocks to test in the search for a solution. It is possible, however, to obtain an eightfold reduction by restricting the motions of the first cube.

The idea is that the first cube need never be rotated through quarter-turns and no reversal of the left–right axis is necessary. The effect of rotating the first cube a quarter-turn on its left–right axis can be achieved, instead, by rotating each of the other three cubes three quarter-turns on their left–right axes. The effect of an axis reversal on the first cube is obtained, instead, by giving each of the other three cubes an axis reversal. Thus, certain rearrangements of the first row are unnecessary.

efficiency achieved through programming

The eightfold reduction by geometry brings the original 331776 combinations down to 41472. Clever programming eliminates the need to consider many of these. The program CUBES nests four FOR–NEXT loops so that the fourth block moves most rapidly and the first block least often. The naïve procedure would be to actually move the fourth block through all of its 24 positions, testing the entire set of four blocks for a solution to the puzzle each time. There is no benefit, however, in moving the fourth block if the first three do not form a "partial solution", that is, if two of the first three blocks have faces in the same direction (not including right and left) that are the same color. The program CUBES avoids a lot of unnecessary motion by using the method of partial solutions.

the solution

The flowchart in Figures 6 and 7 geometrically describes the
solution to the colored cubes puzzle. In fact, the computer is not
really moving blocks but rearranging rows of a matrix. Its goal is to
apply geometrically valid permutations of rows until columns 3
to 6 of the matrix each contain four different numbers, which
corresponds to having four different colors on the sides of the cubes
in each of the four directions: front, back, up, and down.

The DATA statements in lines 140 to 170 code the initial position
of the blocks as given in Tables 1 and 2. Most of the logical details
appear in the nesting of the FOR–NEXT loops based on the
variables K1, K2, K3, and K4.

The program CUBES first tests at lines 224 to 227 to see if the
first two blocks form a partial solution. If not, block 2 is rotated.
Lines 233 to 238 look for a partial solution in blocks 1, 2, and 3.
Lines 260 to 325 test for a complete solution.

Each of the indices K2, K3, and K4 varies from 1 to 24 as the
block it corresponds to moves through all 24 possible positions. The
face that is originally on the left remains there as the block is given
four quarter-turns and the index varies from 1 to 4. Then the
original right face is put at the left for four quarter-turns, and so on,
following column order (as in Table 1) until the original bottom
face is at the left for four quarter-turns and the index reaches 24.
However, the time-saving device of searching for partial solutions
causes considerable skipping ahead within these rules.

When one of the indices K2, K3, or K4 is 4, 12, or 20, the new
left face is obtained by reversing the left–right axis by using lines
2100 to 2170. When one of these indices is 8 or 16, the appropriate
new left face is obtained either by lines 2200 to 2270 or by lines
2300 to 2360.

The index K1 varies from 1 to 3. Line 720 prepares the variable J
so that the subroutine beginning at line 2000 will put the correct
face of the first block at the left.

Lines 211, 212, and 221 are included to trace the progress of the
variables K1 and K2.

looking for errors

The coding of the program CUBES as given here contains no errors,
but if it did, finding them might be somewhat difficult because the
program is long and logically complicated. The way to start

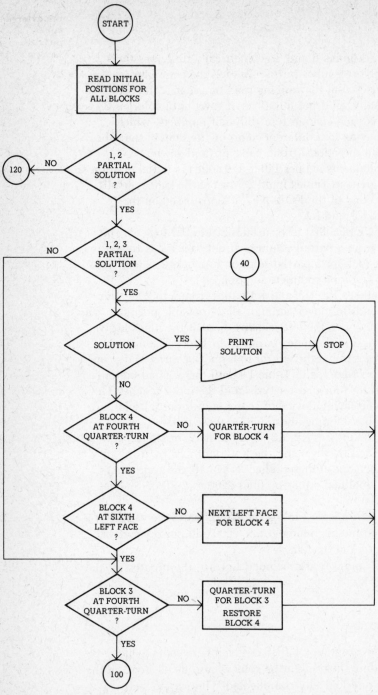

Figure 6   Flowchart of the program CUBES, *part 1.*

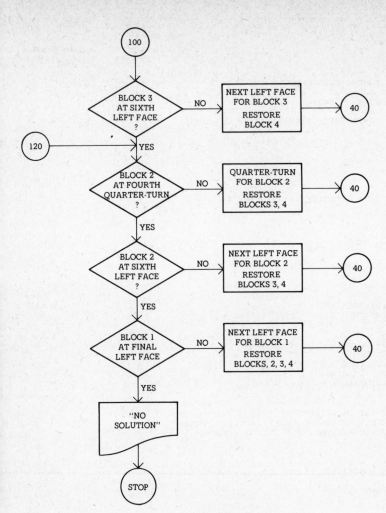

Figure 7   Flowchart of the program CUBES, part 2.

debugging is to replace lines 140 to 170 by data for a hypothetical
set of cubes in such an initial position that to obtain a solution,
only the fourth block must be moved.

```
140    DATA  1,1,1,2,3,4
150    DATA  2,2,2,3,4,1
160    DATA  3,3,3,4,1,2
170    DATA  4,4,1,4,3,2
```

These data are sufficient to check a large portion of the coding,
including the subroutine beginning at line 1000. Inserting additional
tracing instructions at strategic points will help the programmer to

```
70    REM *** SOLVE COLORED CUBES PUZZLE
80    REM FNA(X)=4 IF AND ONLY IF 4 DIVIDES X
90    DEF FNA(X)=X-INT((X-.1)/4)*4
100   DIM A[4,6],S[4,6]
110   REM  MATRIX S CONTAINS INITIAL POSITION OF CUBES
120   MAT   READ S
140   DATA 4,1,2,2,1,3
150   DATA 4,1,3,3,2,3
160   DATA 3,1,2,4,4,3
170   DATA 4,1,3,2,4,2
180   RESTORE
190   MAT   READ A
200   REM ** MAINLINE ** MAINLINE ** MAINLINE **
210   FOR K1=1 TO 3
211   PRINT
212   PRINT K1
220   FOR K2=1 TO 24
221   PRINT K2;
224   FOR J=3 TO 6
225   IF A[1,J]=A[2,J] THEN 600
227   NEXT J
230   FOR K3=1 TO 24
233   FOR J=3 TO 6
235   IF A[1,J]=A[3,J] THEN 500
237   IF A[2,J]=A[3,J] THEN 500
238   NEXT J
240   FOR K4=1 TO 24
250   REM ** TEST FOR SOLUTION
260   FOR J=3 TO 6
290   IF A[1,J]=A[4,J] THEN 400
310   IF A[2,J]=A[4,J] THEN 400
320   IF A[3,J]=A[4,J] THEN 400
325   NEXT J
330   PRINT
340   PRINT "THIS IS THE SOLUTION"
350   PRINT "SIDE ORDER:LEFT,RIGHT,FRONT,BACK,TOP,BOTTOM"
360   PRINT "1 = BLUE, 2 = GREEN, 3 = RED, 4 = WHITE"
370   PRINT
380   MAT   PRINT A;
390   STOP
400   REM **** BLOCK 4 MOTIONS
410   LET I=4
420   IF FNA(K4)=4 THEN 450
430   GOSUB 1000
440   GOTO 470
450   LET J=K4
460   GOSUB 2000
470   NEXT K4
500   REM *** BLOCK 3 MOTIONS
510   LET I=3
520   IF FNA(K3)=4 THEN 550
530   GOSUB 1000
540   GOTO 570
550   LET J=K3
560   GOSUB 2000
570   NEXT K3
600   REM ** BLOCK 2 MOTIONS
610   LET I=2
620   IF FNA(K2)=4 THEN 650
630   GOSUB 1000
640   GOTO 670
650   LET J=K2
660   GOSUB 2000
670   NEXT K2
700   REM * BLOCK 1 MOTIONS
710   LET I=1
720   LET J=8*K1
730   GOSUB 2000
```

```
 740   NEXT K1
 760   PRINT "NO SOLUTION"
 770   STOP
1000   REM ** SUBR ** QUARTER-TURN BLOCK I ON LEFT-RIGHT AXIS
1010   LET Q=A[I,3]
1020   LET A[I,3]=A[I,6]
1030   LET A[I,6]=A[I,4]
1040   LET A[I,4]=A[I,5]
1050   LET A[I,5]=Q
1060   RETURN
2000   REM ** SUBR ** CHANGE AXIS FOR BLOCK I
2010   IF J<24 THEN 2080
2020   REM1 IF J=24 RESTORE BLOCK I TO ORIGINAL POSITION
2030   FOR N=1 TO 6
2040   LET A[I,N]=S[I,N]
2050   NEXT N
2060   GOTO 2399
2080   IF INT(J/8)*8=J THEN 2200
2100   REM2 IF J=4, 12, OR 20 THEN REVERSE LEFT-RIGHT AXIS
2110   REM HALF-TURN ON TOP-BOTTOM AXIS
2120   LET Q=A[I,1]
2130   LET A[I,1]=A[I,2]
2140   LET A[I,2]=Q
2150   LET Q=A[I,3]
2160   LET A[I,3]=A[I,4]
2170   LET A[I,4]=Q
2180   GOTO 2399
2200   REM3 IF J=8 THEN ORIGINAL FRONT BECOMES LEFT PIVOT POINT
2210   IF J <> 8 THEN 2300
2220   LET A[I,1]=S[I,3]
2230   LET A[I,2]=S[I,4]
2240   LET A[I,3]=S[I,2]
2250   LET A[I,4]=S[I,1]
2260   LET A[I,5]=S[I,5]
2270   LET A[I,6]=S[I,6]
2280   GOTO 2399
2300   REM4 IF J=16 THEN ORIGINAL TOP BECOMES LEFT PIVOT POINT
2310   LET A[I,1]=S[I,5]
2320   LET A[I,2]=S[I,6]
2330   LET A[I,3]=S[I,3]
2340   LET A[I,4]=S[I,4]
2350   LET A[I,5]=S[I,2]
2360   LET A[I,6]=S[I,1]
2399   RETURN
9999   END


RUN
CUBES


 1
 1     2     3     4     5     6     7     8     9    10    11    12
13    14    15    16    17    18    19    20    21    22    23    24
 2
 1     2     3     4     5     6     7     8     9    10    11    12
THIS IS THE SOLUTION
SIDE ORDER:LEFT,RIGHT,FRONT,BACK,TOP,BOTTOM
1 = BLUE, 2 = GREEN, 3 = RED, 4 = WHITE

 2     2     1     4     1     3

 3     3     2     3     4     1

 4     3     3     1     2     4

 1     4     4     2     3     2


DONE
```

eliminate any errors which are discovered. But the test data do not cause the program to invoke the big subroutine beginning at line 2000, because a solution can be obtained by two quarter-turns of the fourth block. To test the big subroutine, replace test line 170 by

```
170   DATA 3,2,1,4,4,4
```

elegance achieved through geometry

A reader equipped either with a cube or with good visualization powers will discover that from any starting position of a cube, any other possible position may be obtained by a succession of quarter-turns on the left–right axis and quarter-turns on the top–bottom axis. A slightly shorter and somewhat more elegant program than CUBES is obtained by correct usage of two quarter-turns subroutines, one for left–right axis and one for top–bottom axis. This is left as an exercise.

problems

1   Write a program that arranges the integers from 1 to 16 in a magic square, that is, a 4×4 array so that in each row and column and on both diagonals, the sum of the four numbers is 34.

2   Write a program that arranges the 4 aces and 12 face cards of a deck in a Greco-Latin square, that is, a 4×4 array so that no two cards of the same rank or suit are in the same row, column, or diagonal.

3   A coconut lover finds himself on the first of a cluster of six romantic tropical islands named $I_1, I_2, \ldots, I_6$. Some islands have bridges to other islands, but no two islands have more than one bridge between them. Each island has a supply of coconuts. The coconut lover wants to find a path from island I_1 to island I_6 that allows him to collect the maximum amount of coconuts subject to the condition that it may never cross a single bridge more than once. Assume that the coconut lover is supplied with a matrix B such that $B[P, Q] = 1$ if there is a bridge from island I_P to island I_Q but $B[P, Q] = 0$ otherwise. Also assume that he is supplied with a list of numbers $C[1], C[2], \ldots, C[6]$ such that $C[J]$ is the number of coconuts on the island I_J. Write a program that solves the coconut lover's problem.

4   A salesman must stop in six different cities $C_1, \ldots, C_6$. The distance $D[I, J]$ between each pair of cities C_I and C_J is given as an entry of a 6×6 matrix. The salesman wants to know a route from C_1 to C_6 that stops in all four other cities and requires the least total distance among all such routes. Write a program that solves his problem.

5 A maze can be described as a collection of locations and a collection of passageways between some of them. It can be represented in a computer as a matrix P such that $P[I, J] = 1$ if there is a passageway between locations I and J and $P[I, J] = 0$ otherwise. Write a program that finds a path between the start (location 1) and finish (location 8) of an 8-location maze. That is, write a list of locations starting at 1 and ending at 8 such that any two consecutive locations in the list have a passageway between them.

6 Write a program that solves the colored cubes problem by an "elegant" use of two subroutines that perform different quarter-turns, as discussed in the main body of the section.

suggested readings

Busacker, Robert G., and T. L. Saaty. *Finite Graphs and Networks.* McGraw-Hill, New York, 1965.

Carteblanche, F. de. "Pile of Cubes", *Eureka* (Apr., 1947).

artificial intelligence

COMPUTERS CAN perform a variety of tasks with great speed and
high reliability, but there are many tasks that can be performed
faster and more accurately by people. As an illustration, a human
being can quickly pick out the face of a friend or relative in a
crowd of hundreds of people. Each person can also recognize quite
a number of people by their voice. A dog can do the same thing by
using his nose! A master chess player can often tell from a brief
glance at the chessboard which player will win even though the
game will not end until after many more moves are made. A written
or spoken sentence might be immediately understood even if it
contains many grammatical errors. However, each of these tasks is
difficult for a computer.

The theory of artificial intelligence is derived from the attempts
that have been made to program a machine to perform tasks
which seem to be easier for humans than machines. An important
aspect of many studies in artificial intelligence is the attempt to
learn something about how humans perform these seemingly
complex tasks by carefully analyzing the ways which a machine can
be programmed to perform them.

This chapter briefly discusses a few of the interesting areas of
artificial intelligence and shows in some detail how to program a
machine to learn, a capability that might at first seem to be
restricted to biological organisms. The last section illustrates the
possibility of using a computer to create artistic works.

211

**some
aspects of
artificial
intelligence**
section 1

1 | *some aspects of artificial intelligence*

This section discusses some aspects of artificial intelligence which have interested computer scientists.

pattern matching

Pattern matching is the process by which faces of acquaintances, winning chessboard situations, Picasso paintings, and Mozart symphonies are recognized. Some of the results of research in this area have led to the automation of bank-check processing using machine-readable characters on the check, direct input to a computer by optically reading a typewritten page of text, and the computer analysis of an electrocardiogram.

A typical project in this area involves writing a computer program which will recognize handwritten characters. One approach to this problem is to divide an area in which the character is to be written into a number of smaller regions using a grid of horizontal and vertical lines as shown in Figure 1. All regions crossed by the written character are given the value 1 and all other regions are given the value 0. This information can be stored in a computer as an array of 1's and 0's as shown in Figure 2. The program must then

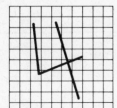 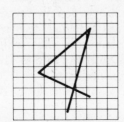

Figure 1   The handwritten versions of the character "4".

```
0 0 0 0 0 0 0 0 0 0          0 0 0 0 0 0 0 0 0 0
0 0 1 0 1 0 0 0 0 0          0 0 0 0 0 0 1 1 0 0
0 0 1 0 1 0 0 0 0 0          0 0 0 0 0 1 1 1 0 0
0 0 1 0 1 1 0 0 0 0          0 0 0 0 1 1 1 0 0 0
0 0 1 0 0 1 1 0 0 0          0 0 0 1 1 0 1 0 0 0
0 0 1 1 1 1 1 0 0 0          0 0 1 1 0 0 1 0 0 0
0 0 1 1 0 1 1 0 0 0          0 0 0 1 1 1 1 0 0 0
0 0 0 0 0 0 1 0 0 0          0 0 0 0 0 1 1 1 0 0
0 0 0 0 0 0 1 0 0 0          0 0 0 0 0 1 0 0 0 0
0 0 0 0 0 0 0 0 0 0          0 0 0 0 0 1 0 0 0 0
```

Figure 2   Arrays of 0's and 1's representing handwritten characters.

decide which character was written by examining the pattern of
1's and 0's in the array. The problem is difficult because of the many
different ways people write the same character.

natural language

A trait which seems to indicate the intelligence of a human is his
ability to communicate in a natural language; therefore, attempts to
program computers to converse in a natural language are considered
a part of the field of artificial intelligence. D. G. Bobrow has written
a program which accepts high school algebra problems in "story"
form ("If John is twice as old as Mary and . . .") and gives the
solution. Another program which will answer all sorts of questions
about the game of baseball has been written by J. R. Slagle. In
these attempts, the programmer's interest is shared by researchers
in linguistics.

An indication of the importance of the ability to converse fluently
is the test proposed by the British mathematician Alan Turing to
determine if a machine is really intelligent. Two teletypewriters are
placed in a room, one connected to a remote teletypewriter operated
by a human, the other connected to a computer. A person in the
room with the two teletypewriters tries to determine which one is
connected to the computer by typing questions on either of the
teletypewriters. The computer may be programmed to purposely
deceive the testor by claiming it cannot do complicated arithmetic
problems, getting wrong answers, and occasionally misspelling
words. The machine passes Turing's test if a smart testor is unable
to determine to which teletypewriter it is connected with greater
certainty than by pure guessing. It is probably safe to say that no
machine has been programmed with the ability to pass Turing's test,
but there is also no reason to believe that it could not be done.

robots

It is possible to build machines that perform quite complicated
mechanical tasks provided they are to perform exactly the same
tasks (or one of some specified group of tasks) each time. It is
extremely difficult to build a machine that will carry out a simple
command, such as "Pick up all of the toys on the floor and put them
in a box". It is difficult because the machine must locate all objects
on the floor and recognize which are toys. Picking them up is not
even easy because there may be several sizes and shapes of toys,
each requiring a different grasp to carry the object without
dropping or crushing it.

Artificial intelligence research groups are working on the problem of programming machines to perform tasks that require a combination of intelligence and manual dexterity.

game playing

Attempts to write programs to play games provide the opportunity to study some of the aspects of artificial intelligence. The rules of most games are simple enough to enable a programmer to easily write a program to play a correct game. The goals of a game are simply defined, so that the success of a program can be easily measured. It might also seem to be an easy task to program a computer to play a perfect game of chess (for example) by allowing the computer to examine all possible moves and select one which is certain to lead to a win or draw. In principle, this can be done, but there are so many different moves in the game of chess that the fastest and largest computers are not capable of making an exhaustive analysis of the game in a reasonable amount of time. Thus, it is an interesting project to try to program a computer to play chess as well as the best human players.

One of the classic studies in artificial intelligence is a program written by Arthur L. Samuel which learned to play checkers. Samuel was able to defeat his program at first, but as the program acquired experience it was able to consistently beat its creator and go on to defeat some of the best checker players. Some techniques for programming a machine to learn are discussed in the next section.

2 | a program that plays NIM

This section discusses a program that will play the game of NIM with a human opponent.

the game of NIM

The game of NIM played by two contestants begins by placing some objects such as coins, beads, or matches in rows. Each player takes a turn by removing some or all of the objects from any single row. The player who removes the last object wins the game. All games discussed will start with three rows containing one, two, and three objects, as shown in Figure 3.

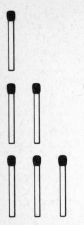

Figure 3   Starting position for NIM.

The first objective is to write a program that plays the game of NIM. The main objective is to construct a program that will learn to play NIM.

When writing a program to play NIM, or any other game, a consideration of primary importance is the method of representing the appropriate information about the status of the game and the rules of play. The methods used in the program described in this section represent a compromise between the two goals of efficiency and ease of understanding.

computer representation of the game

At any stage of the game, the number of objects in each of the rows is represented by a three-digit number called a *position*. Each digit of the position number represents the number of objects in one of the rows. If the rows contain one, two, and three objects, as they would at the beginning of the program, this situation would be represented as position number 123. The number 112 indicates that the first and second rows contain one object and the third row contains two objects. Position number 0 indicates that all rows are empty. There are many three-digit numbers, such as 108 and 972, which do not represent any legal position since no row ever contains more objects than it does at the beginning of the game.

In order to play the game properly, the program must be able to determine which moves are legal. One possibility would be to incorporate a subroutine which, given two position numbers, would decide whether it is possible to move from one to the other by removing some objects from one of the rows. Given a position, the program could then calculate all of the legal moves from that position. Another possibility is to store all possible legal moves as data within the program.

the table of legal moves

It is convenient to have a table of legal moves stored in the program. The program could construct the table itself, given the instructions to test for the legality of a move, but in the program NIM, the table is provided as data and the first instructions of the program read the values for the table of moves M from the data stack. An array P of 24 items is a list of all of the possible positions which may occur in the game. These position numbers appear as the first number of each of the DATA statements 901–924. The remaining six numbers represent the legal moves when the status of the game is given by the first number. The maximum number of legal moves from any one position is 6, which may be made on the first play of the game. The moves are to positions 122, 121, 120, 113, 103, and 23 (023). There are no moves possible when the rows are all empty. The number −1 is used to fill unused entries in the array. The part of the program NIM which sets arrays P and M consists of statements 110–180 and 900–924.

```
110    DIM P[24],M[24,6]
120    REM   SET LIST OF POSITIONS P AND LEGAL MOVES M
130    FOR I=1 TO 24
140    READ P[I]
150    FOR J=1 TO 6
160    READ M[I,J]
170    NEXT J
180    NEXT I

900    REM   LIST OF POSITIONS AND MOVES
901    DATA 0,-1,-1,-1,-1,-1,-1
902    DATA 1,0,-1,-1,-1,-1,-1
903    DATA 2,1,0,-1,-1,-1,-1
904    DATA 3,2,1,0,-1,-1,-1
905    DATA 10,0,-1,-1,-1,-1,-1
906    DATA 11,10,1,-1,-1,-1,-1
907    DATA 12,11,10,2,-1,-1,-1
908    DATA 13,12,11,10,3,-1,-1
909    DATA 20,10,0,-1,-1,-1,-1
910    DATA 21,20,11,1,-1,-1,-1
911    DATA 22,21,20,12,2,-1,-1
912    DATA 23,22,21,20,13,3,-1
913    DATA 100,0,-1,-1,-1,-1,-1
914    DATA 101,100,1,-1,-1,-1,-1
915    DATA 102,101,100,2,-1,-1,-1
916    DATA 103,102,101,100,3,-1,-1
917    DATA 110,100,10,-1,-1,-1,-1
918    DATA 111,110,101,11,-1,-1,-1
919    DATA 112,111,110,102,12,-1,-1
920    DATA 113,112,111,110,103,13,-1
921    DATA 120,110,100,20,-1,-1,-1
922    DATA 121,120,111,101,21,-1,-1
923    DATA 122,121,120,112,102,22,-1
924    DATA 123,122,121,120,113,103,23
999    END
```

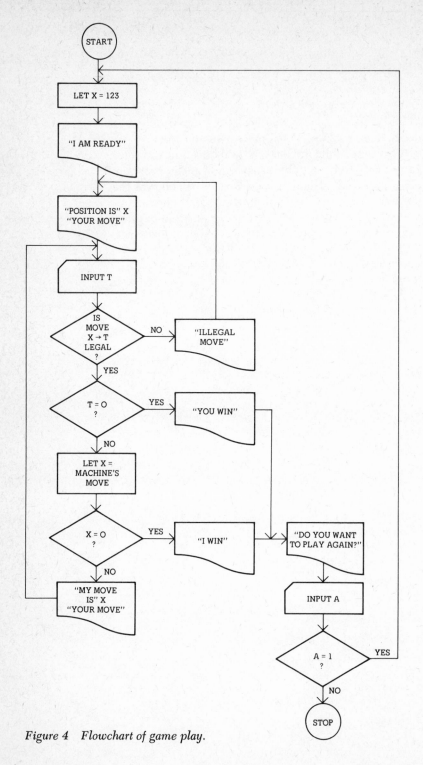

Figure 4   Flowchart of game play.

It might be convenient to have the table of moves M contain 123 rows, so that the moves, given that the rows contain one, one, and three items, for example, would be found in row 113 of M. This would waste quite a lot of space and for a slightly more complicated game, there might not be sufficient computer memory to store such a table. The price paid for the savings in space is the necessity of determining the row containing the possible moves for a particular status of the three rows. This operation is needed in several places in the program and so a subroutine is used. In the subroutine consisting of lines 800–850, the table of possible positions P is searched for the entry X. When it is found, I8 is the number of the row in M which contains the legal moves from position X, since X = P[I8].

```
800   REM  CONVERT POSITION X TO PLACE I8 IN LIST P
810   FOR I8=1 TO 24
820   IF X=P[I8] THEN 850
830   NEXT I8
840   LET I8=-1
850   RETURN
```

playing NIM

From among all of the correct possible moves, the program must select and make a single move. Since the first objective is simply to write a program to play a correct game, a very simple strategy for selecting a move is used. The program always makes the move represented by the first entry in the row of legal moves and so does not play very well.

Statements 400–590 allow the program to play NIM against a human opponent at a teletypewriter. The program does check the legality of each of its opponent's moves and checks to see if the game is won by either player.

```
400   REM  PLAY NIM123
401   PRINT
410   LET X=123
411   LET I6=0
420   PRINT "I AM READY"
430   PRINT "POSITION IS";X;"YOUR MOVE"
440   GOSUB 800
450   INPUT T
460   FOR J=1 TO 6
464   IF M[I8,J]=T THEN 480
468   NEXT J
470   PRINT "ILLEGAL MOVE"
475   GOTO 430
480   IF T=0 THEN 530
490   LET X=T
495   GOSUB 800
```

```
500   REM  DETERMINE NEXT MOVE
505   LET X=M[I8,1]
510   IF X=0 THEN 550
520   PRINT "MY MOVE IS";X;"YOUR MOVE"
525   GOTO 440
530   PRINT "YOU WIN"
540   GOTO 560
550   PRINT "MY MOVE IS 0   I WIN"
560   PRINT "DO YOU WANT TO PLAY AGAIN (IF SO, TYPE 1)";
570   INPUT A
580   IF A=1 THEN 401
590   STOP


RUN
NIM


I AM READY
POSITION IS 123   YOUR MOVE
?122
MY MOVE IS 121   YOUR MOVE
?101
MY MOVE IS 100   YOUR MOVE
?0
YOU WIN
DO YOU WANT TO PLAY AGAIN (IF SO, TYPE 1)?0

DONE
```

The flowchart in Figure 4 indicates the play of the game. The program was easily defeated.

problems

1 Modify the program NIM so that it constructs its own table M of legal moves, instead of reading the table as data.

2 Modify the result of Problem 1 so that the program will accept any given starting position up to 345.

3 The game of hexapawn is described by Martin Gardner in his article "How to Build a Game-Learning Machine and Then Teach It to Play and Win" in the March, 1962, issue of *Scientific American*. It is played on a 3 × 3 board like that used for Tic-Tac-Toe. The play starts with three pawns for each player located as shown in Figure 5.

A player moves one of his pawns either straight ahead one place to an empty square or diagonally one place to a square occupied by an opponent's pawn, capturing that pawn (which is removed from the board). These moves are basic moves for the pawn in chess, hence the name hexapawn. The arrows in Figure 6 show the four possible moves for player X from one position and the resulting board positions.

The game is won by (1) moving into the third row, (2) capturing

X	X	X
O	O	O

Figure 5   Starting position for hexapawn.

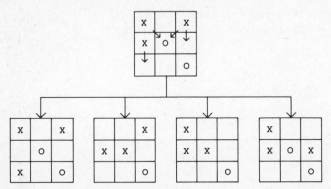

Figure 6   Some hexapawn moves.

all of the opponent's pawns, or (3) placing the opponent in a position from which there is no legal move. There can be no draw in the game.

Write a program that plays hexapawn. Let the human opponent play first.

4   The game tic-tac-toe is played on a board with nine squares. Two players alternate by placing their mark (usually "X" and "O") in an empty square. The game is won by a player who gets three of his marks in a straight line, in a row, a column, or either diagonal. A winning position for player X is illustrated in Figure 7.

X	O	X
O	X	
X		O

Figure 7   A winning tic-tac-toe position.

Write a program that will play tic-tac-toe. The number of different board positions can be considerably reduced by observing that because of symmetry, many different positions are equivalent. For example, the three positions shown in Figure 8 are equivalent.

X		O
O		
X		

O		
X	O	X

X	O	X
O		

Figure 8   Equivalent tic-tac-toe positions.

Tic-tac-toe is different from NIM and hexapawn in that a "tie"
or "draw" is possible, that is, the game may end without either
player winning.

3 | *a program that plays* NIM *perfectly*

The game of NIM is simple enough that it can be completely
analyzed to determine what move should be made in every possible
situation. In fact, the program can make the analysis of the game
itself using only the table of legal moves described in the previous
section. A similar analysis can be made of many games, provided
only that the computer time and memory are available.

the graph of NIM

In order to understand how to analyze the game of NIM, a
schematic diagram called a *graph* will be used. In the graph the
nodes represent the possible game positions and the lines connecting
the nodes (often called *edges*) represent the fact that a move from

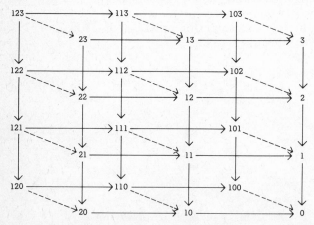

*Figure 9   Structure graph for NIM: To move, travel in any of the three
directions any desired distance.*

221

a program
that plays
NIM
perfectly
section 3

one position to the other is possible.

The graph in Figure 9 should be viewed as a three-dimensional object, typical of something which could be built with a child's toy construction set. A legal move consists of traveling in any one of the three possible directions (representing each of the three rows) any desired distance.

analyzing the game of NIM

The game may be analyzed by assigning a value of "+" or "−" to each possible position according to whether it is "good" or "bad" to move to that particular position. Position 0 is good because a move to position 0 will win the game, so a "+" is placed beside position 0. Any position from which a move to 0 is possible is a bad one because that move will win the game for the opponent. A "−" is placed beside all such positions, which are 1, 2, 3, 10, 20, and 100.

table 1   *table of correct moves
in* NIM 123

position	move
1	0
2	0
3	0
10	0
12	11
13	11
20	0
21	11
23	22
100	0
102	101
103	101
111	101 or 110 or 11
112	110
113	110
120	110
121	101
122	22

Any position from which the only moves are to positions labeled "−" is "good" because the opponent will be unable to make a good move from that position. A "+" should be placed beside all such positions. Then all positions leading to a "+" should be labeled with a "−", and the process is continued until all positions are labeled.

If this procedure is followed, the starting position 123 will receive the label "+". Since the program's opponent starts, he can never win if the machine plays correctly. Correct play for the machine

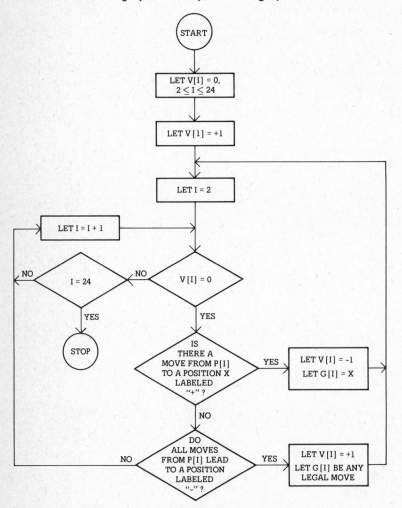

Figure 10   Flowchart for analyzing a game.

223

a program
that plays
NIM
perfectly
section 3

consists of always moving to a position labeled "+", which will always be possible, since the opponent must always move to a position marked "−". The correct moves for the machine are given in Table 1.

The program NIM can now easily be made to play a perfect game by simply rearranging the table of moves so that any correct move given in Table 1 is in the first column of the table M of legal moves.

a program that analyzes NIM

Since this chapter is about artificial intelligence, perhaps the program itself should analyze the game. Figure 10 exhibits a flowchart for the analysis. An array V of values (+1 or −1) is used to hold the labels "+" and "−". Each V is set to 0 at the beginning and the process terminates after all values of V are nonzero. The value V[1] is set to +1, since the first position in the list is 0.

The writing of the program itself is left as a problem.

problems

1 Write a program to analyze NIM 123.

2 Write a program to analyze NIM 555 (starting with five objects in each of three rows) and list all positions labeled "+". These are the positions to which a player should move, if possible.

3 Given a position of NIM, express each digit of the position as a two-digit binary number and write the three numbers in a column. To illustrate, suppose the position is 103, then write

$1 = 01$
$0 = 00$
$3 = 11$

Verify that for each position of NIM 123 labeled "+", namely, 0, 11, 101, 110, and 123, the number of 1's in each column is even and that these are the only positions with that property.

Write a program that will play NIM 123 perfectly using the above observation to determine its playing strategy.

4 Write a program to analyze hexapawn (see Problem 3 of Section 2). A tie is not possible in hexapawn.

5 Write a program that plays hexapawn perfectly.

6 Write a program to analyze tic-tac-toe (see Problem 4 of Section 2). Use 0 to label a position from which neither player can be assured of a win. All terminal positions resulting in a draw game must initially be given the label 0.

7 Write a program to play tic-tac-toe perfectly.

4 | *a program that learns to play* NIM

Games that are too complex to analyze may be played by programs which learn to play well. The program described in this section illustrates one technique for writing such a program. In this program, the value of each position is estimated by the program based on experience obtained from playing games. The value of each position is stored in the array V and each value is initially set to 0. The program keeps track of each move it makes as it plays a game. At the end of each game won by the program the value of each move the machine made is increased by 1. If the machine loses, it subtracts 1 from the value of each of the moves it made. The machine plays by selecting, from all legal moves, the one leading to the position of largest value.

To obtain a program that learns NIM, add to the original program that plays NIM the statements

```
210   DIM V[24],G[24]
215   MAT V=ZER
```

change line 505 to

```
505   GOSUB 600
```

and add a subroutine consisting of lines 600–690 which selects and records a move for the machine.

In the subroutine the variable I6 records the number of moves made and G is a listing of the moves made by the machine. The Ith row of moves represents the legal moves from X. The row is searched for the move with the greatest value. The new move is assigned to the variable X and the index of X in the list P is recorded in the list G.

The statements

```
535   GOSUB 700
555   GOSUB 710
```

together with the subroutine consisting of lines 700–790 are also needed. This subroutine modifies the values V for each move made by the program. If the machine wins, the variable Z has the value $+1$, otherwise it is -1. The value of Z is added to the values of each position played. The complete program is given below.

```
LIST
LEARN

110   DIM P[24],M[24,6]
120   REM   SET LIST OF POSITIONS P AND LEGAL MOVES M
130   FOR I=1 TO 24
140   READ P[I]
150   FOR J=1 TO 6
160   READ M[I,J]
170   NEXT J
180   NEXT I
210   DIM V[24],G[24]
215   MAT V=ZER
400   REM   PLAY NIM123
401   PRINT
410   LET X=123
411   LET I6=0
420   PRINT "I AM READY"
430   PRINT "POSITION IS";X;"YOUR MOVE"
440   GOSUB 800
450   INPUT T
460   FOR J=1 TO 6
464   IF M[I8,J]=T THEN 480
468   NEXT J
470   PRINT "ILLEGAL MOVE"
475   GOTO 430
480   IF T=0 THEN 530
490   LET X=T
495   GOSUB 800
500   REM   DETERMINE NEXT MOVE
505   GOSUB 600
510   IF X=0 THEN 550
520   PRINT "MY MOVE IS";X;"YOUR MOVE"
525   GOTO 440
530   PRINT "YOU WIN"
535   GOSUB 700
540   GOTO 560
550   PRINT "MY MOVE IS 0    I WIN"
555   GOSUB 710
560   PRINT "DO YOU WANT TO PLAY AGAIN (IF SO, TYPE 1)";
570   INPUT A
580   IF A=1 THEN 401
590   STOP
600   REM   SELECT AND RECORD MOVES
610   LET I=I8
615   LET W=-1.E+09
620   REM   FIND LEGAL MOVE WITH LARGEST VALUE
621   FOR J=1 TO 6
630   LET X=M[I,J]
635   IF X<0 THEN 670
640   GOSUB 800
645   IF V[I8] <= W THEN 660
650   LET J6=I8
655   LET W=V[I8]
660   NEXT J
670   LET X=P[J6]
680   REM   RECORD ROW NUMBER OF MOVE MADE
684   LET I6=I6+1
688   LET G[I6]=J6
690   RETURN
700   REM   RECORD LOSS BY DECREASING VALUE OF MOVES MADE
701   LET Z=-1
702   GOTO 720
```

```
710   REM   RECORD WIN BY INCREASING VALUE OF MOVES MADE
711   LET Z=1
720   FOR I=1 TO 16
730   LET V[G[I]]=V[G[I]]+Z
740   NEXT I
790   RETURN
800   REM   CONVERT POSITION X TO PLACE I8 IN LIST P
810   FOR I8=1 TO 24
820   IF X=P[I8] THEN 850
830   NEXT I8
840   LET I8=-1
850   RETURN
900   REM   LIST OF POSITIONS AND MOVES
901   DATA 0,-1,-1,-1,-1,-1,-1
902   DATA 1,0,-1,-1,-1,-1,-1
903   DATA 2,1,0,-1,-1,-1,-1
904   DATA 3,2,1,0,-1,-1,-1
905   DATA 10,0,-1,-1,-1,-1,-1
906   DATA 11,10,1,-1,-1,-1,-1
907   DATA 12,11,10,2,-1,-1,-1
908   DATA 13,12,11,10,3,-1,-1
909   DATA 20,10,0,-1,-1,-1,-1
910   DATA 21,20,11,1,-1,-1,-1
911   DATA 22,21,20,12,2,-1,-1
912   DATA 23,22,21,20,13,3,-1
913   DATA 100,0,-1,-1,-1,-1,-1
914   DATA 101,100,1,-1,-1,-1,-1
915   DATA 102,101,100,2,-1,-1,-1
916   DATA 103,102,101,100,3,-1,-1
917   DATA 110,100,10,-1,-1,-1,-1
918   DATA 111,110,101,11,-1,-1,-1
919   DATA 112,111,110,102,12,-1,-1
920   DATA 113,112,111,110,103,13,-1
921   DATA 120,110,100,20,-1,-1,-1
922   DATA 121,120,111,101,21,-1,-1
923   DATA 122,121,120,112,102,22,-1
924   DATA 123,122,121,120,113,103,23
999   END
```

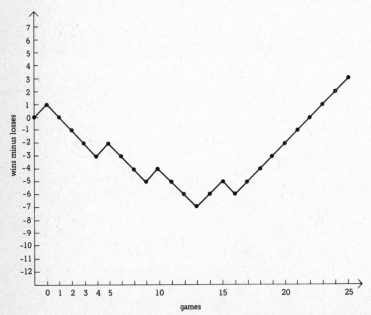

Figure 11   History of a learning session with a human opponent.

The graph in Figure 11 shows the results of a contest between the program LEARN and a human opponent who played each game to win if possible. Any time the program won a game the human opponent avoided, if possible, duplicating the moves which allowed the machine to win. This causes the program to learn quite rapidly. A human opponent can delay the learning process by such tricks as letting the program win after making a poor move. This poor move will then be recorded as a good one and the program will try the move again until it has eventually learned that it is a poor one. Of course, in order to retard the program's learning, the opponent must lose some games.

In Figure 11, a loss by the program is represented by a downward sloping line. A win is indicated by an upward slope. The height of the line after any number of games thus represents the difference between the program's wins and the number of games won by its opponent.

other learning schemes

If a game is too complex to analyze it is likely that it will also not be convenient for a program to retain a "value" for each possible situation. In the Samuel's checkers program mentioned earlier, a value for each position was calculated whenever needed (rather than stored) by examining the location of each of the pieces. Several factors such as the number of pieces, the number of kings, the mobility of the pieces, and the distance of the pieces from the center of the board influenced the value calculated and the weights given to these various factors were the quantities that were modified after each game. The program would make each move by calculating all possible moves based on the current board status, calculating a value for each of the possible moves, and selecting the best one. This method of learning will be illustrated by the investing program discussed in the next section.

heuristics

The program LEARN, Samuel's checkers program, and the program STOCK described in the next section are examples of what is often called a *heuristic* program. To a computer scientist, a heuristic is an aid to decision-making, often associated with learning.

Samuel's program uses the calculated value of a checkers position to learn the appropriate moves to make. The position value is the heuristic.

Another example of a heuristic is the Goren point count used by some bridge players to estimate the value of their cards. Each ace

counts four points, each king counts three, and so forth. Points are
added or substracted for distributions of the suits and other factors.
The point count is then used to help decide what bid to make.

The term "heuristic" is usually applied to procedures which will
not necessarily find a "best" solution, or any solution at all, to a
particular problem. Even if Samuel's checkers program learned
enough to defeat the best players, it still may not play perfectly;
perhaps another program could beat it. There is certainly no
assurance that Goren's methods provide the best bidding strategy.

problems

1 Modify the program LEARN so that it records all moves made
by both players and after the game increases the values of all moves
made by the winner and decreases the value of all moves made by
the loser. Compare the learning rate of the new program with that
of the old program.

2 If a human opponent plays poorly against the program LEARN,
the program may learn to make wrong moves, allowing the
opponent to win later games. Suppose 20 games are played against
LEARN. Try to determine the maximum number that can be won
by the program's opponent.

3 Write a program that learns to play hexapawn (see Problem 3
of Section 2).

4 Write a program that learns to play tic-tac-toe (see Problem 4
of Section 2). Let a draw have a value of +1, a win +2, and a
loss −1.

5 | a program that learns to play the stock market

If the word "game" is interpreted broadly, investing in the stock
market can be considered playing a game. It is therefore reasonable
to consider the possibility of writing a program that learns how
to decide when to buy and sell stocks. In order to obtain a fairly
simple program, the problem of beating the stock market will be
simplified considerably.

a simple investment procedure

Suppose that each month it is possible to buy or sell 100 shares of
one certain stock or do nothing. A speculator has observed that
there is a certain correlation in the change of the market from

229

a program
that
learns to
play the
stock
market
section 5

month to month. If it goes up one month, it seems to go up with
fair regularity the next. Similarly, if the market drops one month,
it is quite likely to do so again. Thus, the speculator decides upon
a specific strategy. If last month's increase was more than a certain
amount B, he buys 100 shares. If the increase was less that S, he
sells 100 shares. If the increase was between B and S, he does
nothing. The question is: What should be used as values for B and
S? The program STOCK attempts to learn the best values for B
and S.

the cost of investing

Each time stock is bought or sold, the stockbroker charges a
commission of $200 plus 1 percent of the price of the stock. The
investor figures this fee should be amortized over a 12-month
period. Thus if the value of the stock is V dollars per share, the cost
of buying 100 shares would be $C = (200 + .01 * 100 * V)/12$
dollars in 1 month.

He also estimates that dividends on the stock would amount to
4 percent, but that he could invest the money in a savings account
which would pay 5 percent per annum. Thus there is an interest
loss of $I = .01 * 100 * V/12$ per month for each 100 shares owned.

If the price of the stock increases by an amount M1 dollars in
1 month, then the gain (or loss) to the investor is $M1 * 100$ for each
100 shares.

the learning program

The program STOCK attempts to learn the optimal values of B and
S, the buy and sell points, by simulating 360 months of activity in
the stock market. Each month the program determines whether or
not the action dictated by the behavior of the market in the
previous month (the value of M) and the values of B and S results
in the most profitable alternative. If not, the value of B or S is
modified according to the following rules.

1 If stock was purchased and the transaction was not profitable,
that is, $100 * M1 \leq I + C$, then B is increased by 5 percent.
2 If stock was sold and it would have been better to keep it, that
is, $100 * M1 \geq I - C$, the value of S, which is negative, is decreased
by 5 percent.
3 If no purchase was made, but it would have been profitable to
buy, that is, $100 * M1 \geq I + C$, then B is decreased by 5 percent.
4 If no stock was sold, but should have been, that is,
$100 * M1 \leq I - C$, then S is increased by 5 percent.

The program also simulates all of the investments and sales that would have been made, recording N, the number of shares owned and R, the cash reserve. These values are initially set to $500 and $950,000, respectively. The initial value V of the stock is $100, so the investor begins as a millionaire.

The generation of the number M1 representing the increase or decrease in the price of the stock, depends in part upon M, the change during the previous month and M0, a long-term market trend, or long-term average increase (or decrease). In the program stock, M0 is .1, which means that the stock price will increase at an average rate of 10¢ per month. The value of M1 is generated by the statement

```
41  LET M1 = (((RND(0)+RND(0)-1)*2+M)*2+M0)/3
```

The value of $RND(0) + RND(0)$ is a number between zero and two, therefore $(RND(0) + RND(0) -1) * 2$ is between -2 and $+2$. This value is added to M, the previous month's increase, so that the value of M1 will be related to the previous month's price change. That result is then averaged with M0 using a weight of $\frac{1}{3}$ for M0 and $\frac{2}{3}$ for the value just generated. This tends to prevent the value of M1 from straying too far from the long-term average M0.

There are many other formulas for generating the value of M1 that might be used which satisfy the requirements that there is a direct correlation between M and M1 and the average of the values of M1 is M0.

```
LIST
STOCK

5    PRINT " YEAR    BUY         SELL        PRICE       ASSETS"
10   READ M0,M,B,S,V,N,R
20   DATA .1,1,.5,-.5,100,500,950000.
30   FOR K=1 TO 360
40   REM   GENERATE CHANGE IN STOCK PRICE FOR NEXT MONTH
41   LET M1=(((RND(0)+RND(0)-1)*2+M)*2+M0)/3
50   REM   D IS DOLLAR VALUE OF 100 SHARES
51   LET D=100*V
60   REM   C IS COST OF BUYING OR SELLING 100 SHARES
61   LET C=(200+.01*D)/12
70   REM   I IS DIFFERENCE BETWEEN INTEREST ON SAVINGS
71   REM      AND DIVIDEND PAID ON VALUE OF 100 SHARES
72   LET I=.01*D/12
100  REM   DECIDE WHETHER OR NOT TO BUY
110  IF M<B THEN 300
120  REM   BUY IF THERE IS SUFFICIENT CASH
130  IF D+C>R THEN 200
140  LET R=R-D-C
150  LET N=N+100
200  REM   DETERMINE IF PURCHASE WAS PROFITABLE
210  IF 100*M1>I+C THEN 600
220  REM   PURCHASE NOT PROFITABLE, INCREASE  B
230  LET B=1.05*B
240  GOTO 600
```

a program
that
learns to
play the
stock
market
section 5

```
300   REM   DECIDE WHETHER OR NOT TO SELL
310   IF M>S THEN 500
320   REM   SELL IF STOCK IS OWNED
330   IF N=0 THEN 400
340   LET R=R+D-C
350   LET N=N-100
400   REM   DETERMINE IF SALE WAS PROFITABLE
410   IF 100*M1<I-C THEN 600
420   REM   SALE NOT PROFITABLE, DECREASE  S
430   LET S=1.05*S
440   GOTO 600
500   REM   DETERMINE IF A PURCHASE WOULD HAVE BEEN PROFITABLE
510   IF 100*M1<I+C THEN 550
520   REM   PURCHASE WOULD HAVE BEEN PROFITABLE, DECREASE  B
530   LET B=.95*B
540   GOTO 600
550   REM   DETERMINE IF SALE WOULD HAVE BEEN PROFITABLE
560   IF 100*M1>I-C THEN 600
570   REM   SALE WOULD HAVE BEEN PROFITABLE, INCREASE  S
580   LET S=.95*S
600   REM   NEW  M   BECOMES OLD  M
610   LET M=M1
620   REM   RECORD INCREASE OR DECREASE IN STOCK PRICE
630   LET V=V+M
640   REM   INCREASE RESERVE CASH BY INTEREST AND DIVIDENDS
650   LET R=R+(.04*N*V+.05*R)/12
700   REM   PRINT RESULTS AT TWELVE MONTH INTERVALS
710   IF INT(K/12) <> K/12 THEN 790
720   PRINT K/12;B;S;V;N*V+R
790   NEXT K
999   END
```

```
RUN
STOCK
```

YEAR	BUY	SELL	PRICE	ASSETS
1	.450122	-.45125	106.695	1.05642E+06
2	.447874	-.427616	110.729	1.11408E+06
3	.469092	-.426547	119.984	1.18488E+06
4	.491315	-.383996	118.541	1.23966E+06
5	.513305	-.402188	122.361	1.30859E+06
6	.510742	-.362975	123.042	1.37386E+06
7	.510742	-.343964	115.11	1.42434E+06
8	.563092	-.342246	113.483	1.49222E+06
9	.506921	-.342246	121.259	1.58022E+06
10	.477972	-.35846	122.185	1.66014E+06
11	.452938	-.291968	120.97	1.73972E+06
12	.451806	-.262843	121.998	1.82809E+06
13	.429215	-.26153	119.684	1.91455E+06
14	.450676	-.247832	116.641	2.00638E+06
15	.406735	-.259573	118.684	2.10912E+06
16	.426004	-.245978	117.749	2.21470E+06
17	.403692	-.244138	119.114	2.32781E+06
18	.422817	-.242312	116.297	2.44424E+06
19	.466156	-.253791	121.179	2.57036E+06
20	.463828	-.240499	125.606	2.70389E+06
21	.416515	-.26515	128.727	2.84374E+06
22	.415473	-.26515	138.61	3.00231E+06
23	.435156	-.26515	145.769	3.16968E+06
24	.432983	-.264487	147.024	3.33105E+06
25	.432983	-.250008	146.509	3.49530E+06
26	.431901	-.249383	147.759	3.67263E+06
27	.452362	-.259893	144.994	3.84902E+06
28	.451231	-.246898	154.052	4.06580E+06
29	.42867	-.233967	159.374	4.28581E+06
30	.426529	-.233382	163.879	4.51588E+06

```
DONE
```

In this particular simulation the value of B is consistently between .4 and .5, and after a few years the value of S stays between −.2 and −.3. The true optimal values for B and S depend upon the value of V and so the values of B and S would gradually change if the simulation were continued for a longer period. The program not only learns good values for B and S but also will adapt its buy and sell strategy as the situation changes. This effect can be observed by changing M0, the average monthly price increase, to a larger value and rerunning the program.

problems

1 Run the program STOCK with larger values of M0 (say, .2 or .3) to observe how the values of B and S change as the market price of the stock changes.

2 Run the program STOCK with M0 = 0 and −.1, observing the assets of the investor, to determine if it is possible to make money on the market even if the long-term trend is stable or even downward. The final assets should be compared with what the assets would be if all money were invested in a savings account paying 4 percent interest.

6 | computers and the arts

Artistic creativity is often regarded as one of the highest forms of intellectual activity, even though there is disagreement as to what is "creative" and what is not. Computers, properly programmed, are capable of producing respectable works of art, music, and even poetry. One of the early computer-produced works to receive some attention was the *Illiac Suite for String Quartet* composed by a program written by L. A. Hiller, Jr. and L. M. Issacson and run on the ILLIAC computer at the University of Illinois. Two drawings produced by computers are shown in Figure 12.

Most works of art produced by a computer depend extensively on a random-number generator. Random numbers generated by a computer can represent notes, colors, or words. Rules imposing restrictions on the way numbers are generated can be applied to produce a certain type of work. For example, a program could be written so that it would produce only music whose structure and harmony is like that of music of the classical period. Another program could be written to generate only six-sided designs that look like snowflakes.

It is important to note that in using even the simplest schemes for generating music, art, or poetry, the programmer will probably be somewhat surprised by the result produced by the program. This contradicts the intended meaning of the cliché stating that "the computer only does exactly what it is told", which is true only in a very narrow technical sense.

a program that composes music

One way to have a computer compose music is to hook the computer directly to a speaker, generate the music, and play it on the speaker. The sound could also be directly recorded. The program described in this section prints its music. The numbers generated are converted into notes. The number 0 represents middle C. The numbers 1, 2, 3, . . . , 7 represent the notes D, E, F, G, A, B, and C above middle C and -1, -2, -3, -4, -5, -6, -7 represent B, A, G, F, E, and D below middle C. The program simply generates a sequence of notes without specifying length or volume. The notes are generated by the statement

```
40   LET N = INT(((RND(0)+RND(0)-1)*9+N)*.667+.5)
```

The formula is similar to the one used to simulate the action of the stock market. The value of $RND(0) + RND(0) - 1$ will be between -1 and $+1$. This value is multiplied by 9 (instead of 2, as before) to give larger changes in consecutive notes. The result of adding the generated change to the previous note is multiplied by .667 to prevent the notes from straying too far from zero (middle C) and then rounded to the nearest integer. If the number generated is less than -7 or greater than $+7$, it is ignored and another note is generated. Ten notes are generated followed by middle C.

```
LIST
MUSIC

1    DIM N$[30]
2    LET N$="C-D-E-F-G-A-B-C D+E+F+G+A+B+C+"
10   LET N=0
20   FOR K=1 TO 10
40   LET N=INT(((RND(0)+RND(0)-1)*9+N)*.667+.5)
50   IF ABS(N)>7 THEN 40
60   PRINT N$[2*N+15,2*N+16];" ";
70   NEXT K
80   PRINT "C"
90   END
```

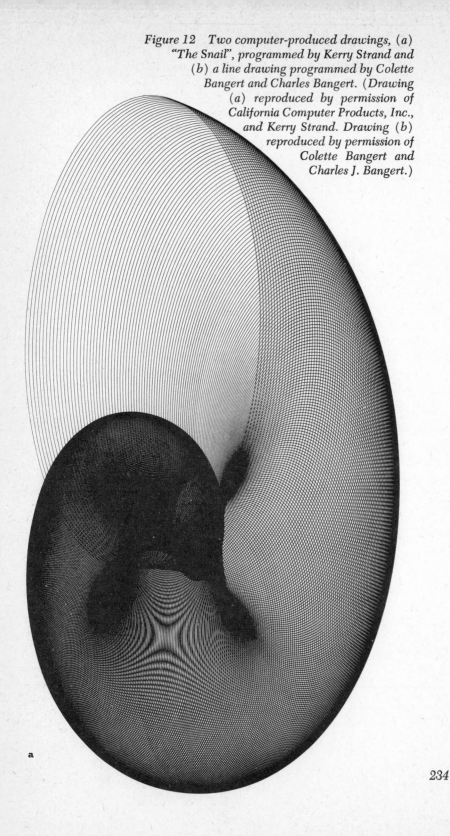

Figure 12 Two computer-produced drawings, (a) "The Snail", programmed by Kerry Strand and (b) a line drawing programmed by Colette Bangert and Charles Bangert. (Drawing (a) reproduced by permission of California Computer Products, Inc., and Kerry Strand. Drawing (b) reproduced by permission of Colette Bangert and Charles J. Bangert.)

a

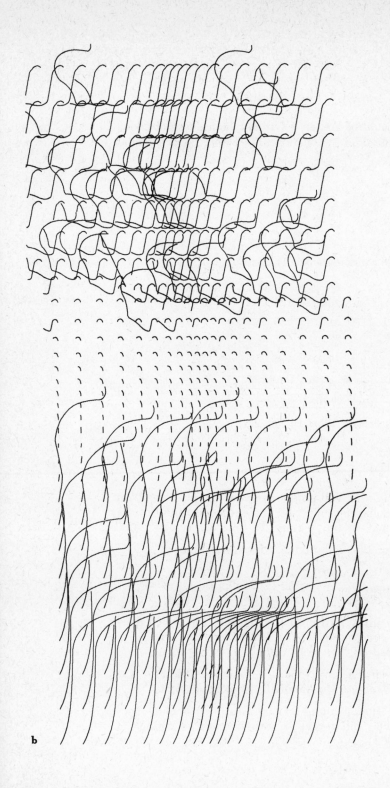

b

```
RUN
MUSIC

D+ E+ E+ A+ E+ D+ E+ B- A- B- C

DONE
```

This program could be run on a system which does not allow character string variables by deleting lines 1 and 2 and changing lines 60 and 80 to

```
60  PRINT N;
80  PRINT O
```

Figure 13 shows one way of scoring the melody generated, producing a simple waltz in the key of C major.

Figure 13   A waltz composed by the computer.

problems

1 Write a program that will produce pictures by printing X's on the output page. Some rules must be imposed concerning the way the X's are printed if the picture is to have some "form".

2 Write a program that will produce rock and roll music.

suggested readings

Feigenbaum, Edward A. "Artificial Intelligence: Themes in the Second Decade", *Proceedings of the IFIP Congress 1968, Edinburgh, Scotland* J10–J24 (Aug., 1968).

Feigenbaum, Edward A. and Julian A. Feldman (Eds.). *Computers and Thought.* McGraw-Hill, New York, 1963.

Gardner, Martin. "How to Build a Game-Learning Machine and Then Teach It to Play and to Win", *Scientific American* **206,** No. 3, 138–152 (Mar., 1962).

Hiller, Lejaren A. "Music Composed with Computers—A Historical Survey", in *The Computer and Music*, H. B. Lincoln (Ed.). Cornell University Press, Ithaca, New York, 1970.

Samuel, Arthur L. "Some Studies in Machine Learning Using the Game Checkers", *IBM Journal of Research and Development* **3**, No. 3, 210–219 (July, 1959).

Sedelow, Sally Y. "The Computer in the Humanities and Fine Arts", *Computing Surveys* **2**, No. 2, 89–110 (June, 1970).

machine language,
assemblers,
and compilers

IT IS possible to drive a car without knowing anything about the function of the carburetor, transmission, or the differential. Similarly, it is possible to write computer programs without understanding the computer or the programming systems which are used. In both cases, however, the machine can be used more intelligently and more efficiently if its functions are understood.

This chapter explores some of the characteristics of a mythical computer called the BRAIN. The organization of the BRAIN computer is described in enough detail to make it possible to write BRAIN *machine language* programs consisting of instructions such as ADD, SUBTRACT, and HALT, which are directly understood by the computer. The purpose of developing a little programming skill in machine language is mainly to obtain a better understanding of how a digital computer works and an appreciation of the tasks performed by a compiler.

1 | computer representation of data

From one point of view a digital computer is a box full of electronic *on–off* or *binary* switches and circuits which connect the switches. The position or value of each switch at any instant depends upon the value of other switches at that instant or at some prior time or upon the signals coming into the switches from some external source, such as a card reader or teletypewriter. Thus, all information, including instructions and data, which is stored in the computer is represented by these binary switches. It is usually not necessary for a programmer to know precisely how instructions and

238

data are stored, or to even know what machine instructions are, but often the programmer can take advantage of that information to write better programs or to understand certain possible errors.

binary numbers

Since the basic element of a digital computer is an "on–off" switch of some kind, most computers represent integers in their binary form. The only digits used in a binary representation are 0 and 1. A binary digit is sometimes called a *bit*. Thus each "on–off" switch can represent one binary digit of an integer. The following is a brief review of the binary number system.

The numeral 742 means $7 \cdot 10^2 + 4 \cdot 10 + 2$ in the decimal system. Analogously, $1011 = 1 \cdot 2^3 + 0 \cdot 2^2 + 1 \cdot 2 + 1$ in the binary system. To convert a binary numeral into its decimal representation, simply expand it as in the above illustration and perform the indicated arithmetic.

$$1011_2 = 2^3 + 2 + 1 = 8 + 2 + 1 = 11_{10}$$

The subscripts 2 and 10 indicate the *base* in which the number is written. If a subscript is omitted, the base is usually 10. To find the binary representation of a decimal number, divide the number by 2. The remainder will be the units (rightmost) digit. The next digit (from the right) may be found by taking the quotient from the previous step, dividing it by 2, and recording the remainder. The conversion of 347 into binary is shown in Figure 1, arranged for easy computation. Remember that the remainder after the first division is the units (rightmost) digit. The computation proceeds from the bottom line to the top. At each step a number is divided by 2, and the remainder is recorded in the column to the right. The binary representation is then obtained by reading the remainders from top to bottom. Thus, $347_{10} = 101011011_2$. Check:

$$2^8 + 2^6 + 2^4 + 2^3 + 2 + 1 = 256 + 64 + 16 + 8 + 2 + 1 = 347$$

	0	
2	1	1
2	2	0
2	5	1
2	10	0
2	21	1
2	43	1
2	86	0
2	173	1
2	347	1

Figure 1 Conversion of 347 into binary representation.

240

machine
language,
assemblers,
and
compilers
chapter 9

The following BASIC program BINARY converts the whole part of any number between 0 and 99999 into its binary form using the process just described. The binary number is stored as a character string B$, which initially contains the binary equivalent of zero.

```
LIST
BINARY

100  REM  **  CONVERTS DECIMAL  M  TO BINARY  B$
110  INPUT M
120  REM  **  CHECK IF M IS AN INTEGER
130  IF M <> INT(M) THEN 110
140  REM  **  CHECK IF M IS IN THE RANGE 0-99999
150  IF M<0 THEN 110
151  IF M>99999. THEN 110
160  DIM B$[17],D$[2]
170  REM  **  B$ IS INITIALLY 0 IN BINARY
180  LET B$="              0"
190  LET D$="01"
200  LET N=M
210  FOR B=17 TO 1 STEP -1
220  IF N=0 THEN 310
230  LET Q=INT(N/2)
240  LET D=N-Q*2+1
250  LET B$[B,B]=D$[D,D]
260  LET N=Q
270  NEXT B
310  PRINT M;"(DECIMAL) = "B$;" (BINARY)"
990  END

RUN
BINARY

?14
  14   (DECIMAL) =                1110 (BINARY)

DONE

RUN
BINARY

?99999
  99999.    (DECIMAL) = 11000011010011111 (BINARY)

DONE
```

hexadecimal numbers

In many computers, the hexadecimal (base 16) number system is also important. It is useful because of its close connection with the binary number system. When writing hexadecimal numbers, the letters "A", "B", "C", "D", "E", and "F" are standard notation for representing the digits 10, 11, 12, 13, 14, and 15.

A binary number may be converted to hexadecimal by grouping the digits by fours from the right and writing one hexadecimal digit for each four binary digits. For example, $101011011_2 = 0001,0101,1011_2 = 15B_{16}$. To determine the units digit, $1011_2 = 8 + 2 + 1 = 11_{10} = B_{16}$.

Table 1 is convenient to have when converting numbers from one base to another.

table 1 *decimal, hexadecimal, and
binary equivalents*

decimal	hexadecimal	binary
0	0	0000
1	1	0001
2	2	0010
3	3	0011
4	4	0100
5	5	0101
6	6	0110
7	7	0111
8	8	1000
9	9	1001
10	A	1010
11	B	1011
12	C	1100
13	D	1101
14	E	1110
15	F	1111

To convert from hexadecimal to binary, write each hexadecimal
as four binary digits. For example, $F02C_{16} = 1111,0000,0010,1100_2$.

Since long binary numbers are cumbersome to write, their
hexadecimal equivalents will often be written instead.

the representation of integers

Typically, some fixed number of switches is used to store each integer
in a computer. The number of switches used to represent an integer
is different for different computers; 12, 15, 16, 24, 32, 36, 48, 60, and
other numbers of switches have been used. The BRAIN computer
uses 16 switches and the number $347_{10} = 0000000101011011_2$ is
represented internally by

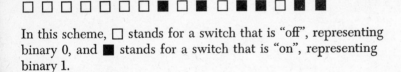

In this scheme, □ stands for a switch that is "off", representing
binary 0, and ■ stands for a switch that is "on", representing
binary 1.

242

machine
language,
assemblers,
and
compilers
chapter 9

It is certainly desirable to represent negative numbers in a computer. One possibility is to reserve one switch (say, the leftmost one) for the sign and let 0 ("off") stand for + and 1 for −. With this scheme using 16 switches, the number −347 would be represented by 1000000101011011. There is another scheme which is widely used, and, in fact, is used by the BRAIN computer. Suppose a car odometer reads 00000 miles and it is driven backward 1 mile. If the odometer can move backward, it would then read 99999. After driving backward 2 miles it would read 99998. By analogy, it is possible to represent −1 in a binary computer using 16 switches by 1111111111111111. Negative 2 would be represented by 1111111111111110. This is called the *two's complement* representation of −2.

If the automobile is driven backward 99999 miles the odometer would read 00001; therefore, there must be some agreement about which possible configurations represent positive numbers and which represent negative numbers. In a binary system, configurations beginning with 0 usually represent positive numbers and those beginning with 1 represent negative numbers.

The following procedure indicates how to find the representation of a number −n.

1 Write down the binary representation of n.
2 Change all 0's to 1's and all 1's to 0's.
3 Add 1.

Using these instructions to find the two's complement representation of −347 in a machine which uses 16 switches to represent each integer, one obtains

1 0000000101011011
2 1111111010100100
3 1111111010100101

arithmetic using complements

One advantage (to the computer designer) of the two's complement representation is that any two integers may be added without any special attention to their sign. Suppose −4 and +7 are to be added on a machine which uses an eight-switch two's complement representation for integers. The representation for +4 is 00000100. Following the procedure with n = 4,

1 00000100
2 11111011
3 11111100

it is determined that 11111100 is the representation of -4. The representation of their sum may be found by adding the two representations without any special consideration for signs.

$$\begin{array}{r} 11111100 \\ +00000111 \\ \hline 00000011 \end{array}$$

The carry from the leftmost column is simply ignored.

Example Find the sum of -4 and -7 using eight-switch two's complement representation; 00000111 is the representation of $+7$, hence 11111001 is the representation of -7.

$$\begin{array}{r} 11111001 \\ +11111100 \\ \hline \end{array}$$

3	11110101
2	11110100
1	00001011

The last three steps reverse the procedure for finding the representation of a negative number, by subtracting 1 and interchanging the 0's and the 1's.

$1011_2 = 8 + 2 + 1 = 11$, hence 11110101 is the representation of -11, which is the correct result.

overflow

The largest and smallest integers which can be represented can be calculated. Suppose a machine uses an eight-switch two's complement representation for integers. The largest number which can be represented is $01111111 = 2^7 - 1$. Adding 1 yields 10000000 which is by agreement the representation of a negative number, in fact, the smallest number which can be represented. In general, the largest number representable in a machine which uses an n-switch two's complement representation is $2^{n-1} - 1$; the smallest representable number is the one represented by $100 \ldots 00$, namely, -2^{n-1}.

It is possible to have two representable numbers whose sum, difference, or product is too large or too small to represent. It is said that an *overflow* occurs when such an arithmetic operation is attempted. On most computers, the machine language allows a programmer to test whether or not an overflow has occurred. One convenience of a language like BASIC is that programs are translated into machine language instructions which include all necessary overflow tests.

characters

The internal representation of characters is quite simple. On most machines, each character has an eight-digit binary code associated with it. Each character can thus be represented by eight switches. Most computers use either an eight-bit code called EBCDIC for Extended Binary Coded Decimal Interchange Code (don't try to make much sense out of that name) or the code called ASCII mentioned in Chapter 4.

As an example, if a machine used the EBCDIC code, the letter "Q" would be stored internally by eight switches set according to the following pattern.

■ ■ □ ■ ■ □ □ □

Two hexadecimal digits are often used instead of eight binary digits to represent the code. Thus, the EBCDIC code for the letter "Q" is 11011000 or D8.

One property of both codes is that the codes for the letters of the alphabet are in order so that the alphabetical order of letters may be checked by the numerical order of their codes.

floating point numbers

To be at all convenient to a user, a computer must be able to calculate with numbers like 3.14159, which is an approximation to π.

One solution is to use 314159 for π. Then the programmer must have some way of keeping track of where the decimal point belongs when two numbers are added or multiplied.

A better solution is to store internally the information corresponding to a number written in what is called scientific or exponential notation. The BASIC constants using the "E" (for exponentiation) correspond to numbers written in this notation. For example, 34 E +13 is the way of writing 34×10^{13} in BASIC. One way of representing such numbers in a computer is to store, as integers, two numbers, one representing 34 and one representing the exponent 13. The number $\pi = 3.14159 = 314159 \times 10^{-5}$ would be represented by the two integers 314159 and -5. Most computers have basic instructions to take two such *floating point* representations and produce the representation of their sum, difference, product, and quotient. In most binary computers, the exponent represents a power of 2 or 16, rather than a power of 10.

problems

1 Convert the decimal number 47 to binary and hexadecimal. Convert the hexadecimal result back to decimal in order to check the answer.

2 If a computer uses eight switches and the complement representation of integers described in this section, what are the representations of -8, 3, and -47? Using the representations obtained, add the numbers -8, 3, and -47. Check the result by complementing and converting to decimal.

3 The ten's complement of a decimal number is found by subtracting each digit from 9 and then adding 1. Find the ten's complement of -8, 3, and -47, using four digits. Add, ignoring carries, and recomplement to check the sum as in Problem 2.

4 a Apply the procedure for complementation to the representations of -8, and -47, getting the representations of 8 and 47. The procedure is its own inverse, meaning that steps (2) and (3) applied in order have the same effect as applying steps (3) and (2) in reverse order.
b What happens when steps (2) and (3) are applied to 10000000?

5 If words are to be sorted by checking the numerical order of their character codes, should the code for the blank character be larger or smaller than the codes for the letters?

6 Two floating point numbers are multiplied by multiplying their integer parts and adding the exponents. For example, $(12 \times 10^{21}) \times (11 \times 10^{17}) = 132 \times 10^{38}$. Explain how to add two floating point numbers.

2 | *the* BRAIN *computer*

The BRAIN computer consists of a memory and a computation section, connected by controlling circuitry. Information goes in and out of the machine via connections between memory and some input/output device, such as a teletypewriter. Figure 2 is a schematic representation of these components.

In some ways the BRAIN is typical of actual digital computers; the instructions of the BRAIN resemble some of the instructions of many computers. However, almost any real computer is considerably more complex than the BRAIN. For example, input/output operations of the BRAIN are very simple, which is not

246

machine
language,
assemblers,
and
compilers
chapter 9

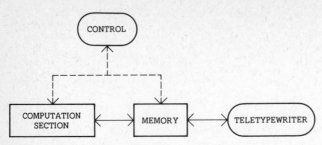

Figure 2   The components of a computer.

at all typical. Most computers can communicate with a variety of devices, such as magnetic tapes, disks, drums, card readers, and printers.

memory

The data and the instructions for a BRAIN program are stored in the memory. The memory can store 256 *words* of information. Each word consists of 16 binary digits, which could represent a 16-digit two's complement integer, two 8-digit character codes, or one instruction. Floating point numbers are not used in the BRAIN computer. The memory of the BRAIN is much smaller than the memories of most actual computers, which can store from a few thousand up to a few million words of information.

Each word in the memory of the BRAIN computer has a number associated with it, called an *address,* a number between 0 and $FF_{16} = 2^8 - 1 = 255$. This allows computer instructions to specify which numbers, characters, or even instructions are to be involved in a certain operation, such as input or output.

On most binary computers the number of memory locations is a power of 2, such as $2^8 = 256$ for the BRAIN computer. This allows each binary number of some particular size (eight bits for the BRAIN) to represent one address.

computation

The computation section consists of sixteen 16-switch registers. Two's complement representation of integers is used so that any integer from $-2^{15} = -32768$ to $2^{15} - 1 = 32767$ may be in a register. One register could also hold two characters.

One reason for having a computation section distinct from the memory is that fast circuits to do arithmetic operations are expensive. On the other hand, it is desirable to have as much memory as possible, so the switches in the memory are of a different type, which operate more slowly and are less expensive. A common switch used for computer memories is a doughnut-shaped ferrite "core", which represents a 0 when magnetized in one sense (say, clockwise) and a 1 when magnetized in the opposite sense. (See Figure 3.)

Figure 3   A portion of a computer memory. (Photograph by the courtesy of IBM.)

problem

How many ferrite cores would be needed to build the memory of the BRAIN computer?

3 | BRAIN *instructions*

Each computer has a set of elementary operations which it can perform. Any program must consist of combinations of these operations. In its most rudimentary form, programming consists of

248

machine
language,
assemblers,
and
compilers
chapter 9

writing lists of machine instructions, each of which causes one of the elementary operations to be performed. The programmer must know exactly how each operation works. The instructions for the BRAIN will be discussed in enough detail to allow programs to be written.

instruction format

Each BRAIN instruction consists of 16 binary digits or 4 hexadecimal digits. The first hexadecimal digit is called the *operation code* and specifies which operation is to be performed, such as add, subtract, print, etc. The other three digits specify which information in the machine is to be involved in the operation by specifying registers, addresses, or constants. Instructions are stored in the memory of the computer.

arithmetic instructions

The first instruction to be considered is the "add" instruction. Its operation code is $A = 1010_2$ and the other three hexadecimal digits of the instructions specify registers. As an example, when the instruction A2F3 is executed, the numbers in registers 15 (or hexadecimal F) and 3 are added and the result is placed in register 2. The contents of registers 15 and 3 are *not* changed when the instruction is executed.

If the instruction A2F3 were one of the instructions of a program to be executed by the BRAIN, it would be stored as one word in memory as

Each hexadecimal digit of the instructions represents four binary digits or four switch settings.

There are three similar instructions "subtract", "multiply", and "divide" with operation codes 2, 5, and D, respectively. Division is integer division; the remainder is ignored: $3/7 = 0$, $9/5 = 1$, and $-7/3 = -3$. If an arithmetic operation is attempted which would produce overflow, that is, a number greater than 32767 or less than -32768, or which would cause division by zero, execution is terminated.

The instruction 2BBB sets register 11 to 0. The instruction DBBA causes the contents of register 11 to be divided by the contents of register 10. The quotient is placed in register 11. The contents of register 11 will, of course, generally be changed by this instruction, but the contents of register 10 will not be changed. The instruction 5999 squares the number in register 9. The instruction AAAA doubles the number in register 10.

The following instructions raise the number stored in register 0 to the fifth power.

```
5100
5111
5010
```

the enter instruction

The "enter" instruction (operation code E) causes a constant to be entered into a register. The second hexadecimal digit of the instruction specifies the register and the third and fourth digits specify an eight-binary-digit constant using two's complement representation. The instruction E452 enters $52_{16} = 82_{10}$ into register 4. The instruction EEFF enters -1 into register 14, since $FF_{16} = 11111111_2$, which is the two's complement representation of -1 using eight switches.

Suppose the numbers a, b, and c are in registers 1, 2, and 3. The following instructions compute $b^2 - 4ac$ and put the result in register 12 without changing registers 1, 2, or 3. Register 11 is used to hold some intermediate results and so its value will be changed.

instructions	comments
5C22	LET R[12] = R[2]*R[2]
EB04	LET R[11] = 4
5BB1	LET R[11] = R[11]*R[1]
5BB3	LET R[11] = R[11]*R[3]
2CCB	LET R[12] = R[12]+R[11]

load and store

The "load" and "unload" (or "store") instructions (operation codes 3 and 4) move data from the memory to a register and vice versa. The instruction 3942 moves the 16-binary-digit word in address 42 into register 9 without changing the contents of address 42. From the programmer's point of view, the 16 bits in the memory may represent an integer, two characters, the answers to 16 true–false questions or even a BRAIN instruction. The instruction 4F9A moves

250

machine
language,
assemblers,
and
compilers
chapter 9

the information in register 15 into address 9A without changing register 15.

input and output

The "output" instruction (operation code 0) prints in *decimal* on the teletypewriter the number whose two's complement representation is stored in the address specified. The "input" instruction (operation code 1) types a question mark on the typewriter, then accepts any integer from -32768 to 32767 typed in decimal and stores it in two's complement form in the memory location specified.

BRAIN machine instructions are written as four hexadecimal digits, which are an abbreviation for 16 switch settings in the machine. The input and output instructions accept and print numbers in decimal.

halt

The "halt" instruction causes execution to terminate. Its operation code is F and the other three digits have no effect. Like the STOP instruction in BASIC, it may appear at any point in a program.

The following is a complete program to compute and print $d = b^2 - 4ac$.

instructions	comments
E504	LET R[5] = 4
1050	INPUT A
1051	INPUT B
1052	INPUT C
3651	LET R[6] = B
5666	LET R[6] = R[6]*R[6]
3150	LET R[1] = A
5551	LET R[5] = R[5]*R[1]
3152	LET R[1] = C
5551	LET R[5] = R[5]*R[1]
2665	LET R[6] = R[6]-R[5]
4653	LET D = R[6]
0053	PRINT D
F000	STOP

summary

Table 2 summarizes the BRAIN instructions. The "branch" (B) and "count" (C) instructions will be discussed later. There are no instructions with operation codes 6, 7, 8, or 9.

table 2 *the* BRAIN *instructions*

instruction	op-code	prototype	description
output	0	00AA	print contents of address AA
input	1	10AA	store number typed into address AA
subtract	2	$2R_1R_2R_3$	put $R_2 - R_3$ in R_1 unless overflow
load	3	3RAA	move contents of AA into R
unload	4	4RAA	move contents of R into address AA
multiply	5	$5R_1R_2R_3$	put $R_2 \times R_3$ in R_1 unless overflow
add	A	$AR_1R_2R_3$	put $R_2 + R_3$ in R_1 unless overflow
branch	B	ECAA	if result of last arithmetic operation satisfies condition C, branch to AA
count	C	CRAA	put $R - 1$ into R, if contents of $R = 0$, branch to AA
divide	D	$DR_1R_2R_3$	put $INT(R_2/R_3)$ in R_1 unless $R_3 = 0$
enter	E	ERNN	put number NN in R
halt	F	FXXX	halt

problems

1 What is the maximum number of instructions that could be stored in the BRAIN computer?

2 Describe the result of executing each of the following instructions.

```
ABAA
DABA
D000
```

3 What is in register 4 after the following three instructions are executed?

```
E222
E310
A432
```

4 Write instructions that will compute $a^2 + 2ab + b^2$, where a and b are the numbers in registers 1 and 2. Leave the result in register 10.

5 Write instructions that compute the BASIC expression $A - B * A \uparrow 2 + 22$, where A and B are the numbers stored in registers 1 and 2. Leave the result in register 10.

6 Write instructions that will place into register 7 the remainder when the number in register 1 is divided by the number in register 2.

7 a Write instructions that will raise the number in register 0 to the sixth power. Use as few instructions as possible.
b What are the largest and smallest numbers that could be in register 0 without causing the instructions in the preceding paragraph to produce an overflow?

4 | *running a* BRAIN *program*

If the BRAIN were an actual computer with a teletypewriter as its input/output device, the instructions for operating the computer might be something like the following.

1 Plug it in and turn the power switch on.
2 Push the button labeled "LOAD" on the console.
3 Type in a program, one hexadecimal instruction per line.
4 Push the button marked "START" on the console.

The program typed in would then be executed. Whenever an input instruction were executed, a question mark would be typed on the teletypewriter and the decimal number typed by the operator would be converted to binary and stored in the appropriate memory location. The output instruction would cause a decimal number to be typed on the teletypewriter. There might be a little red light which comes on when the program halts and another program could be loaded into memory by pushing the LOAD button or the same program could be rerun by pushing the START button again.

the BRAIN *simulator*

There is no BRAIN computer, but a program written for the BRAIN computer may be run using a BASIC program named BRAIN. The program BRAIN will type

```
TYPE 'LOAD' OR 'START' OR 'STOP'
```

The operator responds with one of those commands, which are equivalent to pushing the START button, pushing the LOAD button, or turning the power off.

Typing STOP will halt execution of the BASIC program BRAIN. Typing START will cause the current BRAIN program to be executed with all registers set initially to zero.

If LOAD is typed, the program will type a 2-digit hexadecimal address and request input in the form of a hexadecimal BRAIN instruction. Any number of instructions consisting of up to 64 hexadecimal digits may be typed on one line. The number of digits must be a multiple of 4, since 4 digits are needed to specify each instruction. Any characters following the first blank are ignored and may be used to write comments.

In addition to hexadecimal digits representing machine instructions and data, three "system commands" may be given: SET, SEE, and END. If, for example, SEE-2E is typed, the contents of eight words beginning with the one stored in 2E will be printed. In this way, a part of a program already typed may be examined. SET-50 indicates that the next instruction to be typed is to be placed into address 50. END-B1 indicates that the program is complete and whenever the program is executed, the instruction stored in address B1 is to be executed first. If the dash and 2-digit address are omitted, address 00 is assumed. A system command may not be written on the same line with any BRAIN instruction.

Whenever instructions are loaded into the BRAIN memory, the only memory locations affected are those into which instructions are entered. The memory is *not* cleared (i.e., memory locations are *not* set to 0) at the beginning of the load operation, therefore loading may be used to correct or revise a program already stored in memory. A copy of memory and the program's starting address will be saved each time the LOAD operation is terminated by typing an END command. This copy is then fetched whenever a LOAD or START operation is to be performed.

If the BASIC system being used has a permanent storage capability, then the copy of memory and the starting address will be saved in the permanent memory. It will then be available at a later time or if execution of the BRAIN program is interrupted for some reason. If execution of the BRAIN program begins at statement 2 by typing RUN-2, all memory locations and the starting address are set to 0.

If the program is terminated by any cause other than execution of a halt instruction (e.g., due to overflow), a diagnostic message will be typed and the contents of all registers and memory which do not contain a zero will be given. (Appendix C contains a complete description and a listing of the BRAIN simulator.)

The following example shows how a program to multiply any

254

machine
language,
assemblers,
and
compilers
chapter 9

number by 19 is entered. Note how the constant $19 = 13_{16}$ can be entered in exactly the same way that an instruction is entered. The program is executed twice, then modified so that it will multiply any number by 20, and executed once more.

```
GET-BRAIN
RUN
BRAIN


TYPE 'LOAD' OR 'START' OR 'STOP'
?LOAD

ADDRESS   INSTRUCTIONS/DATA    COMMENTS
00        ?102A                INPUT A
01        ?312A                LET R[1]=A
02        ?3220                LET R[2]=N
03        ?5121                LET R[1]=R[1]*R[2]
04        ?412A                LET A=R[1]
05        ?002A                PRINT A
06        ?F000                STOP
07        ?SET-20
20        ?0013
21        ?END

TYPE 'LOAD' OR 'START' OR 'STOP'
?START

EXECUTION BEGINS WITH INSTRUCTION AT ADDRESS 00

?20
   380

HALT INSTRUCTION AT ADDRESS 06 EXECUTED

TYPE 'LOAD' OR 'START' OR 'STOP'
?START

EXECUTION BEGINS WITH INSTRUCTION AT ADDRESS 00

?-368
  -6992

HALT INSTRUCTION AT ADDRESS 06 EXECUTED

TYPE 'LOAD' OR 'START' OR 'STOP'
?LOAD

ADDRESS   INSTRUCTIONS/DATA   COMMENTS
00        ?SET-20
20        ?0014
21        ?END

TYPE 'LOAD' OR 'START' OR 'STOP'
?START

EXECUTION BEGINS WITH INSTRUCTION AT ADDRESS 00

?-20
  -400

HALT INSTRUCTION AT ADDRESS 06 EXECUTED

TYPE 'LOAD' OR 'START' OR 'STOP'
?STOP

DONE
```

simulating actual computers

The fact that one computer can be used to simulate another is of
great importance to a computer designer. Before undertaking the
expensive and time-consuming task of building a working model of
a new computer, he may use simulation techniques to evaluate his
design.

Simulation can also be an important factor in computer sales. If
a new computer can efficiently simulate the old computer which
it is to replace, the potential buyer will be able to save considerable
reprogramming costs, since all old programs could be run on the
new machine.

problems

1 Write a BRAIN program that will print the sum and difference
of any two numbers.

2 Write a BRAIN program that will convert yards, feet, and inches
into inches.

3 Write a BRAIN program that will convert any number of inches
into yards, feet, and inches.

4 Write a BRAIN program to compute $f(x) = x^3 + 2x^2 + x - 7$,
given any integer x as input.

5 Write a BRAIN program to compute $x^3 + 3x^2y + 3xy^2 + y^3$,
given any two integers x and y.

5 | *branching instructions*

BRAIN instructions are usually executed in sequence. It must be
possible to alter the sequence of instructions that are executed if a
program is to repeat a list of instructions, as in a BASIC
FOR–NEXT loop, or make decisions by taking one of several paths,
depending upon some value that has been typed in or previously
computed.

branch

The basic decision-making instruction for the BRAIN computer is
the "branch" (B) instruction. This instruction tests the result of the
most recent arithmetic operation, which may be in any of the
16 registers and branches conditionally, depending upon whether

256

machine
language,
assemblers,
and
compilers
chapter 9

table 3 *branching condition codes*

second digit of B instruction	branch if result was
0	Never branch
1	<0
2	$=0$
3	≤0
4	>0
5	$\neq0$
6	≥0
≥7	Always branch

that result was positive, negative, or zero. In this instruction, the second hexadecimal digit does not refer to a register, but specifies a combination of conditions to be tested according to the data given in Table 3.

If the condition is satisfied, the next instruction executed is the one stored in the address indicated in the branch instruction. Otherwise, the next instruction (i.e., the one stored in the address following the branch instruction) is executed. Thus, it becomes important to keep track of the address in which each instruction is stored, because, in order to write a branch instruction, the programmer must know the address of the instruction to which the branch is to be made.

The following program computes the absolute value of any number. Since the branch instruction will test only the result of an arithmetic operation, the program contains the instruction A101 which adds 0 to the value of X. Then, the instruction B606 checks the result of the most recent arithmetic operation (in this case the add instruction in address 03). If the result was positive or zero, the instruction in address 06 is executed next, otherwise the next instruction in address 05 is executed. The instruction BA00 at address 08 causes the program to execute repeatedly.

```
GET-BRAIN
RUN
BRAIN


TYPE 'LOAD' OR 'START' OR 'STOP'
?LOAD

ADDRESS    INSTRUCTIONS/DATA    COMMENTS
00         ?1033                S:  I   X
01         ?E000                    E   0,0
02         ?3133                    L   1,X
03         ?A101                    A   1,0,1
04         ?B606                    B   6,Q
05         ?2101                    S   1,0,1
06         ?4133                Q:  U   1,X
07         ?0033                    O   X
08         ?BA00                    B   A,S
09         ?END
```

```
TYPE 'LOAD' OR 'START' OR 'STOP'
? START
```

```
EXECUTION BEGINS WITH INSTRUCTION AT ADDRESS 00

? -34
   34
? 6785
   6785
? 3.75
INPUT MUST BE AN INTEGER BETWEEN -32768 AND 32767
PLEASE RETYPE INPUT
? -32768
OVERFLOW RESULTED FROM INSTRUCTION AT ADDRESS 05

CONTENTS OF REGISTERS
REG   HEX   DECIMAL           REG   HEX   DECIMAL
 1    8000  -32768.            9    0000   0

CONTENTS OF MEMORY IN HEXADECIMAL
00          1033 E000 3133 A101 B606 2101 4133 0033
08          BA00 0000 0000 0000 0000 0000 0000 0000
30          0000 0000 0000 8000 0000 0000 0000 0000

TYPE 'LOAD' OR 'START' OR 'STOP'
? STOP

DONE
```

In this example the comments are simply the BRAIN instructions written in a form that is a little easier to understand. In place of the operation codes, letters suggesting the operation, such as L for load and S for subtract are used. In place of addresses, symbols (the S and Q) are used to label instructions in the way that line numbers are used to identify BASIC statements. These comments look like instructions in a simple assembly language to be discussed in Section 6.

This program also illustrates the *dump* that is given when overflow occurs. The contents of all registers and memory are shown, except some of those which contain zero.

count

There is one BRAIN instruction designed especially for writing loops in programs. The "count" (C) instruction reduces a specified register by one; then if it is *not* zero, a branch is made to the specified address. The instruction CBAA is equivalent to the flowchart shown in Figure 4.

Suppose the number x is stored in address 41 and n is a positive number stored in address F3. The following instructions compute $y = x^n$ and store the result in F1.

```
ADDRESS   INSTRUCTIONS/DATA   COMMENTS
27        ? E001              E   0,1
28        ? 31F3              L   1,N
29        ? 3241              L   2,X
2A        ? 5002          L:  M   0,0,2
2B        ? C12A              C   1,L
2C        ? 40F1              U   0,Y
```

258

machine
language,
assemblers,
and
compilers
chapter 9

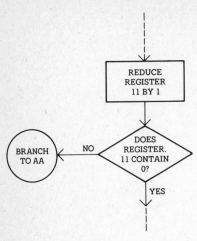

Figure 4   Flowchart for the count instruction.

Register 1 serves as a counter controlling the number of times the
multiply instruction 5002 is to be executed. Since n is placed
initially in register 1, the multiply instruction will be executed
n times.

Suppose the sum $1 + 2 + 3 + 4 + \cdots + n$ is to be computed for
input n. Again, register 1 is used as the counter.

```
ADDRESS   INSTRUCTIONS/DATA    COMMENTS
00        ?109F                    I    N
01        ?319F                    L    1,N
02        ?E000                    E    0,0
03        ?A010                 L: A    0,1,0
04        ?C103                    C    1,L
05        ?409E                    U    0,A
06        ?009E                    O    A
07        ?F000                    H
08        ?END
```

Of course a more efficient program to compute $1 + 2 + \cdots + n$
is the following program.

```
ADDRESS   INSTRUCTIONS/DATA    COMMENTS
00        ?1095                    I    N
01        ?309F                    L    0,N
02        ?E101                    E    1,1
03        ?A001                    A    0,0,1
04        ?5001                    M    0,0,1
05        ?E202                    E    2,2
06        ?D002                    D    0,0,2
07        ?409E                    U    0,A
08        ?009E                    O    A
09        ?F000                    H
0A        ?END
```

Although it has two more instructions than the previous program, it is more efficient because each instruction is executed only once. It uses the fact that $1 + 2 + \cdots + n = \frac{1}{2}(n)(n+1)$.

square roots

It is not possible to compute the square root of 2 precisely, because the BRAIN computer does only integer arithmetic and the square root of 2 is approximately 1.414. With the BRAIN computer it is possible to find the integer part of the square root of any positive integer using the flowchart shown in Figure 5.

If the number N typed in is negative or zero, the same number is

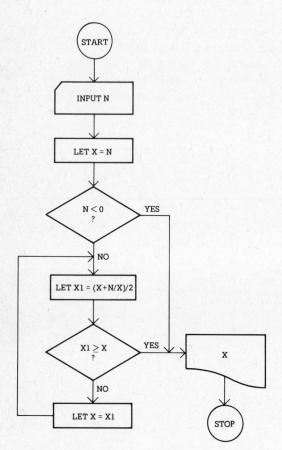

Figure 5   Flowchart for computation of square roots.

260

machine
language,
assemblers,
and
compilers
chapter 9

printed, otherwise the number printed is the largest integer less
than or equal to the square root of N. The answer is computed by
setting X initially to the value of N, then repeatedly recomputing X
according to the formula

LET $X = INT((X + INT(N/X))/2)$

The computation is repeated until one of the values of X is equal
to or larger than the preceding value of X. In the flowchart the
variable X1 is used to temporarily hold the new value of X until the
new and old values can be compared.

It is not at all obvious that the computation shown in the
flowchart will produce the desired answer. One way to be convinced
is to try it for several values of N. It is particularly interesting to
notice what happens when N is one less than a perfect square, such
as 8, 15, 48, or 99.

In the BRAIN program to compute square roots, X is stored in
register 0, X1 is stored in register 1, the constant 2 is kept in
register 2, the value of N is kept in register 3, register 4 holds the
intermediate computational results, and register 15 is used whenever
the constant 0 is needed. The value of X1 is printed at each step in
order to see how the computation is proceeding.

```
GET-BRAIN
RUN
BRAIN


TYPE 'LOAD' OR 'START' OR 'STOP'
?LOAD

ADDRESS   INSTRUCTIONS/DATA   COMMENTS
00        ?1098           S:  I   N
01        ?3398               L   3,N
02        ?A03F               A   0,3,15
03        ?B311               B   3,H     STOP IF N<=0
04        ?E202               E   2,2
05        ?D430           L:  D   4,3,0   N/X
06        ?A404               A   4,0,4   X+N/X
07        ?D142               D   1,4,2   (X+N/X)/2
08        ?4199               U   1,A
09        ?0099               0   A
0A        ?2410               S   4,1,0   X1-X
0B        ?B60E               B   6,P     BRANCH IF X1>=X
0C        ?A040               A   0,4,0   X1=(X1-X)+X
0D        ?BA05               B   A,L     REPEAT
0E        ?4099           P:  U   0,X
0F        ?0099               0   X
10        ?BA00               B   A,S
11        ?F000           H:  H
12        ?END


TYPE 'LOAD' OR 'START' OR 'STOP'
?START
```

EXECUTION BEGINS WITH INSTRUCTION AT ADDRESS 00

? 16
    8
    5
    4
    4
    4
? 3
    2
    1
    2
    1
? 31767
  15884
   7942
   3972
   1989
   1002
    516
    288
    199
    179
    178
    178
    178
? 0

HALT INSTRUCTION AT ADDRESS 11 EXECUTED

TYPE 'LOAD' OR 'START' OR 'STOP'
? STOP

DONE

problems

1   Write a BRAIN program that computes SGN(X), that is, prints +1 if X is positive, 0 if X is 0, and −1 if X is negative.

2   Write a program that calculates $n! = 1 \cdot 2 \cdot 3 \cdots (n - 1) \cdot n$, where n is any integer from 1 to 7.

3   Write a program that computes $1^2 + 2^2 + 3^2 + \cdots + n^2$ for any given $n \geq 1$.

4   Write a program with inputs s and d that finds integers a and b, whose sum is s and whose difference is d. If there are no such integers, print two zeroes.

5 a   Write a program that finds all right triangles, whose sides are whole numbers less than or equal to 100. In other words, find all integers $a, b, c \leq 100$ such that $a^2 + b^2 = c^2$.
  b   Find all integers $a, b, c \leq 100$ such that $a^3 + b^3 = c^3$.

6   Write a program to test if a number is prime. Print 1 if it is and 0 if it isn't.

262

machine
language,
assemblers,
and
compilers
chapter 9

7 Write a program that finds all prime numbers less than 100.

8 Write a BRAIN program that will generate all of the numbers in the Fibonacci sequence

1, 1, 2, 3, 5, 8, . . .

which are less than 32768. Each number in the sequence is the sum of the two preceding numbers. Let the program terminate by getting an overflow when attempting to produce the Fibonacci number bigger than 32767.

6 | *assembly language*

Machine language is obviously a very inconvenient language in which to write programs. It is difficult to remember the operation codes, all constants must be expressed in hexadecimal, and the programmer must keep track of the address in which each variable and constant is stored. Perhaps the greatest inconvenience arises when the programmer attempts to modify the program; if just one instruction is added near the beginning of the program, the address portion of any instruction which refers to a constant or instruction later in the program must be changed.

The comments that have appeared in the examples in the previous section illustrate another language which might be used to specify machine instructions. The language is called *assembly language*. Each assembly instruction usually specifies one machine instruction. In the assembly language, mnemonic (hopefully easy to remember) letter codes replace the hexadecimal operation codes, decimal constants are used instead of hexadecimal constants, and, most importantly, *symbolic addresses* (consisting of a single letter in the examples) are used in place of actual addresses.

assemblers

If a programmer is to be able to write programs in assembly language, a program is needed that will accept assembly instructions as input and produce the corresponding machine instructions. Such a program is called an *assembler*.

A typical assembler will accept a few special instructions in addition to the instructions which correspond to actual machine instructions. Examples are the END instruction, instructions which allow decimal constants or character constants to be entered and instructions which would save 30 addresses in memory for a 5 × 6 array of numbers.

In a simple assembler, the most difficult task performed is that of assigning actual addresses to the symbolic addresses. This task is complicated by the fact that as the assembly language in instructions are scanned, a "branch to X" instruction might be encountered before the assembler has assigned a machine address to the symbolic address X, since X may be the label of a later instruction. Most assemblers resolve this problem by making two or more *passes* through the assembly language instructions. On the first pass, the mnemonics are translated into operation codes and decimal constants, register numbers, etc. are translated into their hexadecimal equivalents. A table of symbolic addresses is constructed. Whenever a symbolic address is encountered as a label, its corresponding address is computed and saved. This is done by keeping track of the number of instructions in the program. The assembler must check to see that every symbolic address used in an instruction is used once and only once as a label. On the second pass the symbolic addresses are replaced by the corresponding hexadecimal machine address by using the values saved during the first pass.

Notice that since both data and instructions are stored in memory, a symbolic address, standing for an actual address, may be used in an assembly language program in the same way that either a line number or a variable name is used in a BASIC program. There is really no need for the assembler to distinguish between these two uses of a symbolic address.

The flowchart in Figure 6 shows some of the important parts of the first pass of an assembler. In it, the symbol A represents the address into which the instruction being translated will be eventually placed when the program is executed.

assembly language versus BASIC

The most sophisticated assembly language is much less convenient to use than even a very simple "higher level" language such as BASIC. Even so, there are some cases in which the use of assembly language is justified. An experienced programmer can usually produce an assembly language program that runs faster than a corresponding higher level language program. That could be important if tomorrow's weather forecast is based on yesterday's weather data, since a prediction program which takes two days to run is not of much use! However, the cost of computing is going down and the cost of programming is going up, which means that there are fewer and fewer occasions which justify the use of assembly language programming.

264

**machine
language,
assemblers,
and
compilers**
chapter 9

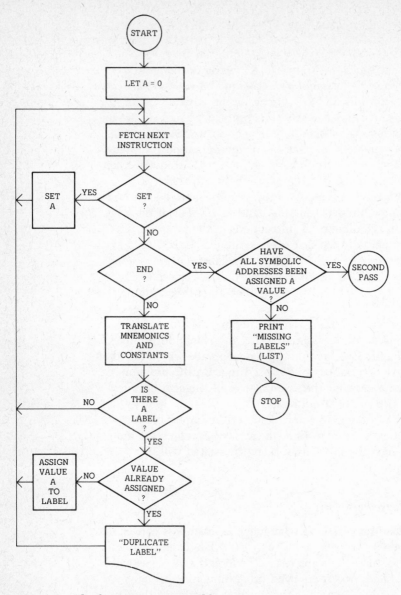

Figure 6   The first pass of an assembler.

An assembly language program is not only difficult to write, it is difficult to modify, even by the person who wrote it. This is important, because almost any large program that is useful must be modified occasionally. Also, an assembly language program can be run on only one type of computer. Hopefully, only minor modifications are needed to run a BASIC program written for one machine on another. The cost of running a somewhat less efficient program will often be saved in reprogramming costs when a new computer or a new programmer is obtained.

project

Describe in detail an assembly language for the BRAIN computer and write an assembler for this language in BASIC.

7 | *compilers and interpreters*

BASIC is obviously a more sophisticated language than an assembly language. There is no direct relationship between the machine instructions and the BASIC statements. The BASIC language is closer to the ordinary language of mathematics. It is one of the many so-called higher level languages. Other widely used languages are FORTRAN, ALGOL, COBOL, LISP, SNOBOL, and PL/I, which are briefly discussed in Chapter 10.

compilers

These higher level languages, as well as assembly languages, must be translated into machine instructions. Such a translating program has traditionally been called a *compiler*. A compiler is usually quite a complicated program. There are many things that a compiler must keep track of, such as which variables are subscripted, which functions FNA, FNB, . . . , FNA have been defined, etc. Consider the BASIC statement

LET X = A + B * (C * D + E) + C * D

A compiler must recognize that the multiplication of C * D must be done before any of the other arithmetic operations. A good compiler should also generate instructions to compute C * D only once when the expression is evaluated.

Compiler writing is both an art and a science. It is interesting that some theorems from a branch of mathematics called "automata theory" or "theory of formal languages" have been of some use to designers of programming languages and compilers. Compiling is a process of translating one language (BASIC, for example) into another language (machine language). Natural languages are vastly more complex than any programming language, but some of the things learned about compiling have contributed to the beginnings of a theory of natural languages which may aid in the writing of programs to translate from one natural language to another.

interpreters

There is another method for executing a BASIC program on a computer. A BASIC *interpreter* is a program that examines each BASIC statement that is to be executed each *time* it is to be executed and carries out the action required by the statement. Thus, roughly, it is the process that a person would use if asked to execute a BASIC program. A person would not translate the BASIC program into machine instructions as a compiler would do. He would step through the program, one statement at a time, keeping track of the values of each of the variables involved in the program.

A program which is interpreted usually runs slower than a program which has been compiled and then executed; however, a language which is to be interpreted may be more flexible than one which is to be compiled. As one simple example, consider the DIM statement in BASIC. One of the tasks of the compiler is to assign memory to each of the variables, both subscripted and unscripted. It would be nice to allow the statements

```
10   INPUT N
20   DIM X[N]
```

in a program, but consider the problem of assigning memory. The compiler would have no way of deciding how much memory to assign for the subscripted variable X because it would not know the value of N which will be typed when the program is executed. On the other hand, an interpreter would know the value of N when executing statement 20 and could allocate the proper amount of memory at the time statement 20 is executed. This is called *dynamic storage allocation,* because the memory assigned to a variable can change as the execution of the program progresses.

Even programming languages which are usually compiled can allow such things as dynamic storage allocation. Most statements are translated into machine instructions, but an instruction like statement 20 causes execution to be interrupted. Control is given to an interpreter, which assigns storage, and then execution of the program resumes. Thus systems which run programs written in sophisticated languages are often, in effect, part compiler and part interpreter.

operating systems

There is one other important type of "system" program. It is the *operating system, monitor,* or *supervisor* program. The operating system schedules all of the types of programs that have previously been discussed: compilers, interpreters, assemblers, and machine language programs. There are special instructions a programmer uses to command the operating system. The GET, LIST, and RUN system commands in BASIC are examples. Operating systems for modern computers are very complex programs. An operating system must not only schedule the compilation and execution of each program, but must usually keep track of many programs, as it must do if it is part of a time-sharing system. The operating system also usually includes an accounting routine which calculates the service charge for using the computer.

A significant percentage of all programmers are systems programmers: they write and maintain assemblers, compilers, interpreters, and operating systems.

projects

1 Devise a floating point representation for the BRAIN computer. One possibility would be to use one hexadecimal digit for the exponent (representing a power of 16) and three digits for the integer part. With this scheme 421A could represent the number $21A_{16} \times 16^4 = 538 \times 16^4$. Include representations for negative numbers and numbers with negative exponents.

2 Modify the BASIC program BRAIN so that operation codes 6, 7, 8, and 9 are floating point add, subtract, multiply, and divide instructions. Modify the input and output instructions to accept and print floating point numbers in a convenient decimal notation (such as the E notation in BASIC) if the second digit of the input/output instruction is C, D, E, or F.

3 Modify the BASIC program BRAIN so that—
  a if the second digit of the input/output instruction is 4, 5, 6, or 7, the number is printed in hexadecimal. Use the subroutines already in the program for conversion.
  b if the second digit of the input/output instruction is 8, 9, 10, or 11, a string of up to 32 characters can be typed or printed. The characters should be stored two per word in memory. Use any codes for the symbols which preserves the order of the codes as shown in Table 1 of Chapter 4, Section 9.

machine
language,
assemblers,
and
compilers
chapter 9

suggested readings

Kemeny, John G., J. Laurie Snell, and Gerald L. Thompson. *Introduction to Finite Mathematics*. Prentice-Hall, Englewood Cliffs, N.J., 1956.

Knuth, Donald E. *The Art of Computer Programming: Volume 1, Fundamental Algorithms*. Addison-Wesley, Reading, Mass., 1968.

Rosen, Saul. "Electronic Computers, A Historical Survey," *Computing Surveys* **1,** No. 1, 7–36 (Mar., 1969).

Rosen, Saul (Ed.). *Programming Systems and Languages*. McGraw-Hill, New York, 1967.

programming languages

THERE ARE two fundamental important steps in the process of solving a problem with the use of a computer. The first is to discover a procedure or sequence of operations which, if followed, will lead to a solution of the problem. Such a procedure is often called an *algorithm*. The second step is to express the algorithm in a language which is understood by a computer.

An algorithm may be described in many ways. Directions for walking to a certain house provide an example. "Walk east from the court house on Main Street for three blocks, turn right onto 3rd Avenue and stop at the fourth house on the left". Cooking recipes are often cited as examples of algorithms, although they often contain ambiguous or imprecise directions, such as "add a pinch of salt". The direction "sauté two onions" may or may not be understood, depending upon the person attempting to follow the recipe. "Sauté" is a reference to a subroutine which may not be accessible to the cook! Algorithms expressed in a programming language may also be imprecise or incomplete, resulting in diagnostic messages or erroneous results.

Once a procedure or algorithm has been discovered which will solve a particular problem, a computer language in which to express the algorithm must be selected. In a sense the computer understands directly only algorithms which are written in machine language, but there are translators available to convert programs written in other languages into machine language.

Flowcharts constitute one language which can be used to express algorithms, but it is one which is not particularly convenient for

computer processing. Assembly language, which was discussed in
Chapter 9, provides another means of expressing algorithms. If a
programmer decides not to write a program in assembly language,
then BASIC and a fairly large choice of other languages are
available. Some of the other commonly used languages will be
discussed briefly here and one of the more exotic languages,
SNOBOL, will be discussed in enough detail to exhibit its special
usefulness.

This chapter does not provide all of the information needed
to write a program in any of the languages. However, the
examples will show that anyone with a good knowledge of BASIC
programming should be able to learn any of these languages if the
need arises.

1 | some programming languages

In order to gain a little familiarity with each of the languages
discussed, a portion of a program written in each language will be
exhibited. The program will be one which corresponds to the
flowchart in Figure 1 and the BASIC statements 10–80 listed below.

```
10   LET A=0
20   FOR I=1 TO 99 STEP 2
30   IF X[I] <= 0 THEN 60
40   LET A=A+2*X[I]
50   GOTO 70
60   LET A=A+X[I]
70   NEXT I
80   LET A=A/50
```

This is a portion of a program which computes an average of the
50 numbers $X[1], X[3], X[5], \ldots, X[97], X[99]$, except that each
positive number in the list is doubled. The program is not complete
(it does not have a DIM, END, or any input/output statements),
but it does illustrate the use of several types of BASIC statements.
The examples in this section show how these statements would be
written in other languages.

When the analogous programs in BASIC, FORTRAN, COBOL,
and PL/I are examined, perhaps the most striking fact is that,
except for the wordiness of COBOL, they are very similar.

FORTRAN

The FORTRAN (for FORmula TRANslation) language was the
first widely used higher level language and is still very popular. It
was developed in the middle 1950s for use in solving scientific and
engineering problems. Programs written in FORTRAN are usually

271

some
program-
ming
languages
section 1

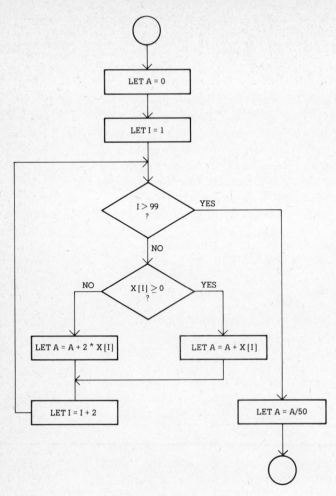

Figure 1   Flowchart for a program segment.

punched on cards for input to a computer. As with most languages
other than BASIC, a line number is not required for every
statement, but any statement may have a number and the size of
the number does not have any effect on the order in which it is
processed. A FORTRAN program segment to carry out the
computation described in Figure 1 is shown below.

```
    A = 0
    DO 42 I = 1,99,2
    IF (X(I) .LE. 0.) GO TO 237
    A = A + 2*X(I)
    GO TO 42
237 A = A + X(I)
 42 CONTINUE
    A = A/50
```

Note that in spite of several minor differences, the language looks very much like BASIC. They are in most respects quite similar.

COBOL

A programming language called COBOL (COmmon Business Oriented Language) was designed to express algorithms typically used to solve problems related to business data processing, such as processing a weekly payroll and maintaining inventories. An attempt to give the language the appearance of English makes it quite clumsy to write simple computation statements, but the language has special features for handling entire files of information as a single unit, such as all information contained in an employee's personnel record.

The algorithm expressed in Figure 1 is not the kind of computation COBOL was designed for, but it might be written in COBOL in the following way.

```
        MOVE 0 TO A.
        PERFORM LOOP VARYING I FROM 1 BY 2 UNTIL I > 99.
        GO TO DIVIDE-A.
LOOP.
        IF X(I) < 0 ADD X(I) TO A.
        OTHERWISE ADD X(I), X(I) TO A.
DIVIDE-A.
        DIVIDE 50 INTO A GIVING A.
```

The names LOOP and DIVIDE-A in the program are called paragraph names.

COBOL became available shortly after FORTRAN and was adopted as a standard language for data processing by the United States Department of Defense, which helped to make it a widely used language. For the same reason, COBOL has become a highly standardized language, contrasting with most other languages which are different in many small ways, depending upon the computer used to run the program.

ALGOL

While FORTRAN was almost universally used in the United States in the late 1950s and early 1960s, ALGOL (for ALGOrithmic Language) was widely used in Europe. It was developed in the late 1950s by an international group of computer scientists. The ALGOL language is more sophisticated than FORTRAN, but due to the earlier development and adoption of FORTRAN, ALGOL has not been used extensively in the United States. Unlike FORTRAN,

273

some
program-
ming
languages
section 1

ALGOL has the capability of handling character strings. It also has more flexible IF and FOR statements and other features not available in FORTRAN.

One of the most interesting things about ALGOL is that the syntax of the language is described in a very concise way which makes it completely clear exactly which kind of statements are legal and which are not.

The algorithm in Figure 1 expressed in ALGOL would appear as follows.

```
A := 0;
FOR I := 1 STEP 2 UNTIL 99 DO
     A := IF X(I)>0 THEN A + 2*X(I) ELSE A + X(I);
DIVIDE:   A := A/50;
```

The words FOR, STEP, UNTIL, DO, BEGIN, IF, THEN, GOTO, ELSE, and END are special symbols in ALGOL. An ALGOL program is treated as one long string of characters. There is no need to begin or end each statement on a line, since statements are separated by a semicolon. Instead of line numbers, a statement may have a *label,* such as DIVIDE in the last statement.

PL/I

In the middle of the 1960s, IBM developed PL/I (Programming Language One), which combines features of FORTRAN, COBOL, and ALGOL with special features not found in any of the earlier languages. The language has excellent facilities for handling character strings, performing operations on entire arrays, establishing arrays and their sizes during execution (dynamic storage allocation), manipulating complex data structures, such as the graph of the game of NIM described in Chapter 8, and describing separate tasks which are to be computed simultaneously. Naturally, none of these features appear in the program describing the algorithm of Figure 1.

```
A = 0;
DO I = 1 TO 99 BY 2;
     IF X(I)>0 THEN A = A + 2*X(I);
               ELSE A = A + X(I);
END;
DIVIDE:   A = A/50;
```

Even though all of these programs look quite similar, there are some programs which could be described much more succinctly in PL/I than any of the other languages using the special features of PL/I.

2 | SNOBOL

Some of the many programming languages do look quite different
from the languages discussed so far in this chapter. Many of them
were developed specially for writing programs of a certain nature.
For example, there are several languages, including GPSS and
SIMSCRIPT, designed for writing simulation programs. The
SNOBOL language is a language designed specifically for
computations involving character strings, is particularly useful for
programming applications in the humanities, and is a very elegant
language. This section will discuss the language just enough that
simple programs can be understood, but not necessarily written.
This will allow a brief discussion of some of its interesting features
and applications.

concatenation and substrings

Since SNOBOL is designed to facilitate the manipulation and
analysis of strings of symbols, one of the fundamental operations in
SNOBOL is concatenation and the basic test is to see if one string
is a substring of another. To *concatenate* two strings, one is simply
written after the other to form a new string. The concatenation of
"FIRE" and "MAN" is "FIREMAN". The concatenation of "WOW"
and the null string is "WOW". If S_1 is a substring of S_2, that means
that the letters of S_1 occur in sequence as a part of S_2. For example
"$X" is a substring of "¢$XT¢" and "AN" is a substring of
"BANANA". Every string is a substring of itself and the null string is
a substring of every string. Another way to express the fact that X is
a substring of Y is to say that there are some strings U and V such
that if U and V are concatenated to left and right of X, the result is
Y, that is, Y = UXV. If Y = "BANANA" and X = "AN", then for
U = "B" and V = "ANA", Y = UXV. It is also true that Y = UXV if
U = "BAN" and V = "A". The characters "AN" occur twice as a
substring of "BANANA".

replacement of substrings

A fundamental operation in SNOBOL consists of replacing one
substring by another. The following complete SNOBOL program
reads and prints one line of characters, replaces the first occurrence
of "COMPUTER" with the characters "MACHINE", and prints the
result.

```
        TEXT = INPUT
        OUTPUT = TEXT
        TEXT "COMPUTER" = "MACHINE"
        OUTPUT = TEXT
END
```

```
COMPUTING REQUIRES A COMPUTER.
COMPUTING REQUIRES A MACHINE.
```

The first line of the program reads one line of data (from
punched cards or a terminal) and the string is assigned as the value
of the variable TEXT. The second statement prints the input data.
The third statement causes the leftmost occurrence of the string
"COMPUTER" in the string called TEXT to be replaced by
the string "MACHINE". Nothing is done if the characters
"COMPUTER" do not occur. The next statement prints the
modified string TEXT. The last line indicates the end of the
program. In any SNOBOL program, the words INPUT, OUTPUT,
and END have special uses, but TEXT is an arbitrarily chosen
variable name. The last two lines show the output produced by the
program.

branching

Like ALGOL and PL/I, SNOBOL statements may have a label.
SNOBOL does not have a "go to" statement, but a transfer or
branch may occur after any statement if a label in parentheses is
placed after a colon in the statement. If the statement contains a
test of some kind (such a test for a substring) a conditional branch
may be made by placing labels in parentheses after the letters "S"
or "F", which indicate where to branch if the test was a Success or a
Failure.

The following program censors all occurrences of a naughty word.

```
MORE        STORY = INPUT    :F(END)
TSKTSK      STORY "DAMN" = "D---"    :S(TSKTSK)
            OUTPUT = STORY   :(MORE)
END
```

```
THE D--- COMPUTERS ARE D--- LIARS.
BUILD THE DAM NOW.
"LE D---ATION OF FAUST" IS A CANTATA WRITTEN BY HECTOR BERLIOZ.
```

The first line of the program reads one line of characters and
assigns the string to the variable STORY. This operation will fail if
there is no more data and a branch will be made to the label END,

terminating execution of the program. The second statement checks the data for "DAMN" and if it occurs the A, M and N are each replaced by dashes. If the test succeeds, that is, "DAMN" does occur, then a branch is made to the statement labeled TSKTSK, so that the same statement is executed over and over until all occurrences of "DAMN" have been censored. Then the censored line is printed and control is given to the statement labeled MORE in order to process the next line of text.

counting

Even in programs which manipulate strings of characters, some arithmetic operations are often essential. The following program counts the number of times the letter "Z" occurs in some data.

```
              N = 0
READ          TEXT = INPUT   :F(PRINT);   OUTPUT = TEXT
TEST          TEXT "Z" =  :F(READ);   N = N + 1   :(TEST)
PRINT         OUTPUT =
              OUTPUT = "THE ABOVE TEXT CONTAINS " N " Z'S."
END


THE BEES BUSILY BUZZED---BZZZ.
HOW NOW, BROWN COW?

THE ABOVE TEXT CONTAINS 6 Z'S.
```

The variable N which counts the number of Z's is first set to zero. The statement with label READ causes one line of text to be assigned to the variable TEXT. The next statement prints the input data. The string is then checked for the letter "Z". If it occurs, it is replaced by the null string, N is increased by one, and the test is made again. If there are no more Z's, a new line of text is read. When all input data has been read and all Z's counted, the value of N is printed by the last line of the program.

3 | *the towers of Hanoi*

There is a legend that there is a temple in Hanoi containing three large poles. When the temple was built, 64 golden disks, all of different diameters, were placed on one of the poles, with the largest at the bottom, the smallest at the top, and the other disks between according to their size.

The sole task of the monks residing at the temple is to move the disks from their original position onto pole 3 in Figure 2. They

Figure 2   The towers of Hanoi.

must follow two simple rules: They must move only one disk at a time and no disk may ever be placed on a pole above a smaller disk. The legend says that the completion of their task will signal the end of the world.

The goal of this section is to write a SNOBOL program which will print a list of instructions for the monks to follow, so that they will not get mixed up in the middle of their task and make some erroneous move.

recursion

In order to write the program, a programmer must make an analysis of the problem to understand something about how the moves are made. A complete understanding of exactly which move to make at any point is not really necessary in this case, if the language allows a subroutine to be defined *recursively* or *inductively*. A recursive subroutine is one which contains an instruction (such as GOSUB in BASIC) which transfers control to that same subroutine. Recursive subroutines are not allowed in FORTRAN and COBOL but may be used in ALGOL, PL/I, and SNOBOL.

It is possible to write a recursive subroutine in BASIC. The instructions 90–94 constitute a very inefficient subroutine which divides X by 2 until the result is between -1 and $+1$.

```
90   REM   SUBROUTINE TO MAKE X SMALL
91   IF ABS(X)<1 THEN 94
92   LET X=X/2
93   GOSUB 90
94   RETURN
```

To understand how the subroutine works, recall that the GOSUB works exactly like a GOTO except that the line number of the next instruction is added to the return-address stack. The RETURN statement is also like a GOTO except that the next statement to be executed is the one whose line number appears on top of the return-address stack.

In any BASIC system, there is a limit to the number of items that may be placed on the return-address stack, and hence a limit to the "depth of nesting" of subroutines in any computation.

The SNOBOL subroutine HANOI to be described shows that recursion can be a very useful technique.

instructions for moving the disks

Let N represent the number of disks to be moved from pole 1 to pole 3. If N = 1, then the only instruction to be printed is

```
MOVE DISK 1 FROM POLE 1 TO POLE 3
```

For N = 2, the instructions are

```
MOVE DISK 1 FROM POLE 1 TO POLE 2
MOVE DISK 2 FROM POLE 1 TO POLE 3
MOVE DISK 1 FROM POLE 2 TO POLE 3
```

For N = 3, the instructions could be as follows: Use the previous instructions to move the top N − 1 disks from pole 1 to pole 2. Move the bottom disk (disk N) from pole 1 to pole 3. Use the previous instructions to move the N − 1 disks on pole 2 to pole 3. It is important to realize that to "use the previous instructions to move the top N − 1 disks from pole 1 to pole 2", the pole numbers in those instructions must be changed because they are instructions to move disks from pole 1 to pole 3.

For N = 4, the directions are exactly the same as the directions for N = 3. When N is 4, the "previous instructions" will refer to the instructions for N = 3. Looking back, it is possible to see that the case N = 2 can also be described in terms of the instructions for N = 1.

The complete list of instructions for moving N disks from pole 1 to pole 3 using pole 2 could thus be:

For N > 1, use these directions to move the top N − 1 disks from pole 1 to pole 2.

Move disk N from pole 1 to pole 3.

If N > 1, use these directions to move the N − 1 disks from pole 2 to pole 3.

subroutine arguments

Almost all languages have more extensive facilities for writing subroutines than BASIC. Most programming languages are more flexible than BASIC in that they allow the computation of a

subroutine to depend upon several arguments. This capability is
essential when writing a subroutine to print directions for moving
the disks, since the pole numbers in the instructions are not the
same each time the instructions are used. The arguments for the
SNOBOL subroutine are N, the number of disks to be moved and
A, B, and C, character strings representing names for the three
poles.

A complete SNOBOL program to print directions for moving four
disks is given below.

```
        DEFINE("HANOI(N,A,B,C)")
        HANOI(4,"POLE 1","POLE 2","POLE 3")   :(END)
HANOI   GT(N,1)  HANOI(N - 1, A, C, B)
        OUTPUT = "MOVE DISK " N " FROM " A " TO " C
        GT(N,1)  HANOI(N - 1, B, A, C)   :(RETURN)
END
```

```
MOVE DISK 1 FROM POLE 1 TO POLE 2
MOVE DISK 2 FROM POLE 1 TO POLE 3
MOVE DISK 1 FROM POLE 2 TO POLE 3
MOVE DISK 3 FROM POLE 1 TO POLE 2
MOVE DISK 1 FROM POLE 3 TO POLE 1
MOVE DISK 2 FROM POLE 3 TO POLE 2
MOVE DISK 1 FROM POLE 1 TO POLE 2
MOVE DISK 4 FROM POLE 1 TO POLE 3
MOVE DISK 1 FROM POLE 2 TO POLE 3
MOVE DISK 2 FROM POLE 2 TO POLE 1
MOVE DISK 1 FROM POLE 3 TO POLE 1
MOVE DISK 3 FROM POLE 2 TO POLE 3
MOVE DISK 1 FROM POLE 1 TO POLE 2
MOVE DISK 2 FROM POLE 1 TO POLE 3
MOVE DISK 1 FROM POLE 2 TO POLE 3
```

The first statement declares that HANOI is the name of a
subroutine with arguments N, A, B, and C. The second statement
executes the subroutine with N = 4, A = "POLE 1", B = "POLE 2",
and C = "POLE 3". It is equivalent to a GOSUB statement in
BASIC. The next three statements constitute the subroutine. The
first and third statements of the subroutine recursively invoke the
subroutine HANOI provided that N is greater than 1.

execution of recursive programs

The way in which the computation is actually performed can be
understood by imagining that there are lots of clerks available, each
of whom can perform the computation described by the subroutine
HANOI. Whenever one of the clerks is working and comes to an
instruction which invokes the subroutine HANOI, he gives the task
of making this computation to another clerk, also giving him the

values of the four arguments, with which he is to work. When a clerk finishes a computation (indicated by a branch to RETURN), he signals the clerk who assigned him the task that it is complete and that clerk can then continue his computation. The computation of HANOI (3, "X", "Y", "Z") is illustrated by Figure 3. Each box represents the work of a single clerk, the values of the parameters

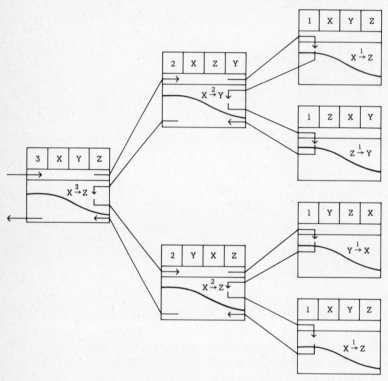

Figure 3   Computation of HANOI (3, "X", "Y", "Z").

N, A, B, and C are shown within each block. The center portion of the box indicates the printing operation. For example, $X \overset{2}{\to} Z$ means to print "MOVE DISK 2 FROM X TO Z".

The ability to write a recursive subroutine has made it easy to express an algorithm which expressed in another language could be fairly complicated. It is noteworthy that the programmer could write this program without really understanding which moves are necessary at each point in the operation.

the number of moves

An interesting question about the towers of Hanoi is how long it would take to move 64 disks if one disk were moved each second. It is possible to determine the number of moves needed for N disks by examining the subroutine HANOI. For $N = 1$ the number of moves is $M(1) = 1$. For each value of $N > 1$, the number of moves $M(N) = M(N-1) + 1 + M(N-1) = 2 * M(N-1) + 1$. From this formula it is possible to construct the table of values for M.

N	M(N)
1	1
2	$2 \cdot 1 + 1 = 3$
3	$2 \cdot 3 + 1 = 7$
4	$2 \cdot 7 + 1 = 15$

It can be seen by looking at the values for $M(N)$ that $M(N) = 2^N - 1$.

If there are 64 disks, the number of moves needed is $2^{64} - 1$, which is approximately 1.8×10^{19}. To calculate the time needed:

$$1.8 \times 10^{19} \text{ moves} \times \frac{1 \text{ sec}}{1 \text{ move}} \times \frac{1 \text{ min}}{60 \text{ sec}} \times \frac{1 \text{ hour}}{60 \text{ min}} \times \frac{1 \text{ day}}{24 \text{ hours}} \times \frac{1 \text{ year}}{365 \text{ days}}$$

which is approximately 6×10^{12} or 6 trillion years. Assuming a printer could produce 1000 lines per minute, the computer program to print the instructions would run for

$$1.8 \times 10^{19} \text{ lines} \times \frac{1 \text{ min}}{1000 \text{ lines}} \times \frac{1 \text{ hour}}{60 \text{ min}} \times \frac{1 \text{ day}}{24 \text{ hours}} \times \frac{1 \text{ year}}{365 \text{ days}}$$

$= 3.5 \times 10^{10}$ or 35 billion years!

suggested readings

Dijkstra, E. W. *A Primer of ALGOL 60 Programming*. Academic, New York, 1962.

Griswald, Ralph E., James F. Poage and Ivan P. Polonsky. *The SNOBOL4 Programming Language*, 2nd ed. Prentice-Hall, Englewood Cliffs, N.J., 1971.

Higman, Bryan. *A Comparative Study of Programming Languages.*
Elsevier, New York, 1967.

McCracken, Daniel D. *A Guide to ALGOL Programming.* Wiley,
New York, 1962.

McCracken, Daniel D. *A Guide to FORTRAN IV Programming.*
Wiley, New York, 1965.

Rice, John K. and John R. Rice. *Introduction to Computer Science.*
Holt, Rinehart & Winston, New York, 1969.

Rosen, Saul (Ed.). *Programming Systems and Languages.*
McGraw-Hill, New York, 1967.

Sammet, Jean. *Programming Languages: History and Fundamentals.*
Prentice-Hall, Englewood Cliffs, N.J., 1969.

Sprowls, R. Clay. *Introduction to PL/I Programming.* Harper &
Row, New York, 1969.

Stern, Nancy B. and Robert A. Stern. *COBOL Programming.* Wiley,
New York, 1970.

appendix A

CALL/360-OS BASIC

THE IBM Corporation has developed a version of BASIC designed for use at IBM 2741 Communications Terminals (or at Teletype Units, Types 33 and 35) under Operating System 360. The purpose of this appendix is to enable a person who has CALL/360 BASIC available to use this book. A description of the extensive additions of CALL/360 BASIC to the standard BASIC language discussed in this book appears in IBM publication GH20–0699.

Programs in CALL/360 BASIC are largely identical to programs in standard BASIC except that X to the power N is denoted by X ** N instead of by X ↑ N. The instructions discussed in Chapters 1 and 2 will all operate correctly under CALL/360. The system commands LIST, RUN, SAVE, and CATALOG will also operate correctly under CALL/360 if they are used as detailed in Chapter 1. Features of the 2741 Terminal, other CALL/360 system commands, and CALL/360 string variables are described below in the order of the descriptions in the main text of their parallel features in standard BASIC.

The reader is forewarned that some CALL/360 systems use lower case alphabetic characters.

logging in

First type LOGON (instead of HELLO). The computer will respond in the form

```
ON AT 14:30   7/24/70   LINE 3
USER NUMBER,PASSWORD--
```

The programmer supplies a user number, then a comma, then a password after the hyphens. It is forbidden to place any blank characters between the comma and the password or elsewhere on this line.

giving a name

To give a name (e.g., PROG4) to the program in the scratch area, type the command

```
NAME PROG4
```

The computer will either respond READY or else

```
FILE NAME--
```

In the latter case, type the program name after the hyphens. Up to eight letters are allowed for a program name in CALL/360 BASIC.

erasing a line

To erase a line which has been typed but not entered by the RETURN key, press the SHIFT key and the J key, and then the ATTN key.

backspacing

To correct a line which has been typed but not entered, press the BACKSPACE key until the carriage returns to the point of the error. Pressing the ATTN key will now cause the carriage to feed a line. Then type the correct character and the rest of the line, including the characters backspaced over.

logging out

To log out, type OFF (instead of GOODBYE).

scratch

To clear the scratch area, type CLEAR.

retrieving programs

To transmit a copy of a saved program (e.g., PROG4) into the scratch area, type

```
LOAD PROG4
```

killing programs

To remove a program (e.g., PROG4) from disk storage, type

```
PURGE PROG4
```

public library

CALL/360 BASIC includes three levels of public library. To list the names of the programs stored therein, type the following commands.

```
CATALOG *
CATALOG **
CATALOG ***
```

To run a program (e.g., ***FTBALL) in a public library, type

```
RUN ***FTBALL
```

It may be impossible to LIST or LOAD certain public programs. The protection feature is described in IBM publication GH20–0699.

deleting lines

A systems command of the form

```
DELETE 120, 200 THRU 310, 1050 THRU 2080
```

will delete line 120, lines 200 through 310, and lines 1050 through 2080 from the program in the scratch area.

renumbering

The systems command

```
RENUMBER 100, 50, 10
```

will renumber line 50 and all subsequent lines with numbers starting at 100 and incrementing by 10.

appending

The CALL/360 systems command MERGE serves the purpose of the standard command APPEND. The form

```
MERGE  MNPROG, SBPROG, 580
```

will insert the lines of SBPROG sequentially into MNPROG immediately after line 580 of MNPROG. The side effects are numerous. The old version of MNPROG in disk storage is irretrievably lost. The new version is renumbered, 10 lines apart, beginning at line 100. The END statement of SBPROG does not appear in the new version of MNPROG.

arrays of strings

To specify an array of strings (e.g., 24 strings) issue a declaration of the form

```
100  DIM A$(24)
```

Each of the components A$(1), A$(2), . . . , A$(24) will be a string variable of maximum length 18. This is a convenient device for sorting strings. Observe that the number 24 in the example does not specify string length.

substrings

To the authors' deep regret, CALL/360 BASIC presently has no substring capacity.

testing a random-number generator

SUPPOSE X is a random variable that could assume any one of the values $v_1, v_2, \ldots, v_n$. Let $p_i = \Pr(X = v_i)$, $1 \leq i \leq n$. If the value of X is observed N times, let f_i be the number of times that X has the value v_i. One should expect f_i, the frequency with which v_i occurred, to have a value approximately equal to $p_i \times N$, the appropriate percentage of the N cases observed.

It is desirable to have a test to determine if the value of X observed is really a "fair" sample of the distribution that X is assumed to have.

A number which attempts to measure this property is the χ^2 (chi square) statistic. It is calculated by the formula

$$\chi^2 = \sum_{i=1}^{n} \frac{(f_i - p_iN)^2}{(p_iN)}$$
$$= \frac{(f_1 - p_1N)^2}{p_1N} + \frac{(f_2 - p_2N)^2}{p_2N} + \cdots + \frac{(f_n - p_nN)^2}{p_nN}$$

The value of $(f_i - p_iN)^2$ will be small when f_i has a value close to that expected, namely, p_iN. Thus, large values of χ^2 indicate that the random variable X does not have the distribution indicated by the values of P_i.

Table B.1 shows, for some values of n and χ^2, the probability that if a fair sample were taken of the variable with probability distribution given by the p_i, the χ^2 computed on the fair sample would be greater than that indicated by the value actually obtained.

Suppose the BASIC function RND is tested by computing 1000

table B.1 *probability that a random sample gives no better fit*

n \ x^2	1	2	3	4	6	8	10	15	20
3	.607	.368	.223	.135	.050	.018	.007	.001	.000
4	.801	.572	.392	.261	.112	.046	.019	.002	.000
5	.910	.736	.558	.406	.199	.092	.040	.005	.000
6	.963	.849	.700	.549	.306	.156	.075	.010	.001
7	.986	.920	.809	.677	.423	.238	.125	.020	.003
8	.995	.960	.885	.780	.540	.333	.189	.036	.006
9	.998	.981	.934	.857	.647	.433	.265	.059	.010
10	.999	.991	.964	.911	.740	.534	.350	.091	.018
11	1.000	.996	.981	.947	.815	.629	.440	.132	.029
12	1.000	.998	.991	.970	.873	.713	.530	.182	.045

n \ x^2	8	10	12	14	16	18	20	25	30
10	.534	.350	.213	.122	.067	.035	.018	.003	.000
11	.629	.440	.285	.173	.100	.055	.029	.005	.001
12	.713	.530	.363	.233	.141	.082	.045	.009	.002
13	.785	.616	.446	.301	.191	.116	.067	.015	.003
14	.844	.694	.528	.374	.249	.158	.095	.023	.005
15	.889	.762	.606	.450	.313	.207	.130	.035	.008
16	.924	.820	.679	.526	.382	.263	.172	.050	.012
17	.949	.867	.744	.599	.453	.324	.220	.070	.018
18	.967	.904	.800	.667	.524	.389	.274	.095	.026
19	.979	.932	.847	.729	.593	.456	.333	.125	.037
20	.987	.953	.886	.784	.657	.522	.395	.161	.052

SOURCE: *C.R.C. Standard Mathematical Tables,* 12th ed., Chemical Rubber Co., Cleveland, 1959, p. 395. Used with permission.

values of FNR(10). In this case, $n = 10$, $N = 1000$, and $p_i = .1$ for each i. If the computed value of x^2 obtained from the test is 6, then the table indicates that 74 percent of all samples taken from a perfect random generator would yield a x^2 value greater than 6, thus the distribution is close to what is desired. On the other hand, if the value of x^2 computed from the test data were 15, the table indicates that a χ^2 computed from a truly uniform distribution would be 15 or more only 9.1 percent of the time, indicating that the function FNR may not generate the digits from 1 to 10 uniformly.

In this case all of the probabilities p_i are the same, namely $1/n$. When all values of p_i are $1/n$, $p_i \times N$ is N/n and it is possible to simplify the computation of χ^2 to the following formula.

$$\chi^2 = \frac{n}{N} \sum_{i=1}^{n} f_i^2 - N$$

$$= \frac{n}{N} (f_1^2 + f_2^2 + \cdots + f_n^2) - N$$

The program CHKRAN generates 1000 integers between 1 and 10 and computes the χ^2 statistic based on the observed distribution. In the program F[R] records the number of times the number R is generated. The variable I counts the 1000 numbers which are generated by statements 40–44. The distribution is printed by lines 50–52. The variable S records the sum of the squares of the frequencies F[I] and X2 is the value of χ^2.

```
LIST
CHKRAN

10    DIM F[10]
20    DEF FNR(N)=INT(N*RND(0))+1
30    MAT F=ZER
40    REM  **  GENERATE 1000 NUMBERS
41    FOR I=1 TO 1000
42    LET R=FNR(10)
43    LET F[R]=F[R]+1
44    NEXT I
50    FOR I=1 TO 10
51    PRINT F[I];
52    NEXT I
60    REM  **  COMPUTE CHI SQUARE
61    LET S=0
62    FOR I=1 TO 10
63    LET S=S+F[I]↑2
64    NEXT I
65    LET X2=S/100-1000
70    PRINT
71    PRINT "X2 =";X2
90    END


RUN
CHKRAN

 115    106    88    117    103    90    95    84    104    98
X2 = 11.04

DONE
```

The value of χ^2 computed is a little larger than would be expected from a perfect uniform random-number generator, but the sequences generated are probably acceptable for most simulation programs.

the BRAIN simulator

THIS APPENDIX documents a BASIC program named BRAIN, which simulates the mythical computer, also called the BRAIN, described in Chapter 9.

abstract

There are two principal sections of the program BRAIN. The *load* phase of the program allows the operator to type BRAIN instructions which are stored. The *execute* phase is a deterministic simulation of the execution of the BRAIN instructions stored. The program begins by requesting of the operator which phase is to be used.

If the operator types the request "LOAD", the program fetches from the disk the permanent copy of memory and the first address into which instructions are to be stored. After the operator has typed BRAIN instructions, the new version of memory is saved on the disk.

If the operator types the request "START", the program fetches from the disk the copy of memory and the address of the first instruction to be executed and simulates execution of the BRAIN program. A maximum of 10000 BRAIN instructions will be simulated and execution will be terminated by an overflow, divide by 0, attempt to execute the illegal instructions 6, 7, 8, or 9, or a halt instruction. In all but the last case, the contents of the registers and memory will be printed. Any values not printed are 0.

After either the load or execute phase, the program will again ask the operator for instructions. Either phase of the program may then be run again. After the execute phase, the status of the memory is *not* saved, so if the same program is rerun, the memory will contain the original values.

flowchart

A flowchart for the BRAIN simulator is shown in Figures C.1, C.2, and C.3. Numbers within the connecting circles represent line numbers in the program.

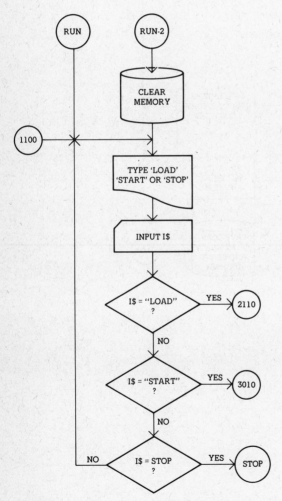

Figure C.1   Flowchart for BRAIN simulator.

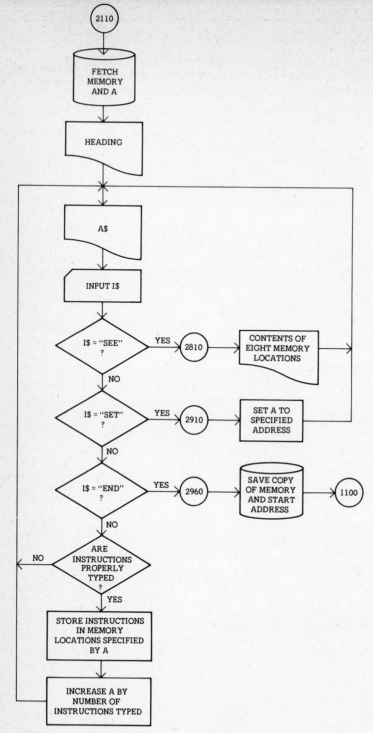

Figure C.2   Flowchart for BRAIN *simulator.*

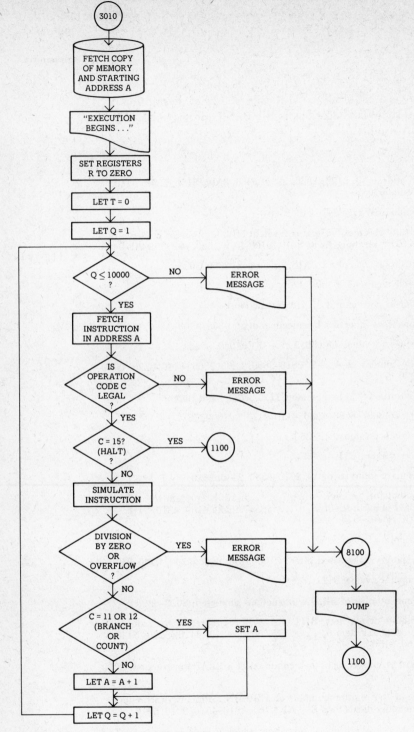

Figure C.3   Flowchart for BRAIN *simulator.*

variable names

The following is a list of all variable names, a brief description of their use, and some key locations in the BASIC program BRAIN where they are used.

A	an address; 8, 2120, 2830, 2930, 2980, 3012, 5130, 5250, 6210, 9840, 9950
A1	temporarily saves A; 2240–2520
A$[4]	usually the hexadecimal equivalent of an address or contents of a memory location; 8250–8410, 9100–9150, 9200–9290, 9461–9463
C	operation code of a BRAIN instruction; 3050–3095
C$	single character; 9300–9320
E	address portion of a BRAIN instruction; 3040
H	numerical value of a hexadecimal digit; 9300–9360
H$[16]	the hexadecimal digits 012 . . . EF; 1020, 9320
I	loop counter; 2–4, 5–7, 2610–2680, 2860–2866, 8140–8220, 9910–9930
I$[64]	input line typed by operator; 1110, 2230, 9400–9490
J	loop counter; 8260–8280, 9110–9115, 9270–9275
J5	temporary value of J; 8350
K	loop counter; 8340–8395
L	length of input string I$; 2310–2330, 2440, 2610
M[256]	contents of memory, M[1], . . . , M[256] represent the values stored in locations 0, . . . , 255; 5–7, 2650, 4160, 4310, 4410, 8360, 9830, 9940
M7	temporary value; 2850
N	temporary value used often; 9100–9150, 9200–9290, 9400–9490
N1	temporary value; 9111
Q	counts number of BRAIN instructions simulated; 3029–6220
R[16]	contents of registers, R[1], . . . , R[16] represent the values stored in registers 0, . . . , 15; 3020, 4310, 4410, 5230, 5430, 6160, 8150
R0	register number or branch condition of a BRAIN instruction; 3030, 3061
R1	one of the register numbers of a BRAIN arithmetic instruction (the other one is then E − R1 * 16); 4210, 4510, 5010, 5310
T	result of any arithmetic operation, which is used as test value for branch instruction; 3025, 4220, 4520, 5020, 5110, 5340, 6110

comments

1 The program BRAIN can only be run on a BASIC system that allows string variables.

2 The keyword LET is optional on most BASIC systems and has been omitted.

3 A dump may be obtained after the execution of any BRAIN program by using one of the illegal instructions with operation codes 6, 7, 8, or 9 instead of the halt instruction (operation code F).

4 A way to list a BRAIN program is to use the "SEE" instruction.

5 The instructions that read and write on a disk in lines 2–9, 9800–9850, and 9900–9960 are not standard BASIC and probably need modification. The instructions 2–9 store 257 zeros on the disk. Subroutine 9800–9850 reads 256 numbers into the array M and the value of A from the disk. Subroutine 9900–9860 stores the 256 values of M and the value of A onto the disk. Consult an instruction manual for the system being used.

6 On most systems, some system commands to establish space on a disk must be executed before the program can be run the *first* time.

7 If a disk is not available, modify the program in the following ways.

  a Replace lines 2–8 with

```
3    DIM D[256]
5    MAT D=ZER
7    D2=A
```

  b Replace lines 9800–9850 with

```
9800    REM  ***   FETCH VALUES OF M AND A
9810    MAT M=D
9820    A=D2
9830    RETURN
```

  c Replace lines 9900–9960 with

```
9900    REM  ***   SAVE M AND A
9910    MAT D=M
9920    D2=A
9930    RETURN
```

listing

```
LIST
BRAIN

1     GOTO 1020
2     FOR I=9 TO 1 STEP -1
3     PRINT #1,I
4     NEXT I
5     FOR I=1 TO 256
6     PRINT #1;0
7     NEXT I
8     PRINT #1;0
9     PRINT "MEMORY HAS BEEN CLEARED"
1010  DIM M[256],R[16],A$[4],H$[16],I$[64]
1020  H$="0123456789ABCDEF"
1100  PRINT
1101  PRINT "TYPE 'LOAD' OR 'START' OR 'STOP'"
1110  INPUT I$
1120  IF I$="LOAD" THEN 2110
1130  IF I$="START" THEN 3010
1140  IF I$ <> "STOP" THEN 1100
1160  STOP
2000  REM   ***   LOAD   ***
2110  PRINT
2120  GOSUB 9800
2140  PRINT "ADDRESS  INSTRUCTIONS/DATA  COMMENTS"
2210  N=A
2220  GOSUB 9100
2225  PRINT A$[3,4];"       ";
2230  INPUT I$
2240  A1=A
2250  IF I$[1,3]="SEE" THEN 2810
2260  IF I$[1,3]="SET" THEN 2910
2270  IF I$[1,3]="END" THEN 2960
2310  FOR L=1 TO LEN(I$)
2320  IF I$[L,L]=" " THEN 2440
2330  NEXT L
2440  L=L-1
2450  IF L/4=INT(L/4) THEN 2610
2460  PRINT "NUMBER OF DIGITS IS NOT A MULTIPLE OF FOUR"
2510  PRINT "PLEASE RETYPE INSTRUCTION"
2520  A=A1
2530  GOTO 2210
2610  FOR I=1 TO L STEP 4
2620  A$=I$[I,I+3]
2630  GOSUB 9200
2640  IF N>1.E+08 THEN 2710
2650  M[A+1]=N
2660  A=A+1
2670  IF A<256 THEN 2680
2675  A=0
2680  NEXT I
2690  GOTO 2210
2710  PRINT "ILLEGAL CHARACTER IN INSTRUCTION ";A$
2720  GOTO 2510
2810  GOSUB 9400
2820  IF N>255 THEN 2510
2830  A=N
2840  I$=I$[5,6]
2845  I$[3,8]="       "
2850  M7=7
2851  IF A<249 THEN 2860
2852  M7=255-A
2860  FOR I=0 TO M7
2861  I5=I*5
2862  I$[9+I5,9+I5]=" "
2863  N=M[A+I+1]
2864  GOSUB 9100
2865  I$[10+I5,13+I5]=A$
2866  NEXT I
2870  PRINT I$
```

```
2880    GOTO 2210
2910    GOSUB 9400
2920    IF N>255 THEN 2510
2930    A=N
2940    GOTO 2210
2960    GOSUB 9400
2970    IF N>255 THEN 2510
2980    A=N
2990    GOSUB 9900
2995    GOTO 1100
3000    REM   ***   START   ***
3010    PRINT
3012    GOSUB 9800
3016    N=A
3017    GOSUB 9100
3018    PRINT "EXECUTION BEGINS WITH INSTRUCTION AT ADDRESS ";A$[3,4]
3019    PRINT
3020    MAT R=ZER
3025    T=0
3029    FOR Q=1 TO 10000
3030    R0=INT(M[A+1]/256)
3040    REM   E IS THE ADDRESS PORTION OF THE INSTRUCTION
3041    E=M[A+1]-256*R0
3050    REM   C IS THE OPERATION CODE
3051    C=INT(R0/16)
3060    REM   R0 IS THE REGISTER NUMBER IN THE INSTRUCTION
3061    R0=R0-16*C
3070    IF C >= 0 THEN 3090
3080    C=C+16
3090    IF C>7 THEN 3095
3091    GOTO C+1 OF 4000,4100,4200,4300,4400,4500,4600,4700
3095    GOTO C-7 OF 4800,4900,5000,5100,5200,5300,5400,5500
4000    REM   **   OUTPUT
4010    PRINT " ";M[E+1]
4020    GOTO 6210
4100    REM   **   INPUT
4110    INPUT N
4120    REM   IF N=INT(N) AND N>=-32768 AND N<=32767 THEN 4160
4121    IF N-INT(N)+SGN(32767.6-ABS(N+.5))=1 THEN 4160
4130    PRINT "INPUT MUST BE AN INTEGER BETWEEN -32768 AND 32767"
4140    PRINT "PLEASE RETYPE INPUT"
4150    GOTO 4110
4160    M[E+1]=N
4170    GOTO 6210
4200    REM   **   SUBTRACT
4210    R1=INT(E/16)
4220    T=R[R1+1]-R[E-R1*16+1]
4230    GOTO 6110
4300    REM   **   LOAD
4310    R[R0+1]=M[E+1]
4320    GOTO 6210
4400    REM   **   UNLOAD(STORE)
4410    M[E+1]=R[R0+1]
4420    GOTO 6210
4500    REM   **   MULTIPLY
4510    R1=INT(E/16)
4520    T=R[R1+1]*R[E-R1*16+1]
4530    GOTO 6110
4600    REM   **   OP-CODE 6 NOT USED
4700    REM   **   OP-CODE 7 NOT USED
4800    REM   **   OP-CODE 8 NOT USED
4900    REM   **   OP-CODE 9 NOT USED
4901    N=A
4902    GOSUB 9100
4903    PRINT "ILLEGAL OP-CODE IN INSTRUCTION AT ADDRESS ";A$[3,4]
4904    GOTO 8110
5000    REM   **   ADD
5010    R1=INT(E/16)
5020    T=R[R1+1]+R[E-R1*16+1]
5030    GOTO 6110
```

```
5100    REM  **  BRANCH
5110    N=INT(RO/2↑(SGN(T)+1))
5120    REM  IF N IS EVEN AND RO<7 THEN 6210
5121    IF N/2-INT(N/2)+SGN(7-RO)=1 THEN 6210
5130    A=E
5140    GOTO 6220
5200    REM  **  COUNT
5210    N=R[RO+1]
5220    IF N=-32768. THEN 6140
5230    R[RO+1]=N-1
5240    IF N=1 THEN 6210
5250    A=E
5260    GOTO 6220
5300    REM  **  DIVIDE
5310    R1=INT(E/16)
5320    N=R[E-R1*16+1]
5330    IF N=0 THEN 5360
5340    T=INT(R[R1+1]/N)
5350    GOTO 6110
5360    N=A
5370    GOSUB 9100
5380    PRINT "ATTEMPT TO DIVIDE BY ZERO AT ADDRESS ";A$[3,4]
5390    GOTO 8110
5400    REM  **  ENTER
5410    IF E<128 THEN 5430
5420    E=E-256
5430    R[RO+1]=E
5440    GOTO 6210
5500    REM  **  HALT
5510    PRINT
5520    N=A
5530    GOSUB 9100
5540    PRINT "HALT INSTRUCTION AT ADDRESS ";A$[3,4];" EXECUTED"
5550    GOTO 1100
6100    REM  **  CHECK FOR OVERFLOW
6110    REM  IF T>=-32768 AND T<=32767 THEN 6160
6111    IF ABS(T+.5)<32767.6 THEN 6160
6120    N=A
6130    GOSUB 9100
6140    PRINT "OVERFLOW RESULTED FROM INSTRUCTION AT ADDRESS ";A$[3,4]
6150    GOTO 8110
6160    R[RO+1]=T
6210    A=A+1
6211    IF A<256 THEN 6220
6212    A=0
6220    NEXT Q
6230    PRINT "10000 INSTRUCTIONS HAVE BEEN EXECUTED"
8100    REM  **  MEMORY DUMP
8110    PRINT
8120    PRINT "CONTENTS OF REGISTERS"
8130    PRINT "REG   HEX    DECIMAL           REG    HEX    DECIMAL"
8140    FOR I=1 TO 8
8150    REM  IF R[I]=0 AND R[I+8]=0 THEN 8220
8151    IF ABS(R[I])+ABS(R[I+8])=0 THEN 8220
8160    N=R[I]
8170    GOSUB 9100
8180    I$=A$
8190    N=R[I+8]
8200    GOSUB 9100
8210    PRINT I-1;I$;"   ";R[I],I+7;A$;"   ";R[I+8]
8220    NEXT I
8230    PRINT
8240    PRINT "CONTENTS OF MEMORY IN HEXADECIMAL"
8250    FOR A=0 TO 255 STEP 8
8260    FOR J=A+1 TO A+8
8270    IF M[J] <> 0 THEN 8300
8280    NEXT J
8290    GOTO 8410
8300    N=A
8310    GOSUB 9100
8320    I$=A$[3,4]
8330    I$[3,8]="        "
8340    FOR K=0 TO 7
8350    J5=K*5
```

```
8360    N=M[A+K+1]
8370    GOSUB 9100
8380    I$[9+J5,9+J5]=" "
8390    I$[10+J5,13+J5]=A$
8395    NEXT K
8400    PRINT I$
8410    NEXT A
8420    GOTO 1100
9100    REM  ***  CONVERTS N INTO 4 HEX DIGITS A$  ***
9101    A$="    "
9110    FOR J=4 TO 2 STEP -1
9111    N1=INT(N/16)
9112    H=N-N1*16+1
9113    N=N1
9114    A$[J,J]=H$[H,H]
9115    NEXT J
9120    IF N >= 0 THEN 9140
9130    N=N+16
9140    A$[1,1]=H$[N+1,N+1]
9150    RETURN
9200    REM  ***  CONVERTS 4 HEX DIGITS A$ INTO N  ***
9210    C$=A$[1,1]
9220    GOSUB 9300
9230    IF H<0 THEN 9280
9240    IF H<8 THEN 9260
9250    H=H-16
9260    N=H
9270    FOR J=2 TO 4
9271    C$=A$[J,J]
9272    GOSUB 9300
9273    IF H<0 THEN 9280
9274    N=N*16+H
9275    NEXT J
9276    RETURN
9280    N=1.E+09
9290    RETURN
9300    REM  ***  CONVERTS CHARACTER C$ INTO HEX DIGIT H  ***
9310    FOR H=1 TO 16
9320    IF H$[H,H]=C$ THEN 9350
9330    NEXT H
9340    H=0
9350    H=H-1
9360    RETURN
9400    REM  ***  SETS N TO NEW ADDRESS BY I$[4,6]
9410    IF LEN(I$)=3 THEN 9450
9420    IF I$[4,4]=" " THEN 9450
9430    IF LEN(I$)<6 THEN 9440
9431    IF I$[4,4]="-" THEN 9460
9440    N=999
9441    GOTO 9480
9450    I$[4,6]="-00"
9460    N=0
9461    A$[1,2]="00"
9462    A$[3,4]=I$[5,6]
9463    GOSUB 9270
9470    IF N<256 THEN 9490
9480    PRINT "AFTER THE THREE LETTER COMMAND SHOULD BE"
9481    PRINT "      EITHER NOTHING OR ELSE '-HH' WHERE"
9482    PRINT "      EACH H IS A HEXADECIMAL DIGIT"
9490    RETURN
9800    REM  ***  READ M AND A FROM DISC  ***
9810    FILES MEM
9820    READ #1,1
9830    MAT READ #1;M
9840    READ #1;A
9850    RETURN
9900    REM  ***  PUT M AND A ONTO DISC  ***
9910    FOR I=9 TO 1 STEP -1
9920    PRINT #1,I
9930    NEXT I
9940    MAT PRINT #1;M
9950    PRINT #1;A
9960    RETURN
9990    END
```

index

72 73 74 75 76 9 8 7 6 5 4 3 2 1